Dear Researcher-to-Be,

Having trouble getting high-quality articles from the Internet? Can't organize the information that you do find? Break out in a cold sweat when your instructor says, "There's a research paper required for this class"? Worst of all, have you ever dropped a class just because of the term paper requirement? If so, this book is for you. No more confusion, fear, or bailing on my watch!

Learning any new skill is daunting and difficult. Learning how to write a research paper is no exception; but you've learned many other skills, and you'll learn this one, too. I'm going to take you point-by-point through the process. You'll find out how to develop a thesis, use primary and secondary sources, and evaluate what you find. I'll show you how to draft the document, too, including parenthetical documentation, footnotes, and endnotes. You'll explore how to prepare the final copy as well. Along the way, I'll show you how to integrate source material to make your point. By the end of this book, you'll write research papers with skill and success.

After earning my B.A. in English and American literature, my M.A. in English and American literature, and my Ph.D. in English and American Literature, I've written *far more* than my share of research papers. I sure wish that I knew *then* what I know *now* about research! Fortunately, I can teach all my hard-won knowledge to my college students. And I can share it with you as well, so that you don't have to bang your head against the wall in frustration because you can't find the facts that you need, arrange them in a logical form, and make your point cogently. (It hurts your head and often damages the wall. We don't want that!)

Remember: Mastering the basics of research and writing is well within your abilities.

Best wishes,

Laurie E. Rozakis, Ph.D.

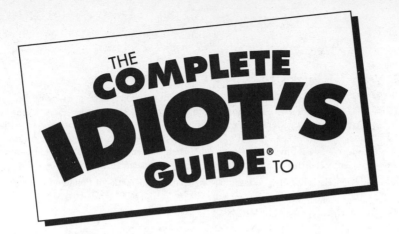

THE COMPLETE IDIOT'S GUIDE® TO

Research Methods

by Laurie E. Rozakis, Ph.D.

ALPHA

A member of Penguin Group (USA) Inc.

To Robert from Farmingdale, now and always.

Publisher: *Marie Butler-Knight*
Product Manager: *Phil Kitchel*
Senior Managing Editor: *Jennifer Chisholm*
Senior Acquisitions Editor: *Randy Ladenheim-Gil*
Development Editor: *Michael Thomas*
Senior Production Editor: *Billy Fields*
Copy Editor: *Keith Cline*
Illustrator: *Richard King*
Cover/Book Designer: *Trina Wurst*
Indexer: *Heather McNeil*
Layout/Proofreading: *Angela Calvert, Donna Martin*

Contents at a Glance

Appendixes

Contents

Foreword

So you've been sitting in class all semester waiting for the day to arrive, the day you have to start writing your research paper. This is the paper that's going to determine your final grade. The paper for which you have a subject and a topic but no clue how to begin researching.

In my twenty years of working in libraries, I have seen the frantic patron, be it a high school or college student, trying to find information to support a thesis. With deadlines looming, they try to twist and fit information from journals or books to support an idea, like pushing a square peg into a round hole.

Today, most K-12 school districts integrate information literacy skills into the curriculum. Colleges and universities offer information literacy courses and workshops, thereby teaching students the skills necessary to tackle a research paper. The American Library Association defines information literacy as "a set of abilities requiring individuals to recognize when information is needed and … locate, evaluate, and use effectively the needed information."

With the massive amounts of information available in print and through the Internet, it is extremely important that people have the ability to locate needed information, analyze it, and evaluate it so that it can be used to form an opinion, create a product such as a research paper, or make a decision. Being information-literate helps people become lifelong learners.

Research is about planning, then doing, and then reviewing what has been done. When confronted with a research project, most people just think of the "do" part of research. They run to the library, search the Internet, gather lots of books and articles, and jump right in only to find that they have collected a lot of nothing.

Part of the planning in the research process is identifying the topic and locating the information sources you'll need. In this book, Laurie Rozakis helps you plan by identifying information sources, examining their strengths and weaknesses, and telling you when to apply them. Dr. Rozakis provides tips on note taking, which makes completing the research paper so much easier. In addition, she provides the reader with a time-management chart to reduce anxiety and prevent the deadline blues. As a library director, I found the best part of the book to be her discussion of libraries. Your library is the gateway to information; from print, to electronic, to artifacts, the library has it all. Your librarian is there to assist in finding appropriate materials. All you have to do is ask.

You can breathe a sigh of relief after reading this book, knowing that Dr. Rozakis has armed you with the tools necessary to tackle your research project.

—Deborah Podolski

Deborah Podolski began her career in libraries as a volunteer in 1982, then received her Masters degree in Library Science in 1989. She has worked as a librarian at the Port Washington Public Library and at the Nassau Library System. She is also a certified teacher with a Masters in Secondary Education and a certificate in School District Administration. She worked as a Program Coordinator for the Nassau BOCES School Library System and is currently the director of the Farmingdale Public Library.

Introduction

You know you have the intelligence, ambition, and resilience to succeed, but one problem holds you back. "I'm afraid of writing research papers," you say to yourself. When it comes to finding and organizing scholarly material, you just don't know where to start. Or you can get started, but then you get lost in the stacks, online, or during the writing. By the time the deadline smacks you in the face, your paper is only half-done.

You know you need to know how to find high-quality references and use them to make your point in writing. Being able to do research and write a research paper will help you earn that degree, get a raise and promotion at work, and achieve your goals within your community. That's why you bought this book.

Aimlessly surfing the web isn't the answer. Printing out stacks of articles and trying to wade through them won't work, either. Using someone else's words as your own is immoral as well as illegal.

You know you need to do the following:

♦ Understand how to craft a thesis statement that suits your purpose and audience.

♦ Learn how to manage your time.

♦ Know the different types of libraries and how to use them.

♦ Find what you need on the Internet, especially by using proprietary databases.

♦ Evaluate your research.

♦ Use research to make your point.

♦ Give proper credit to all your sources and thus avoid plagiarism.

What You'll Learn in This Book

You know that if you want to get ahead in almost any business or profession, you must know how to do research and write up your findings. That's what this book can help you achieve. You'll learn that research is not a mysterious activity at which only a few people can succeed. Rather, writing effective research papers is a craft that can be learned by almost anyone willing to invest the required time and energy.

This book is divided into four sections that teach you all the practical, hands-on research skills you need to succeed. You'll understand how to locate the authoritative information you need and how to use it to make your point in writing. Most of all, you'll finish this book convinced that writing a research paper is fun as well as useful and important.

Part 1, "Basic Training," starts by exploring the origin of the research paper and comparing and contrasting the two main types of research papers. Then I discuss different types of research sources and the advantages and disadvantages of each one. Next, you'll learn how to write a thesis statement, the backbone of every research paper. This section also includes a chapter on time management to help you stay on track. You'll learn how to keep track of your findings, too, and refine your search by using search engines, Boolean logic, and key words. In addition, you'll discover the easiest and most effective ways of taking notes, including techniques for summarizing, paraphrasing, and documenting direct quotations. This section concludes with a survey of libraries—public libraries, university libraries, and specialized libraries—so you can see what services they each provide.

Part 2, "Seek and Ye Shall Find," opens with an explanation of the different ways that books are classified in a library to make sure that you can find the books you need. Next, you'll discover the different types of reference books (almanacs, atlases, dictionaries, and encyclopedias are just the start!) and when to use each one. Then extend your knowledge of reference sources by delving into periodicals and academic journals so you'll know how to use these important reference sources. I cover interviews, media sources, surveys, government documents, archives, and vertical files as well. There's a complete section devoted to researching with electronic media.

Part 3, "Evaluate Your Research," emphasizes a key point in research: the difference between commercial databases and those available through libraries. This will help you get the highest-quality reference material. Then I cover how to evaluate your research on the basis of quality, bias, appropriateness, and reliability, paying special attention to evaluating electronic sources.

Part 4, "Use and Document Research to Make *Your* Point," teaches you how to integrate research into your paper. Here, you'll practice using cue words and phrases, exact quotes, paraphrases, and summaries so you can use your research to support your persuasive argument. I cover plagiarism (literary theft) in detail, as well as MLA, APA, and CMS documentation style. You'll learn all about the different forms of documentation and when to use each one. The section concludes with guidelines for writing a Works Cited page (MLA) or a References page (APA) so your reader can locate your sources quickly and easily, an essential aspect of responsible research.

Last, there's a glossary of terms, model research papers, and a handy-dandy guide to grammar and usage.

More for Your Money!

In addition to all the explanation and teaching, this book contains other types of information to make it even easier for you to master writing a research paper. Here's how you can recognize these features:

You Could Look It Up

Like every other skill worth knowing, research has its own terminology. These definitions explain all those terms.

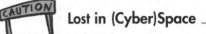

Lost in (Cyber)Space

These warnings help you stay on track—so you don't end up lost in space.

Ask the Librarian

These are little expert tips that make writing a research paper much easier.

From the Reference Desk

You could skip these tasty tidbits, but you won't want to because they're too much fun!

Acknowledgments

Special thanks to the brilliant and generous people who contributed their research papers to this book:

Elisabeth Sara Fink   Elizabeth Landau

Charles Rozakis   Jessica Swantek

And my deepest appreciation to my wonderful editor Randy Ladenheim-Gil. Randy, I am blessed to work with someone of your insight, intelligence, and kindness. Also, much thanks to all the hard-working and dedicated people "behind the scenes" who make me look so good: Michael Thomas, Billy Fields, and Keith Cline.

Trademarks

All terms mentioned in this book that are known to be or are suspected of being trademarks or service marks have been appropriately capitalized. Alpha Books and

Part 1

Basic Training

There was an engineer who had a gift for fixing all things mechanical. After serving his company for 30 years, he retired. Years later his company contacted him regarding a problem they were having with one of their machines. They had tried everything to get the machine fixed, but to no avail. The engineer studied the machine. Then he marked a small x in chalk on a particular component and stated, "This is where your problem is." The part was replaced and the machine worked again.

The company received a bill for $50,000 from the engineer. They demanded an itemized accounting of his charges. He responded:

One chalk mark	$1
Knowing where to put it	$49,999

In this part, you'll learn how to build the foundation of your research paper: writing a solid thesis statement, tracking your findings, and taking notes. By the end of this section, you'll know just where to put the chalk mark … and why.

What Is Research?

In This Chapter

- ◆ Discover the origins of the research paper
- ◆ Define the "research paper"
- ◆ Explore expository and persuasive research papers
- ◆ Distinguish between primary and secondary sources
- ◆ Read excerpts from sample research papers and primary sources

Parent: "What do you want to be when you grow up, Little Sally?"

Child: "A researcher, of course."

Yes, every child dreams of becoming a researcher. Not very likely, eh? However, the odds *are* great that all students will do some hard time in the library or in cyberspace hunting for the facts they need. They will be standing right next to every adult in town, too. That's because research is essential to our lives.

In this chapter, you'll discover the two main types of research papers: the expository paper and the persuasive research paper. You'll read examples of each type of research paper so you can see specific examples of the similarities and differences.

Next, you'll explore different sources for your research, focusing on primary and secondary sources. You'll read two famous primary sources to help you understand the strengths and weaknesses of this type of research material. This will help you decide on the appropriate mix of primary and secondary sources to use in your own research papers.

The Origins of the Research Paper

In America, the research paper has noble origins. It began around 1870, when young college teachers who had studied in Germany began to assign what they called a "scholarly thesis" to their students. At that time, German universities were very involved with research, not a commonplace course of study on our side of the Atlantic. Because research papers helped students learn about topics in depth, the idea caught on quickly: Only ten years later, many colleges had begun to require seniors to write a thesis of 1,000 to 3,000 words as a condition for graduating. (That's four to twelve pages, double-spaced.) By the turn of the century, a "graduating thesis" was often assigned in seminar classes for advanced students.

At first, professors who assigned research papers concentrated more on content than form. But by the early 1900s, students were required to include a list of works in their research paper to document the sources of their facts, along with footnotes, charts, and diagrams. A few years later, realizing that they had stumbled upon a good way to prepare students to be critical thinkers and responsible citizens, instructors decided to require underclass students to churn out research papers as well. By the 1930s, research papers were routinely being assigned to high school students. Today, students as young as the first grade are learning the basics of research and how to write a research paper.

Employees in the public as well as private sectors are often required to write research papers, especially in hot fields where information is flying around at dizzying speeds. The logic is strong: If you can gather the facts in a readable format, then you've got the power to make logical decisions and reasonable judgments. That's why you need to know how to write a research paper.

What *Is* a Research Paper?

In everyday life, you may need to research information about a van's safety record, a town's schools, or a company's stocks. In a classroom, you may delve into a controversial topic such as cloning or a tame one such as chocolate. No matter what your topic and aim, when you research you need to know how to gather, sort, and track the facts and opinions available to you. You must also know how to present the information you find in a form that suits your purpose and audience (your reader or readers). That's what this book is all about.

A research paper reports a writer's research findings. In a classroom, a research paper takes a specific form. The length of the paper will be determined by the professor's guidelines, the requirements for the class, and the topic. Ditto on the format and citation form. Therefore, always make sure that you understand your parameters from the get-go. Much more on this in Chapter 3.

Take a close look at the word *research*. You'll see that the word contains the prefix "re" and the root "search." When you write a *research paper*, you are "searching again" through material that other people have written to find the facts you need to write your paper. As you sift through the material, you evaluate what you find to judge its quality.

The facts you gather can be presented in two forms: as an *expository research paper* or a *persuasive research paper*. The two types of writing are often confused, which is a serious issue because the two forms are so radically different.

> **You Could Look It Up**
>
> A **research paper** reports a writer's research findings. A research paper can also be called a library paper, a term paper, or a thesis. If it is very long (usually book length, as mine was) and written to partially satisfy the requirements for the degree of Doctor of Philosophy, it is called a dissertation.

An Expository Research Paper

Exposition is writing that explains. The word *exposition* comes from the Latin word *exponere*, which means "to place out." When you write exposition, you try to place out or set forth specific information. Exposition shows and tells by giving information about a specific topic. The topic can be anything—computers and the Internet, medicine, economics, social studies, history, math, science, or music, for example. In addition to term papers, expository writing can be found in business letters, personal letters, news stories, press releases, textbooks, and wills.

> **You Could Look It Up**
>
> **Exposition** is writing that explains. An **expository research paper** summarizes facts about a topic. The writer does not argue a point or prove a thesis.

An expository research paper summarizes the relevant information about a topic. When you write this kind of research paper, you synthesize into a cohesive whole what you read in different sources. You are serving as a conduit, reporting what others have said. Expository research papers are a great way to present a lot of data in an organized and easy-to-use form. That's why government employees often write research papers about the economy, demographics, transportation, and so forth.

Because your thesis will be original and creative, you won't be able to merely summarize what someone else has written. Instead, you'll have to synthesize information from many different sources to create something uniquely your own.

Ask the Librarian

You can remember that exposition is writing that explains by this memory trick: *exposition = explain.* Both words starts with the same three letters, "exp."

In brief, an expository research paper …

♦ Presents data.

♦ Reports what others said.

♦ Explains or describes.

♦ Summarizes.

♦ Considers *what*.

Model Expository Research Paper

Here is the beginning of an expository research paper on the composer Felix Mendelssohn. The paper was written by Charles Rozakis.

Jakob Ludwig Felix Mendelssohn-Bartholdy was born on February 3, 1809, to Abraham and Lea Mendelssohn in Hamburg, Germany (*Oxford Companion* 1162). He was the second of four children, but he was closer to his older sister Fanny than any of his other siblings. The two of them studied music and played together for many years, and Fanny also composed. Several of the *Songs Without Words* were her works, published under Felix's name because of the family's feeling that it was unbecoming for a woman to engage in public life (Harris 1368).

The family moved to Berlin in 1812, where Felix, at the age of four, began to receive regular piano lessons from his mother. In 1816, Abraham Mendelssohn went to Paris on business and brought his family with him. Throughout their stay, Felix and Fanny had piano lessons with Madame Marie Bigot, who was highly esteemed by both Haydn and Beethoven (*Grove Dictionary* 135). When they returned to Berlin, Abraham put into effect a systematic plan of education for his children.

Under this plan, Karl Wilhelm Ludwig Heyse (father of poet and short story writer Paul Heyse) taught the children general subjects and classical languages; Johann Gottlob Samuel Rosel taught drawing; Ludwig Berger taught piano;

Carl Wilhelm Henning taught violin; and Carl Zelter gave lessons in musical theory and composition. The children were up at 5 A.M. and began their lessons right after breakfast. Abraham Mendelssohn never considered his children too old for his discipline and correction, and Felix could not consider himself his own master until he was twenty-five years old (Harris 1368).

Felix made his first public appearance as a pianist at the age of nine. He debuted with a *Concert militaire* by F. X. Dusek and was met with great success (*Grove Dictionary* 135). On April 11, 1819, he entered the Singakademie as an alto, and on September 10 of that year they performed his setting of the Nineteenth Psalm. He remained a member for many years, even after he became a tenor at age sixteen (Harris 1368).

On March 7, 1820, Felix's piano piece *Recitativo* was published. It is his oldest surviving work. From then until he was thirteen, Felix entered a phase of composing in which he mastered counterpoint and classical forms of music, especially in sonata form (*Grove Dictionary* 135–136).

You see how the writer summarizes information from various sources. This makes it easy for readers to get an authoritative account in an easy-to-read format.

From the Reference Desk

There are four types of writing, often called the "Four Modes of Discourse." They are *exposition, persuasion, description,* and *narration.* Although the "Four Modes of Discourse" are often explained separately in textbooks, they are usually combined in a piece of writing. As you are learning in this chapter, you will base your research paper on either exposition or persuasion (depending on your assignment), purpose, topic, and audience. In addition, you will use description and narration to explain or persuade. *Description* is writing that uses details drawn from the five senses: sight, taste, touch, sound, and smell. *Narration* is storytelling—writing that contains a plot, characters, setting, and point of view. You will most likely use anecdotes (brief narratives) that illustrate and support your point.

A Persuasive Research Paper

Persuasion is writing that appeals to reason, emotion, or ethics (or the sense of right and wrong). Writing that appeals specifically to reason is often called *argumentation*. When you argue a point in writing, you analyze a subject, topic, or issue in order to persuade your readers to think or act a certain way. *The Declaration of Independence* is a persuasive essay; so is the letter to the editor you read this morning in the newspaper. Persuasive writing is also found in critical reviews, editorials, job evaluations, resumés, cover letters (letters written to accompany resumés), and letters of recommendation.

A persuasive research paper argues or proves a thesis, the writer's hypothesis, a theory, or an opinion. Therefore, this type of research paper evaluates a position. When you write a persuasive research paper, you use authoritative evidence to persuade your readers that your argument is valid or at least deserves serious consideration.

You Could Look It Up

Persuasion is writing that appeals to reason, emotion, or ethics (or the sense of right and wrong). A **persuasive research paper,** also called an argumentative research paper, argues or proves a thesis, the writer's hypothesis, a theory, or an opinion.

In brief, a persuasive research paper …

♦ Is organized around a thesis or assertion.

♦ Argues a point.

♦ Supports the assertion with appropriate and relevant details and examples.

♦ Considers *why* and *how*.

Model Persuasive Research Paper

Below is an excerpt from a persuasive research paper on the following thesis statement: *People should make edible insects part of their diet.* The writer argues that insects have a nutritional content superior to many other food sources, that raising insects rather than other protein sources is better for the ecosystem, and that insects taste good. I wrote this paper one night after I swallowed a bug during a bike ride.

Butterflies in My Stomach

In Japan, gourmets relish aquatic fly larvae sautéed in sugar and soy sauce. Venezuelans feast on fresh fire-roasted tarantulas. Many South Africans adore fried termites with cornmeal porridge. Merchants in Cambodia sell cooked cicadas by the bagful. Diners cut off the wings and legs before eating them. People in Bali remove the wings from dragonflies and boil the bodies in coconut milk and garlic.

Insect cuisine may not be standard food in the United States, but Miguel Vilar notes in *Science World* that 80 percent of the world's population savors bugs, either as staples of their everyday diet or as rare delicacies. *Entomophagy* (consuming insects intentionally) has yet to catch on in America and Europe in spite of the superior nutritional content of edible insects compared to other food sources. It's time that changed.

Bugs and Burgers

For example, even fried rather than broiled, grasshoppers contain more than 60 percent protein with about 6 percent of fat per 100 grams (a quarter pound). By comparison, the same sized broiled quarter-pound hamburger contains 18 percent protein with 18 percent fat.

Grasshoppers are the most commonly consumed insect, but wasps have the highest protein content—81 percent—of all edible insects. They are widely consumed in Mexico, and the insect larvae is a popular food in Thailand and Laos. Fried wasps, mixed with boiled rice, sugar, and soy sauce, was a favorite dish of Emperor Hirohito of Japan.

The following chart compares the nutritional content of raw insects with cooked animal food. Protein and fat are listed as the amount in grams per 100 grams (a quarter pound) of meat. Carbohydrates, calcium, and iron amounts are measured in milligrams.

Food	Protein	Fat	Carbohydrates	Calcium	Iron
Crickets	38.7	5.5	5.1	75.8	9.5
Grasshoppers (small)	61.8	6.1	3.9	35.2	5
Grasshoppers (large)	42.9	3.3	2.2	27.5	3
Red ants	59.4	8.3	2.1	43.5	13.6
Giant water beetles	41.7	3.5	2.9	47.8	5.7
Lean beef	18.0	18.3	0	9	2.1
Cod fish	22.9	0.9	0	0.03	1.0

Source: The Eat-a-Bug Cookbook by David Gordon, Ten Speed Press, 1998

Further, insects are rich in necessary vitamins and minerals. As the above chart shows, crickets are packed with calcium, a mineral crucial for bone growth and a key element in the prevention of osteoporosis. Termites and caterpillars (not listed on the chart) are a rich source of iron, a key element in the formation of bone marrow and red blood cells.

Many Advantages

Raising insects is far easier and requires much less space than raising conventional Western protein sources such as cattle, pork, and chicken. For example, thousands of edible termites can be raised in a 6-foot mound; the same number of cattle requires hundreds of acres of grassland.

Consuming insects can also help the ecosystem. "Humans are polluting the earth by using pesticides to eliminate insects," notes retired University of Wisconsin entomologist Gene DeFoliart, reiterating Rachel Carson's findings in her landmark study *Silent Spring*. Not surprisingly, he advocates consuming edible insects that attack plants and keeping artificial chemicals off plant food.

In addition, the amount of food gained from insects is much higher than from a comparable number of cattle and hogs. For every 100 pounds of feed, farmers can raise 10 pounds of beef. Using the same amount of feed, farmers can raise 45 pounds of crickets. It also takes far less time to raise a comparable amount of insects: It requires more than two years to raise a cow from birth to slaughter, but a cricket can lay nearly 2,000 eggs that mature in six weeks. With the mushrooming human population around the world and the prospect of diminishing livestock and fish, insects may be our best hope of feeding everyone.

Finally, we may think of insects as dirty, but they are actually cleaner than other creatures. Grasshoppers and crickets eat fresh, clean plants whereas crabs and lobsters are bottom feeders who eat foul, decomposing materials.

Bugs: They're What's for Dinner

Despite our revulsion at the thought of chomping down on a cricket, there's nothing new about entomophagy. "As long as humans have lived, people have picked up insects and eaten them," says Faith Thayer, an entomologist at the University of Massachusetts, Amherst. More than one million species of insects and worms exist and humans can eat about 1,400 of these species. In many cultures, people also relish the taste of arthropods, especially scorpions and spiders. Our ancestors learned which insects were edible by observing which ones animals chose. Early humans quickly learned that red ants and monarch butterflies were toxic, for example.

Scientists have theorized that entomophagy declined about 4,000 years ago with the rise of agriculture. At that time, insects took on a negative connotation in America and Europe as the destroyers of crops. As a result, what had previously been considered a foodstuff came to be regarded as a pest.

Man Eating Bugs

Will Americans and Europeans catch on to the advantages of eating bugs? The January 2, 1996 *Wall Street Journal* reported on a "small energetic group of entomologists, farmers, and chefs" who are promoting edible insects, a foodstuff known in academic circles as "Microlivestock."

"Food choices are arbitrary," argues food scholar and professor Robert Leonard. What some people consider appropriate foods are simply foods they are used to eating, he maintains. In his research, Leonard has identified what he calls three levels of food.

First, there's a culture's "essential" food. "This is the food without which you have not eaten," says Leonard. To the Chinese, it's rice; to most Americans, it's meat. Next comes "emblematic" food. That's the food that people associate with your culture. Here's where distinctions become less clear. Americans, for example, consider the egg roll the emblematic food of China, while a Chinese person would not agree. The last category is "insider" foods. These are the foods that people inside a culture believe outsiders won't eat—organ meats, seaweed, raw fish, sheep's eyeballs, and insects, for example.

Leonard polled recent immigrants to learn what they classify as American "insider" foods. Among the foods they considered too disgusting to eat were mayonnaise, cheese, grits, breakfast sausages, and the combination of a hamburger, French fries, and a milk shake. Those polled were most repulsed about American fast food because they had difficulty with the concept of washing down ground beef with melted ice cream. Most Americans, in contrast, consider these foods perfectly matched.

American Way, the official magazine of American Airlines, recently carried an article on eating insects. Jane Homan, professor and an entomologist at the University of Washington, takes this as a sign that eating insects is becoming acceptable, even haute cuisine. Dick Reavis, contributing editor of *American Way*, agrees that entomophagy is chic: "It's in style. Now that Mexican restaurants are popular from Bangor to San Diego, the cognoscenti of real Mexican food are seeking out restaurants that serve unadulterated un-European food from Central America and Mexico. Pre-Hispanic or pre-Columbian food it's called, the kinds of dishes Mexicans ate before the region was subdued by the Spanish. Worms [insect larvae] cooked or live, are a big part of pre-Hispanic cuisine, and eating them has become a rite of passage for those who would be intimate with the Mexican past."

The Primal Feast

Manfred Kroger, professor of food science at Penn State University, agrees with Robert Leonard's food classification. "Right now we're driven by the look of what we eat," he notes. However, Kroger sees a change in Americans' perception of what is and is not appropriate to eat. Kroger claims that Americans are in the midst of a food revolution, a change fueled by the craving for more inventive as well as healthful foods. Insects fit the menu on both counts. You know that insects are healthful, but what do they taste like?

Because insects don't have much muscle, the texture is similar to that of a clam. Not surprisingly, each type of insect has its own taste. One type of caterpillar has been compared to a mushroom omelet; a Mexican stinkbug has a pleasant cinnamon flavor despite its unappealing name. Catherine Fowler, a professor of anthropology at the University of Nevada, Reno, described the taste of Pandora moth caterpillars as "very good—like a scrambled egg omelet with mushrooms." Tom Turpin, a professor of entomology at Purdue University, enjoys "chocolate chirpy cookies," chocolate chip cookies with roasted crickets. Gene DeFoliart likes greater wax moth larvae, which taste like bacon when deep fried.

Ready for something delicious as well as nutritious? If so, here's an easy recipe for Grasshopper Tacos.

Ingredients:

$^1/_2$ pound grasshoppers

2 cloves minced garlic

1 lemon

salt

2 ripe avocados, mashed

6 tortillas

Preheat oven to 350°. Roast grasshoppers in a shallow pan for 10 minutes. Toss with garlic, lemon juice, and salt to taste. Spread mashed avocado on tortillas. Sprinkle on grasshoppers. [Source: Department of Entomology, Iowa State University, Ames, Iowa]

Reread this research paper and you will see that the writer considers *why* and *how* as she evaluates. Notice how the writer reaches her own conclusions about the topic. She has formulated a thesis, "Insects are a nutritious, beneficial, and tasty food." She then argues the point by using research. What kind of research? Read on to find out!

What Makes an Effective Research Paper?

Whether you're writing an expository or a persuasive research paper, all research papers share the same qualities. With apologies to Dave Letterman, here are my top 10 characteristics of an effective research paper.

1. Focuses on an appropriate and interesting subject
2. Narrows the subject to a topic that suits the purpose and audience
3. Contains a clear thesis (main idea)
4. Supports the thesis with authoritative evidence
5. Presents the evidence as direct quotations, paraphrases, and summaries
6. Gives credit for all evidence in the correct format
7. Follows a clear method of organization
8. Shows evidence of original thinking
9. Is typed and formatted according to the conventions of the research paper
10. Includes a Works Cited page

You'll learn more about each of these characteristics in subsequent chapters.

Different Sources for Research

"Just the facts, ma'am," the detectives say, and when it comes to research, there are a lot to choose from. Possible sources include the following:

- Websites
- Books
- Reference books
- Periodicals (magazines and newspapers)
- Journals and diaries
- Government documents
- Surveys
- Interviews

These sources can be divided into two categories: *primary* and *secondary sources*. It's important to know the distinction between these two types of sources because each one has its advantages and its disadvantages. In addition, teachers and professors will often specify a mix between the two types. Let's look at each type of source in greater detail.

Primary Sources: Information Straight from the Horse's Mouth

Primary sources are created by direct observation. The writers participated in or observed the events they describe. Primary sources include the following:

- Autobiographies
- Diaries
- Eyewitness accounts
- Experiments (especially scientific experiments)
- Government documents
- Historical records and documents
- Interviews
- Journals
- Letters
- Oral histories
- Maps prepared by direct observation
- Photos taken at the scene
- Surveys

> **You Could Look It Up**
>
> **Primary sources** are based on direct observation or participation, while **secondary sources** are created from primary sources.

Secondary Sources: Reported After the Fact

Secondary sources are written by people with indirect knowledge. These writers had to rely on primary sources or other secondary sources for their information. Secondary sources include the following:

- Abstracts
- Almanacs
- Biographies

- Book reviews

- Books written by nonparticipants

- Encyclopedias

- Government documents

- Literary criticism

- Most newspaper and magazine articles

- Textbooks (some textbooks may contain primary sources)

From the Reference Desk

Currently, about 50,000 books and 10,000 magazines are published every year in America alone. Every day, 7,000 scientific studies are written; *one* daily edition of the *New York Times* contains more information than an educated person in the sixteenth century absorbed in his or her entire life. There is so much information that even the huge Library of Congress in Washington, D.C., fears the downpour. To deal with the onslaught of new information, the library is converting much of its holdings into digital form. The new collection, called the "National Digital Library," will become the most extensive source of information for the National Information Infrastructure, the so-called "Information Superhighway." It is estimated that the amount of information produced will double every two years.

The Strengths and Weaknesses of Primary and Secondary Sources

The words *primary* and *secondary* can be misleading. The word *primary* may make you think that primary sources are better than secondary sources; after all, they're the ones called "primary." However, both primary and secondary sources have their strengths and weaknesses. The following chart lays it all out for you.

	Strengths	Weaknesses
Primary sources	May provide facts not available from other sources	May be affected by author's bias
	Often have an immediacy and freshness not available from other sources	May lack critical distance
	Present thrill of discovery	May contain inaccuracies

continues

continued

	Strengths	**Weaknesses**
Secondary sources	May offer a broader perspective than primary sources	Tend to be less immediate
	May be easier to use because of editing, footnotes, and indexes	May be affected by author's bias
	May resolve inaccuracies	May contain inaccuracies

Lost in (Cyber)Space

When you work with old primary sources or those written in foreign languages and then translated, be sure to get a scholarly edition. Look for a book produced by a reputable publishing house such as W.W. Norton. Their critical editions of major literary works are carefully done.

Although primary sources are not necessarily historically accurate, they do give you as a researcher some strong advantages, including …

◆ The rare opportunity to get acquainted with a historical figure and time through the person's own words

◆ Exposure to the way in which language was used during a period in history

◆ Alternate ways of thinking about events and interpreting them

The following examples show the advantages and disadvantages of using primary sources.

Fame, Fortune, and Food

John Smith wrote one of the most famous primary sources in American literature. His read is utterly fascinating … and it illustrates many of the strengths and weaknesses of primary sources. On one hand, Smith's work gives us a thrilling first-hand account of America before British settlement; on the other hand, his reporting is not always reliable.

John Smith (1579–1631) led the expedition that established in 1607 the first permanent British colony in America, in Jamestown, Virginia. Now, we can't exactly blame Smith for some inaccuracies because he wasn't setting out to write a historical account. Rather, his purpose was to encourage colonization—and not just any colonization.

Smith's main purpose was to attract settlement to the New World for the Virginia Company. He wanted to attract young, strapping men to the vast wilderness of the New World. So Smith provided wild tales of adventure, filled with lots of flying arrows, dramatic rescues, beautiful women, and bountiful feasts. Roll it all into one and you get the sensational story of the lithe Indian princess Pocahontas rescuing John Smith from an especially nasty death.

Describing Smith's account, a literary critic has written: "Of all the Indian tales of early America, that of Captain John Smith's rescue by Pocahontas is the most famous and the most symbolic. That Smith probably made it up matters little; it tells us still what the English wanted us to think about themselves and about the people they were to displace." Although Pocahontas was a real person, Smith's account of this dramatic rescue at her hands is suspect because he did not mention it in two earlier accounts of the same events.

Below is an excerpt from this famous primary source, Smith's rescue by Pocahontas.

> At his entrance before the King, all the people gave a great shout. The Queen of Appamatuck was appointed to bring him a bunch of feathers, instead of a towel, to dry them. Having feasted him after their best barbarous manner they could, a long consultation was held, but the conclusion was, two great stones were brought before Powhatan; then as many as could laid hands on him, and being ready with their clubs to beat out his brains, Pocahontas, the King's dearest daughter, when no entreaty could prevail, got his head in her arms, and laid her own upon his to save him from death; whereat the emperor was contented he should live to make them hatchets, and her bells, beads, and copper, for they thought him as well of all occupations as themselves. For the King himself will make his own robes, shoes, bows, arrows, pots; plant, hunt, or do anything as well as the rest. (from Smith, John. *Generall Historie of Virginia, New England, and the Summer Isles*, 1624)

How can you use this account in your research paper? You balance it with scholarly and trustworthy secondary accounts. Weigh the information in the primary account and the information in the secondary accounts to decide what information is verifiable.

A Not-So-Secret Diary

Now, I don't want you to think that all primary sources are suspect. Consider the case of the diary of Samuel Pepys (pronounced "peeps"). A successful public official in London, Pepys lived from 1633 to 1703. He hobnobbed with the rich and famous, made himself a tidy bundle, and loved to dish the dirt on everyone.

Ask the Librarian

Diaries that have passed into literature are not merely records of what the writer ate for dinner. Rather, these important primary sources provide insight into key historical events and periods. *The Diary of Anne Frank,* for example, gives readers an emotional look into a young Jewish girl's tragic fate at the hands of the Nazis in Nazi-occupied Netherlands during World War II.

Pepys is an unusual figure in the annals of primary sources not only because his fame rests on a single work, but also because he never intended that one work, his *Diary,* to be published. To make sure that no one read his diary, Pepys wrote it in his own private code. The *Diary* was not deciphered until the nineteenth century!

Pepys' diary is important because it gives us firsthand information about life in London during the seventeenth century. Published in 1825, Pepys's *Diary* (all six manuscript volumes of it!) is a spellbinding mix of candid private revelations and astute public commentary. Among other events, Pepys describes the coronation of King Charles II, the Great Plague of 1665, and London's Great Fire of 1666. His diary is an invaluable primary source for its honesty and perceptive detail. Intelligent researchers who want to learn more about life in seventeenth-century London turn first to Pepys. Below is an excerpt from his account of the Great Fire, which he saw up close and personal.

> … At last I met my Lord Mayor in Canning Street, like a man spent, with a handkerchief about his neck. To the King's message he cried, like a fainting woman, "Lord! What can I do? I am spent: people will not obey me. I have been pulling down houses; but the fire overtakes us faster than we can do it." That he needed no more soldiers; and that, for himself, he must go and refresh himself, having been up all night. So he left me, and I him, and walked home, seeing people all almost distracted, and no manner of means used to quench the fire. The houses, too, so very thick thereabouts, and full of matter for burning, as pitch and tar, in Thames Street; and warehouses of oil, and wines, and brandy, and other things. … By this time it was about twelve o'clock: and so home. Soon as dined, and walked through the city, the streets full of nothing but people and horses and carts loaden with goods, ready to run over one another, and remove goods from one burned house to the other ….

Ask the Librarian

Works of art from historical periods can sometimes provide valuable primary sources for researchers. As you research, consider paintings and sculpture as well as photographs and etchings.

Choices, Choices

Primary sources versus secondary sources. Secondary sources versus primary sources. What's a researcher to do? *All* sources are suspect until verified. This concept is so important to the success of your research paper that I devote an entire chapter to it: lucky Chapter 13.

Effective research papers often use a mix of both primary and secondary sources. For example, a research paper arguing the beneficial effects of chocolate might include primary sources such as interviews with physicians and medical researchers as well as secondary sources such as scientific studies, scholarly websites, and journal articles on the subject. You will need to evaluate each source individually, of course.

Some topics, in contrast, require more of one type of material than the other. Always check with your teacher or professor before you start your research to see what mix of primary and secondary materials he or she requires you to use.

The Least You Need to Know

- ◆ The research paper began in America around 1870; today, writing original research papers is mandatory in most high schools and colleges (even some elementary schools!).

- ◆ An expository research paper summarizes information about a topic.

- ◆ A persuasive research paper argues a point or proves a thesis.

- ◆ There are many different sources for research, including websites, reference books, and periodicals.

- ◆ Primary sources (such as diaries, eyewitness accounts, and historical records and documents) are created by direct observation.

- ◆ Secondary sources (such as encyclopedias, literary criticism, and textbooks) are written by people with indirect knowledge.

- ◆ Effective research papers often use a mix of both primary and secondary sources.

Craft a Thesis

In This Chapter

- ◆ Define research paper subjects and topics
- ◆ Choose appropriate subjects for your audience and purpose
- ◆ Evaluate the subjects you choose
- ◆ Narrow your subject into a topic
- ◆ Write thesis statements

Question: What do you call a boomerang that doesn't work?

Answer: A stick.

Question: What do you call a thesis that doesn't work?

Answer: A big disaster.

It's not too often that we're tossed a boomerang, but life *does* throw us a lot of opportunities to write research papers. To make sure that every one of your research papers returns to you with a big "A+" on the top, we'll start the process by laying the groundwork for choosing and evaluating winning subjects and topics.

You'll first learn how to distinguish between subjects and topics. Next, you'll explore which subjects are appropriate for a research paper and which ones aren't—and why. I'll help you find a research paper topic that suits your audience, purpose, and parameters. Then I'll show you how to shape your ideas and write a thesis statement.

Subjects vs. Topics

A *subject* of a research paper is the general content. Subjects are broad and general. For example:

- Health
- Television

- Stocks and bonds
- Travel

You Could Look It Up

A **subject** of a research paper is its general content. A **topic** is the specific issue being discussed.

The *topic* of a research paper, in contrast, is the specific issue being discussed. The following chart shows some possible topics for a research paper developed from the previous subjects. (Not to worry; later in this chapter, you'll learn specific ways to narrow subjects into topics.)

Subject	Possible Topics
Health fad diets	The effect of exercise on longevity
Television	The V-chip in televisions
	The development of television from its beginnings to the present
Stocks and bonds	Day trading, e-trades
Travel	Surcharges for solo travelers
	The effects of airline deregulation

Some of us have greatness thrust upon us; the rest of us have to settle for subjects. If you are given the subject of your research paper (a common occurrence in business and government jobs), you're all set. If not, the ball is in your court. You must decide what subject to research and write about.

Ask the Librarian _____

If you've been assigned a subject you *do not* like, see if you can find an aspect of the subject that you *do* like. Nearly all subjects can be tweaked a bit here and there. Of course, always clear those "tweaks" with the person who assigned the topic *before* you start researching and writing.

Subject to Change

Understand that nearly every subject *can* be researched, but not every subject *should* be researched. After all, why waste your time finding information about a subject that's been ground into meaningless pap? Banal and boring subjects often lead to banal and boring research papers. Give yourself (and your readers) a break by starting with an original subject or an original way of looking at a familiar subject.

Further, don't deliberately choose a subject that you know will antagonize your reader. For instance, if you know that your reader is a vegetarian, you'll probably want to avoid writing a paper on the joys of hunting and eating deer. Likewise, if your reader is a feminist, it's probably not a good idea to choose "Why women should stay home and raise their babies rather than working" or "Women don't belong in the military."

I'm not saying that you should pander to your reader. I *am* saying that you should avoid insulting, degrading, or upsetting your reader by choosing boring or inappropriate subjects.

Audience Analysis

Your audience is the people who are reading your writing. Your research paper is likely to have a *primary audience* and a *secondary audience*.

- The **primary audience** is the person or the group of people to whom you are deliberately aiming and addressing your research paper.

- The **secondary audience** is people who are likely to read your writing as well, although you are not intentionally aiming your writing at their needs.

Your *primary audience* is likely to be your instructor, an advisor, and perhaps a thesis committee. Thus, your primary audience is likely to have considerable expertise in the field. For instance, anyone writing a research paper for me in American literature,

British literature, or Shakespeare better have those ducks in a row because my Ph.D. is in those areas. I know the research material, so I'm a much more critical audience with these papers. Remember that your primary audience is judging your paper. They are the ones grading and evaluating it.

Your *secondary audience* may be your classmates. They are expected to be part of an educated elite who frequently read newspapers, books, and magazines. They attend movies and concerts, too, and are culturally knowledgeable. As a result, your secondary audience is likely to have some general information about the subject you have chosen, and because of your fine research and writing, they will enjoy having a chance to learn something new or to see the subject from a different perspective.

To help you pinpoint your audience, ask yourself the following questions every time you prepare to write a research paper:

◆ Who is my primary audience? For whom am I writing this research paper?

◆ How much do they already know about this topic?

◆ How do they feel about my topic? Are they likely to be receptive, hostile, or somewhere in between?

◆ Who is my secondary audience? Who else is likely to read this paper?

◆ How much do they already know about this topic?

Writing a research paper without identifying your audience is like sending e-mail without an address. How do you know the writing will hit its mark? How do you know it will accomplish your purpose? Always pinpoint your audience before you choose a research subject or write a word of your paper.

From the Reference Desk

A surprising number of famous people worked as librarians between their forays into other fields. For instance, the infamous Casanova (1725–1798) toiled as a private librarian to the royal family for thirteen years. Pope Pius XI (1867–1939) spent nineteen years as the chief librarian at the Ambrosian Library in Milan, Italy. Before he ruled China, Mao Zedong (1893–1976) served as the assistant to the chief librarian at the University of Beijing. J. Edgar Hoover (1895–1972) was a messenger and cataloger at the Library of Congress long before he took over the reigns of the Federal Bureau of Investigation.

Stale Subjects

The right subject can make your paper; the wrong one can break it. How can you tell if you've picked a stinker? Unsatisfactory subjects …

- ◆ Can't be researched because the material doesn't exist or can't be located within a reasonable period of time.

- ◆ Can't be completed within your time frame.

- ◆ Bore you before you've even gotten started.

- ◆ Are certain to bore your reader.

- ◆ Have been beaten to death in countless other research papers.

- ◆ Are inappropriate, offensive, or vulgar.

> **CAUTION**
>
> **Lost in (Cyber)Space**
>
> Beware of hot subjects. "Hot" subjects—very timely, popular issues—often lack the expert attention that leads to reliable information. The books, articles, and interviews on such subjects have often been produced in great haste. As a result, they're not carefully fact-checked.

Stupendous Subjects

"I don't have anything to write about," you moan. "All the good subjects are taken." Quit your kvetching; you know far more than you think you do. Besides, I'm here to help. So take two of the following ideas for the top ten ways to get great research paper subjects, and thank me in the morning!

1. Read subject headings. You can skim the multivolume *Library of Congress Subject Headings* (a reference text) and check the subjects listed on your web browser. Let your fingers do the walking to find interesting and suitable topics.

2. Browse through encyclopedias. Skim online, book, or CD-ROM encyclopedia headings for a rich list of topics. If you see something you like, print or photocopy the page for later reference.

3. Stroll the stacks. Walk around the shelves and see what topics catch your eye. Or spend an afternoon in a bookstore to see what topics strike your fancy.

4. Consider textbooks. Pick a field that intrigues you and check out a few textbooks on that topic. Read the table of contents; leaf through the pages. Find an idea that piques your interest and delve into it.

5. Ask for suggestions. Talk to other people about research papers they have written. Fellow students, doctors, lawyers, accountants, real estate salespeople,

computer programmers, and other business people are all excellent sources for ideas. Don't crib their ideas, but see where they lead you.

6. Make a list and check it twice. If you've been assigned the paper in a class, jot down all the ideas linked to the subject of the class. For example, if you're taking a sociology class, you might list *working women*, *divorce laws*, *immigration regulations*, and *eating disorders*. One of these might make a good paper.

7. Create graphics. Many writers find that charts, webs, graphs, and other pictures help them generate a slew of ideas. If you are a visual person, write a general topic in the middle of a web and list subtopics that come to mind.

8. Ask questions. If you are given an issue or come up with one on your own, use the five *W*s and *H* (*who*, *what*, *when*, *where*, *why*, and *how*) to help you consider all sides of the topic.

9. Tap your personal interests. If you have a genuine passion for a subject, odds are good that your reader will catch your enthusiasm. For instance, this semester one of my students wrote a persuasive research paper on why all public places such as malls, libraries, and sports arenas should be equipped with portable defibrillators. I knew nothing at all about the topic but found myself entranced by her enthusiasm. And she convinced me that all public places *should* be equipped with portable defibrillators.

10. Read, listen, and watch. Read everything and anything: newspapers, magazines, journals, critical reviews, essays, and matchbook covers. Watch TV, listen to the radio, go to the movies. Inspiration is all around; just tap into it.

Ask the Librarian

The media is an excellent source of research for paper subjects, but rather than focusing on the side everyone else sees, probe a little deeper for the story behind the story. This can help you get an intelligent and unusual slant.

If none of these suggestions work for you, speak to your instructor, teacher, or professor. They are paid to help you learn. By contract, teachers and instructors are often required to offer extra help after school or during office hours, so these are good times to visit. You might also want to visit the tutoring center or writing center and speak to the instructors to see what research topics have worked well for their clients.

You shouldn't pick a subject in a second, but you're not going to have time to dally. If you're stuck in third gear, try these three suggestions to get your engine revving:

♦ Focus on your purpose. Some subjects work best for expository papers; others, for persuasive papers.

◆ Look for topics that have enough information available, but not so much information that you can't possibly dig through it all.

◆ Recognize that not all questions have answers. Dealing with questions that don't have definitive answers can make your paper provocative and intriguing.

Trust me: Choosing a subject isn't as difficult as it may seem because there's so much out there that's interesting.

Evaluating Your Subject

So now you have some ideas for subjects—how can you tell if they're keepers? Ask yourself these questions as you evaluate your catch:

1. How much time do I have? The amount of time you have to write a research paper is vital because it's all too easy to get caught in your research and make it a career choice. I've had students spend so much time delving into their subject that they never actually got around to drafting their paper. So choose a subject that you can complete in the time you've been allotted.

2. How long must my paper be? It will obviously take you much longer to write a 50-page research paper than it will to write a 10-page one. Weigh this consideration as you select a subject. The longer the paper and the less time you have to write, the less leeway you'll have to select a challenging subject that will require more research. And the inverse is equally true: The shorter the paper and the more time you have to write, the more leeway you'll have to select a challenging subject that will require more research.

3. What type of research must I do? As you learned in Chapter 1, there are two main kinds of sources: primary sources and secondary sources. Primary sources include firsthand material such as letters, interviews, and eyewitness accounts. Secondary sources include almanacs, biographies, and encyclopedias. Sometimes, you'll have to use a specific type of source, or a mix. If that's the case, factor it into your subject/choice equation.

4. What are my reader's expectations? As we've already discussed in this chapter, some subjects play better than others. You don't want to parrot back the instructor's own words, but neither do you deliberately want to antagonize your reader. I'm always astonished at the number of times I explain, "I'm fed up to *here* with papers on gun control, euthanasia, and the death penalty"—and I still get papers on gun control, euthanasia, and the death penalty. I crave papers on new topics,

such as cloning, filtering the Internet, and a flat tax. Heck, I'd even be delighted to receive a paper that argues the merits of artificial turf over natural grass.

5. Can I live with this subject? You'll be spending considerable time cuddling up to your subject. Make sure you like each other. For example, when it came time to write my Ph.D. dissertation, I was coerced into writing about a subject that I detested. I knew the topic didn't suit my interests, but my advisor insisted that it was "perfect." It wasn't—and it wasn't even close. I had a miserable two years researching a topic that bored and baffled me. When I graduated and started researching my own books, I chose topics that I found fascinating, such as Laura Ingalls Wilder of *Little House on the Prairie* fame, antiques and collectibles, and the NBA. The research and writing have been a pleasure ever since.

> **Lost in (Cyber)Space**
>
> Warning: Your teacher may make selecting and narrowing a subject part of the research paper process itself. As a result, you may be assessed on how well you choose a subject and narrow it into a topic.

Evaluate your subject carefully to make sure that it fits these criteria. Few things are as disheartening as discovering half-way through your research that your subject just doesn't work. You may want to share your subject with your instructor before you go any further to make sure that you are on the right track.

Narrowing the Subject

So now you have a subject, and it's a lulu. The only problem is size—this baby's as big as a tractor trailer. So you *narrow the subject into a topic* by finding smaller aspects of the topic within the subject area to use as the basis of your research paper.

Earlier I promised you practice in narrowing subjects into topics. And here it is! Following are some subjects that have been narrowed into topics suitable for a research paper of 7 to 10 pages.

Subjects	Topics
Space exploration	The *Challenger*, John Glenn
Social services	Workfare, food stamps
Violence	Gangs in New York City, date rape
Antidepressants	Prozac, antidepressants and children
Intelligence	Intelligence tests, Gardner's Seven Intelligences

Having trouble? To tame that beast of a subject, list subdivisions of the subject to create topics. For example:

Subject	Topics
Special education	Diagnosis and testing
	Placement issues
	"Dump and hope"
	"Inclusion" of special education students in regular classrooms
	Gifted education
	Social promotions
	Summer school
	Costs of special education
	Federal and state laws
	History of special education

Fine-Tuning Your Topic

So the topic still seems too broad. So the topic still seems too narrow. How can you make sure your topic is just right for your purpose and audience? Ask yourself the following questions as you evaluate your topic:

1. Is my topic still too broad? Check your sources. How many pages do they devote to the topic? If it takes other writers a book to answer the question you've posed, your topic is still too big.

2. Is my topic *too* limited? Is the topic perfect for a 350- to 500-word essay? If so, it's too narrow for the typical research paper.

3. Is my topic tedious? If your topic doesn't light your fires before you start writing, you can bet it will bore your audience.

4. Is my topic too controversial? If you're afraid you're going to offend your audience with your topic, don't take the risk. Start with a new topic that suits both your audience and purpose.

5. Is my paper one-sided? If there's only one opinion about your topic or the vast

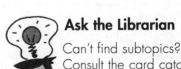

Ask the Librarian

Can't find subtopics? Consult the card catalog, reference books, and textbooks for ideas.

majority of people think the same way as you do, there's no point in arguing the issue.

Practice Makes Perfect

Narrowing your subject into a topic is one of the key elements in writing a successful research paper. Think of your research paper as a house and the topic as the foundation. If the topic is flawed (too big or too small), the house will fall down.

Following are some subjects that need to be narrowed into topics. Try your hand at it now.

Subject	Topic
Africa	
Natural resources	
Food	
Customs	
Smoking	
Genetic engineering	

Here are some possible answers. Compare them to your versions.

Subject	Topic
Africa	Ancient West African kingdoms of Ghana
Natural resources	Rain forests
Food	Chocolate

Subject	Topic
Customs	Personal space
Smoking	Second-hand smoke
Genetic engineering	Genetically engineered foods

The Heart of the Matter: Writing a Thesis Statement

After you've narrowed your topic, it's time to turn your attention to your *thesis statement*, what you are proving in your research paper. An effective thesis statement …

♦ States your main idea, the topic of your research paper.

♦ Reveals your purpose (to explain or persuade).

♦ Shows how your essay will be structured.

♦ Is clear and easy to understand.

♦ Is interesting and will intrigue your reader.

As you draft your thesis statement, consider what you want to explain or prove.

Here are some terrific thesis statements:

♦ Much of the conflict between men and women results from their very different way of using language.

♦ Fairy tales are among the most subversive texts in children's literature.

♦ The brief economic boom of the 1920s had a dramatic impact on the U.S. economy.

♦ The computer revolution has done more harm than good.

♦ Everyone wins with a flat tax: government, business, accountants, and even consumers.

♦ There are striking similarities between the 1920s and the present.

Try several variations of your thesis statement until you have one that says all you need to say. Don't panic: Remember that you're very likely to revise your thesis statement several times as you research, draft, and revise your paper.

You Could Look It Up

The **thesis statement** is the central point you're proving in your research paper.

Try it now. Complete the following worksheet by narrowing each of the topics we looked at before into a thesis statement.

Topic	Thesis Statement
Ancient West African kingdoms of Ghana	_____
Rain forests	_____
	_____
Chocolate	_____
	_____
Personal space	_____
	_____
Second-hand smoke	_____
	_____
Genetically engineered foods	_____

Following are some possible thesis statements. Some are persuasive; others, expository.

Topic	Thesis Statement
Ancient African kingdoms of Ghana	Ancient Ghana was the land of gold. *or* Ancient Ghana was the first of the great West African trading empires.
Rain forests	Rain forests provide us with many irreplaceable resources.
Chocolate	Chocolate has so many beneficial qualities that it can be considered a health food.
Personal space	Accepted distances for personal space are determined by culture.

Topic	Thesis Statement
Second-hand smoke	Smoking should be banned in all public places. *or* Second-hand smoke is far less dangerous than previously thought.
Genetically engineered foods	Genetically engineered foods can help increase crops and alleviate hunger. *or* The benefits of genetically engineered foods outweigh their disadvantages.

CAUTION

Lost in (Cyber)Space

When you write a research paper, you are attempting to find an answer to the question you have posed (or the one that has been given to you). Remember that not all research questions lead to definitive answers. Rather, some questions invite informed opinions based on the evidence you have gathered from research. Dealing with questions that don't have definitive answers can make your paper provocative and intriguing.

Bending the Rules

You've no doubt noticed that I'm showing you a clear, effective, proven way to write a fine research paper. The steps are arranged in chronological order, from start to finish. Be aware, however, that writers rarely move in such neat steps. Although I recommend that you follow the steps in order, don't worry if you find yourself repeating a step, doing two steps at the same time, or skipping a step and then returning to it.

For example, let's say you select and narrow your topic to create a thesis statement. Then you set off to find the information you need. After you start looking at sources, however, you discover that there is a) too much material on the topic or b) not enough material on the topic. In this case, you might go back to the previous step and rework your thesis to accommodate your findings and the new direction your work has taken.

Here's another common occurrence. You may think you have found all the material you need and so have started writing. But half-way

Ask the Librarian

Research may lead you to revise your thesis, even disprove it, but framing it at the very beginning of your research will focus your thinking.

through your first draft, you find that you are missing a key piece of information, a crucial fact, an essential detail. To plug the hole, you'll go back and find the material—even though you are, in effect, repeating a step in the process. That's okay.

I use the method I teach here in my own classes and when I write my own research papers, but remember that one size may not fit all. As a result, you may find yourself adapting the information here to fit your particular writing style.

Study Fine Writing

One of the most effective ways to learn how to research and write a research paper is to study examples of fine writing. Below is the beginning of a persuasive research paper on the following thesis statement: Is language innate in humans? The writer argues that language is innate, at least in part. To decide if language is innate, the writer first examines whether grammar is innate. The writer argues that if a major component of language—grammar—is innate, then language itself should follow. The paper was written by Charles Rozakis.

> Is language innate in humans? I say, at least in part, yes it is. We can say that if a major component of language—grammar—is innate, then language itself should be as well. "Complex language is universal because *children actually reinvent it*, generation after generation," says Pinker. Based on this, I will examine several cases of spontaneous grammar formation by children. If children are capable of creating grammar without any instruction, then such grammar must pre-exist in their brains.

> A new language can come into being as a pidgin. A pidgin is a makeshift jargon containing words of various languages and little in the way of grammar. Some of the best examples of the innate formation of a grammar system are linguist Derek Bickerton's studies of such pidgins. Bickerton noted that indentured workers on plantations in the South Pacific needed to communicate with each other in order to carry out practical tasks. However, the slave masters of the time were wary of their laborers being able to communicate with each other, so they formed mixed groups of laborers who spoke different languages. These laborers created their pidgin from rough mixtures of their own language and the language of the plantation owners. But this formation was not a sudden, conscious act. The formation of a pidgin is a gradual shift from speaking a few words of the owner's tongue to speaking a new language. Pidgins typically have "… no consistent word order, no prefixes or suffixes, no tense or other temporal and logical markers, no structure more complex than a simple clause, and no consistent way to indicate who did what to whom," according to Pinker. A pidgin is not a full, complex, grammatically specific language.

The leap into a "true" language is made when the pidgin speakers have children. These children learn the pidgin as their native language. Amazingly, though, the language they speak has much greater grammatical complexity. Such children use a consistent word order, prefixes or suffixes, tenses to indicate past or future events, complex sentence structures, and similar grammatical devices the pidgin lacked. This newly formed, "true" language is called a creole.

According to Bickerton, since the children have created the creole largely on their own, without formal training or even complex language input from their parents, they must have some innate mental machinery that forms grammar. As evidence of this, he also notes that creoles that are mixtures of different languages tend to be uncannily similar, sometimes even to the point of having the same basic grammar. Additionally, the mistakes some children make while learning more established languages show this basic grammar as well, suggesting that there is an underlying grammatical structure imprinted on the human mind—one that children "default" to.

While there are currently no societies where we can observe creolization occurring with a spoken language, we can observe the creolization of sign languages for the deaf. Since 1979, in Nicaragua, children at schools for the deaf have essentially formed a pidgin. None of them had a real signing system, so they pooled their collections of makeshift gestures into what is now called the Lenguaje de Signos Nicaragüense (LSN). Like any spoken pidgin, LSN is a collection of jargon that has no consistent grammar, and everyone who uses it uses it differently.

When younger children joined the school, after LSN existed, they creolized it into what is called Idioma de Signos Nicaragüense (ISN). While LSN involves a lot of pantomime, ISN is much more stylized, fluid and compact. And children who use ISN all use it the same way—the children had created a standardized language without need for textbooks or grammar classes. Many grammatical devices, such as tenses and complex sentence structures, that didn't exist in LSN, were introduced by the children into ISN.

Jenny Singleton and Elissa Newport's study of a deaf boy they called Simon, who was born of two deaf parents, shows that only one child is needed to creolize a language. Both of Simon's parents had learned American Sign Language later in life, and had not fully mastered many of the complex grammatical features of the language. Simon grew up being exposed to his parents' problematic signing. Simon was very similar to the child of pidgin speakers, and true to Bickerton's theories, he essentially created grammar where there was none. His signing was far better than his parents', including grammatical devices they had never mastered but he used perfectly and effortlessly. For example, while his parents were unable to properly combine verb inflections, Simon essentially reinvented the ASL system of superimposing two inflections onto a single verb in a specific order.

As these examples show, children can create grammar—and the grammar created by different children is very similar. If this is possible, the grammar must exist in their minds from birth, hard-wired into the complex computer that is the human mind. And if grammar pre-exists in the brain, the basis of complex language must as well.

Reread this research paper and you will see that the writer considers *why* and *how* as he evaluates. Notice how the writer reaches his own conclusions about the topic.

From the Reference Desk

I interviewed the writer (one of the advantages of hiring your son to hand over his A+ college papers). Here's what he said: "When I revised this brief research paper, I clarified my thesis statement and removed the term 'instinct,' as it wasn't really what I wanted to say. I moved the topic sentence of the second paragraph to the beginning of that paragraph. I added several examples to the third paragraph and tried to clarify my sentences throughout the essay. And I almost completely rewrote my closing paragraph to make it more clear and concise."

The Least You Need to Know

- A subject of a research paper is its general content. A topic is the specific issue being discussed.

- Choose a subject you like. Be practical, shun overly timely subjects, and recognize that not all questions have answers (but that's okay).

- Every subject *can* be researched, but not every subject *should* be researched. Choose appropriate subjects for your audience and purpose.

- Narrow your subject into a topic that fits the assignment by finding smaller aspects of the topic within the subject area to use as the basis of your research paper.

- The thesis statement is the central point you're proving in your research paper. Effective thesis statements state your main idea, reveal your purpose (to explain or persuade), and show how your essay will be structured.

- Adapt my method to fit your individual writing style.

Chapter 3

Manage the Project

In This Chapter

- ◆ Discover how to allocate your time efficiently
- ◆ Create a schedule
- ◆ Draft working outlines for persuasive research papers
- ◆ Draft working outlines for expository research papers

Research has a way of taking a lot longer than anyone imagines. One web page leads to another and another and another … and suddenly, you've been staring at that screen for two hours and you don't have anything but a backache to show for it. Leafing through scholarly journals, viewing an educational video, conducting an interview—all aspects of research eat up your days and nights.

In this chapter, you'll learn how to budget your time so you can get your research paper completed by the deadline. The handy-dandy time schedules I provide here will make it easier for you to allocate your time from the beginning of your project. That way, you'll work smarter, not harder. This chapter covers potential problems so you can learn how to deal with emergencies, too. Then I'll show you how to plan your research paper through a working outline—whether you're writing a persuasive or an expository research paper. By the end of this chapter, you'll be ready to hit the ground running!

Time Flies When You're Writing a Research Paper

You don't have enough time to do your laundry (how *does* it pile up so fast?), so how are you going to find the time to write your research paper? Here's the brutal truth: You *won't* have the time you need. Nonetheless, the task has to get done—and within a set time frame. That's why it's especially important that you plan the task from the get-go.

I'm presenting the steps involved in writing a research paper in chronological order, but don't worry if you don't follow the steps in order. Remember that all writers compose differently. You may double-back, combine two steps, or even omit a step or two. That's okay, if it works for you.

Here are the steps you'll complete as you write a research paper:

1. Select a topic.

2. Narrow the topic.

3. Write the thesis statement.

4. Outline your paper.

5. Research material.

6. Take notes on material.

7. Draft rough copies.

8. Find more sources, if necessary.

9. Integrate source materials.

10. Document sources.

11. Do Works Cited page.

12. Write frontmatter, backmatter, title page.

13. Revise, edit, proofread.

14. Keyboard your paper.

15. Deal with catastrophes.

That last step is a dilly, so it's crucial that you build in time to deal with it. Computers crash; the dog eats your rough draft. People get sick and you have to help out. Work in other classes piles up; perhaps you are forced to take a job to make ends meet.

Sometimes the *one* book you really need isn't available from the library; more than one website has been known to mysteriously vanish into the Bermuda Triangle of cyberspace.

To help you deal with these problems and all the emergencies that crop up, I've worked out some time-allocation plans that you can follow as you prepare your research paper. Each plan includes some "air," that crucial extra time, so your back won't be up against the wall as the deadline looms.

In the spaces provided, note the day you started and completed each step. You may want to photocopy these plans so you can use them again as you write different research papers.

Just because you are given eighty days or sixty days or forty days to complete your paper does not mean that you must use all of that time to work on it. Choose the plan that works best for you. Weigh the importance of the paper, your level of experience, and the difficulty of the topic as you decide which schedule to follow.

When You're Given Sixteen Weeks

Many professors (yours truly included) assign their research papers the first day of class to give clever well-organized students like *you* the opportunity to get a leg up on the crushing college workload. Because the average semester runs about sixteen weeks, that gives you the longest possible lead time on a college research paper. Figure you have about eighty days in which to produce a first-class term paper.

If you have the entire semester in which to write a research paper, don't get too comfortable. With that much time, it's human nature to get a little complacent. "This paper will be a piece of cake because I have so much time," you might think. Not so fast, my friend.

With a long lead time, it's tempting to leave the assignment to the last minute. After all, you do have *plenty* of time. But "plenty of time" is relative, like "having *plenty* of money" and "losing a *little* hair." Time, like money and hair, goes faster than you think. To prevent serious problems later in the semester, use my little chart below. Follow the chart to make sure that you work at a steady pace.

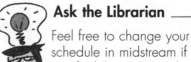
Ask the Librarian

Feel free to change your schedule in midstream if you find that you need more time or less time. If in doubt, err on the side of allowing more time.

Task	Days	Date Started	Date Ended
1. Select topic	3 _____	_____	_____
2. Narrow topic	1 _____	_____	_____
3. Write thesis statement	1 _____	_____	_____
4. Outline	2 _____	_____	_____
5. Research	14 _____	_____	_____
6. Take notes	13 _____	_____	_____
7. Draft	15 _____	_____	_____
8. Find more sources	5 _____	_____	_____
9. Integrate materials	2 _____	_____	_____
10. Document sources	2 _____	_____	_____
11. Write Works Cited	1 _____	_____	_____
12. Write frontmatter	1 _____	_____	_____
13. Revise, edit, proofread	5 _____	_____	_____
14. Keyboard	5 _____	_____	_____
15. Extra time	10 _____	_____	_____

When You're Given Twelve Weeks

We're talking three months, so you have no excuse for not getting started immediately … after you finish reading this chapter. Far too many of my students think, "I've got time to spare, so instead of working on my research paper, I'll pump iron/catch up on my Napster backlog/take a nourishing snack to my grandmother who lives in the woods." Come semester's end, I get the excuses: "My muscles ached too much to type," "I got arrested for illegally downloading music," and "A wolf ate my grandmother."

And my personal favorite: "I just lost track of the time."

CAUTION

Lost in (Cyber)Space

Do not count weekends as working days. First, you need time to recharge your batteries and have a life. Second, if you do find yourself really pressed for time, you'll still have Saturday and Sunday in your pocket as insurance.

Now that you've been warned, if you have three months in which to write a research paper, why not use it this way?

Task	Days	Date Started	Date Ended
1. Select topic	3 _____	_____	_____
2. Narrow topic	2 _____	_____	_____
3. Write thesis statement	1 _____	_____	_____
4. Outline	2 _____	_____	_____
5. Research	8 _____	_____	_____
6. Take notes	8 _____	_____	_____
7. Draft	10 _____	_____	_____
8. Find more sources	4 _____	_____	_____
9. Integrate materials	3 _____	_____	_____
10. Document sources	2 _____	_____	_____
11. Write Works Cited	1 _____	_____	_____
12. Write frontmatter	2 _____	_____	_____
13. Revise, edit, proofread	6 _____	_____	_____
14. Keyboard	3 _____	_____	_____
15. Extra time	5 _____	_____	_____

When You're Given Eight Weeks

If you have eight weeks (forty days) in which to complete a research paper, I suggest that you allocate your time this way.

Task	Days	Date Started	Date Ended
1. Select topic	2 _____	_____	_____
2. Narrow topic	2 _____	_____	_____

continues

continued

Task	Days	Date Started	Date Ended
3. Write thesis statement	1 _____	_____	_____
4. Outline	1 _____	_____	_____
5. Research	4 _____	_____	_____
6. Take notes	5 _____	_____	_____
7. Draft	7 _____	_____	_____
8. Find more sources	3 _____	_____	_____
9. Integrate materials	3 _____	_____	_____
10. Document sources	1 _____	_____	_____
11. Write Works Cited	1 _____	_____	_____
12. Write frontmatter	1 _____	_____	_____
13. Revise, edit, proofread	1 _____	_____	_____
14. Keyboard	2 _____	_____	_____
15. Extra time	2 _____	_____	_____

Ask the Librarian

Using a laptop computer can shave days off the time it takes to write a research paper. It's especially helpful for taking notes and organizing information. More on this later.

When You're Given Six Weeks

If you have six weeks (thirty working days) in which to complete a research paper, try the following timetable.

Task	Days	Date Started	Date Ended
1. Select topic	1 _____	_____	_____
2. Narrow topic	1 _____	_____	_____
3. Write thesis statement	1 _____	_____	_____
4. Outline	3 _____	_____	_____
5. Research	3 _____	_____	_____
6. Take notes	4 _____	_____	_____
7. Draft	3 _____	_____	_____
8. Find more sources	2 _____	_____	_____
9. Integrate materials	1 _____	_____	_____
10. Document sources	1 _____	_____	_____
11. Write Works Cited	1 _____	_____	_____
12. Write frontmatter	1 _____	_____	_____
13. Revise, edit, proofread	2 _____	_____	_____
14. Keyboard	2 _____	_____	_____
15. Extra time	10 _____	_____	_____

When You're Given Four Weeks

If you have one month (twenty working days) in which to complete a research paper, the following schedule works well. How can I be so smug? Many of my most successful students report good results from using this timetable!

Task	Days	Date Started	Date Ended
1. Select topic	$^1/_2$ _____	_____	_____
2. Narrow topic	$^1/_2$ _____	_____	_____
3. Write thesis statement	$^1/_2$ _____	_____	_____

continues

continued

Task	Days	Date Started	Date Ended
4. Outline	$^{1}/_{2}$ _____	_____	_____
5. Research	2 _____	_____	_____
6. Take notes	2 _____	_____	_____
7. Draft	3 _____	_____	_____
8. Find more sources	2 _____	_____	_____
9. Integrate materials	1 _____	_____	_____
10. Document source	$^{1}/_{2}$ _____	_____	_____
11. Write Works Cited	$^{1}/_{2}$ _____	_____	_____
12. Write frontmatter	1 _____	_____	_____
13. Revise, edit, proofread	3 _____	_____	_____
14. Keyboard	1 _____	_____	_____
15. Extra time	2 _____	_____	_____

Plan Ahead

At this stage of the game, you're probably not totally sure where you're going with your research paper. You've found a subject, narrowed it into a topic, and narrowed it further still into a thesis statement. But odds are that you've yet to firm up your thinking. Relax. You're right where you're supposed to be.

Ask the Librarian

In many instances, it's actually easier to have *less* time in which to write a research paper, because you know that you're under pressure to produce.

If you're writing a persuasive research paper, you might even end up switching sides in the debate that you've set up! For example, if you plan to argue that juvenile offenders should be tried as adults, you might find that after you complete much of your research, you feel that just the opposite is true. That's fine—your goal is to write a logical and persuasive research paper, not to stick to a side that you can't support.

Before you begin your research, I recommend that you draft a *working outline*.

A working outline …

◆ Provides you with a general plan for your research paper.

◆ Gives you an easy way to improve your method of organization.

◆ Lets you change and revise your thinking.

◆ Allows you to get feedback easily from your instructor, classmate, co-worker, or supervisor at different stages in the process.

◆ Helps you begin your research in a logical direction.

◆ Saves you time.

You Could Look It Up

A **working outline** shows how you will organize the information in your research paper. Revise the outline as you re-search and draft to accommodate new information and your rethinking on the topic.

So don't throw up your hands in despair and moan, "Where *do* I start?" Start with a working outline.

And not to worry: No one expects you to have all the information you need at this stage. Far from it! When you don't know what to write for a specific entry, just leave it blank. You will go back later and fill it in.

I strongly suggest that you draft your working outlines on your computer. That way, you can revise easily, refer to previous versions, and produce clean copies. *Do not* erase each previous outline; rather, save each file as follows: outline1.doc, outline2.doc, outline3.doc, outline4.doc, and so on. Print out each outline with its header (such as outline1.doc) and staple them together. That way, you can refer to the older outlines as you refine your topic.

Working Outlines for Persuasive Research Papers

There are several ways to arrange the information in a persuasive research paper. My two favorite ways are the "chunk" method and the "slice" method. Let's look at each method now.

The "Chunk" Method

I call this the "chunk" method because you deal with the main points in chunks. Use the following order:

◆ All of *their* side (the opposition)

◆ All of *your* side

Notice that you present the opposing points first. This way, you acknowledge that there *is* another side. You use the rest of your paper to persuade the reader that the opposition is wrong or that the opposition has some merit, but that your side is stronger.

Use the "chunk" method when …

◆ You have more points on your side than the opposition.

◆ The opposition is rather weak.

◆ Your audience is neutral or receptive to your ideas.

The following model outline shows a persuasive research paper developed through the "chunk" method.

Persuasive Essay Structure 1: "Chunk" Method

I. Introduction

     A. Intriguing opening (such as a quote or anecdote)

     B. Thesis sentence

     C. Summary of the opposition

     D. Summary of your side

     E. Transition or lead-in sentence to the next paragraph

II. Background (if necessary)

III. Opposition (one to two points)

     A. Point 1

     B. Point 2

IV. Your side of the argument (two to four points)

     A. Refute opposition point 1

     B. Refute opposition point 2

     C. Point 3

     D. Point 4

V. Conclusion

     A. Summarize the opposition

     B. Summarize your side

     C. Make your point

From the Reference Desk

When you are addressing readers who disagree with your thesis, start with common ground, areas of agreement. For example, if you are arguing that prescription drugs are overpriced and your readers are shareholders in a pharmaceutical company, you might argue that such companies have a moral responsibility to help indigent people in third-world countries get access to crucial medications, such as HIV "cocktails." Because most readers would agree with this statement, they are likely to be more inclined to consider your argument that prices for prescription drugs must be reduced.

The "Slice" Method

I call this the "slice" method because you deal with the main points in slices, as follows:

◆ Point one

   Their side (the opposition)

   Your side

◆ Point two

   Their side (the opposition)

   Your side

◆ Point three

   Their side (the opposition)

   Your side

The following model outline shows a persuasive research paper developed through the "slice" method.

Persuasive Essay Structure 2: "Slice" Method

I. Introduction

   A. Intriguing opening (such as a quote or anecdote)

   B. Thesis sentence

   C. Summary of points to follow

   D. Transition or lead-in sentence to the next paragraph

II. Background (if necessary)

III. Your first main point

    A. Opposition

    B. Refute the opposition and present your side

IV. Your second main point

    A. Opposition

    B. Refute the opposition and present your side

V. Your third main point

    A. Opposition

    B. Refute the opposition and present your side

VI. Conclusion

    A. Summarize the opposition

    B. Summarize your side

    C. Make your point

If you're having a hard time finding the most suitable organizational plan for your ideas, try jotting each main topic on scraps of paper or index cards. Arrange the scraps in various ways to see which arrangement makes the most sense, given your purpose and readers.

Use the "slice" method when …

◆ You have the same number of points on your side and on the opposition's side.

◆ The opposition is rather strong.

◆ Your audience is likely to be hostile to your ideas.

Variations on a Theme

Now that you know the basic format for a persuasive research paper, you can vary it. For example, you may choose to play down the opposition or devote far more space to your strongest points. Obviously, your strongest points will be backed up by the most persuasive research, including statistics and facts.

In addition, the placement of your points can increase the effectiveness of your argument. Many writers place their strongest point last for emphasis. The format looks like this:

second strongest point

↓

weaker points

↓

strongest points

Another variation involves building your argument to its strongest point, like this:

weakest point

↓

stronger points

↓

strongest point

There are numerous variations. Always choose the one that suits your purpose and audience.

Working Outlines for Expository Research Papers

Expository research papers (as with any expository essays) can be organized in many different ways. You've heard my mantra before: Choose the method that suits your topic and audience. For example, you may want to use chronological order (the order of time) if all the ideas are of equal rank. By arranging your points in time order, you sidestep the issue of which ones are most important.

The following chart summarizes the most common methods of organization for expository research papers.

Method of Organization	Definition
Cause and effect	Explains why something happened; shows the results
Chronological order	Traces events in time order
Classify and divide analysis	Sorts topics by categories and analyzes each class

continues

continued

Method of Organization	Definition
Compare and contrast	Shows similarities and differences
Order of importance	Arranges details from most to least important, least to most important, and so on
Problem and solution	Defines an issue and presents answers
Process analysis	Explains "how to" complete a process

The following generic outline shows how to arrange your details point by point.

General Expository Outline Format

I. Introduction

      A. Intriguing opening (such as a quote or anecdote)

      B. Thesis sentence

      C. Summary of your main points

      D. Transition or lead-in sentence to the next paragraph

II. Your first point

      A. Topic sentence

      B. Examples from your research

      C. Examples from your research

      D. Conclusion

III. Your second point

      A. Topic sentence

      B. Examples from your research

      C. Examples from your research

      D. Conclusion

IV. Your third point

      A. Topic sentence

      B. Examples from your research

      C. Examples from your research

      D. Conclusion

V. Conclusion

    A. Topic sentence

    B. Summary of first point

    C. Summary of second point

    D. Summary of third point

    E. Conclusion

Whichever outline you use to organize your material, you'll find it an invaluable way to organize your thoughts and track your research.

The Least You Need to Know

- Research has a way of taking a lot longer than you think, so budget your time carefully.

- Create and use a schedule to help you get your research paper completed on time.

- Before you begin your research, draft a working outline. Choose the method of organization that best suits your purpose, audience, and topic.

- Use the "chunk" or "slice" method for persuasive research papers.

- Expository research papers (as with any expository essays) can be organized in many different ways.

Chapter 4

Record, Refine, and Research

In This Chapter

- ◆ Make bibliography cards to track your findings
- ◆ Create a working bibliography and an annotated bibliography
- ◆ Learn ways to make your search easier, faster, and better
- ◆ Use key words
- ◆ Use Boolean logic

Lost those car keys? They're probably somewhere in the kitchen. Or the dining room. Or maybe in your coat pocket. Lost the luggage on a connecting flight? You're in deep trouble, kiddo. As you've learned the hard way, some searches are easy, but others don't go quite as well. In this chapter, you'll learn the basics of searching for research material. These include keeping track of what you find, refining your search, identifying key words, and using Boolean logic. Many of these ideas will be developed in later chapters, but an overview always helps put things into perspective.

Keeping Track of Your Research

In Chapter 3, we discussed the steps you'll complete as you write a research paper. The first four steps go like this:

1. Select a topic.

2. Narrow the topic.

3. Write the thesis statement.

4. Research the material.

Zero in on Step 4: *Research material.* Now you're almost ready to begin researching. Soon you'll find relevant and reliable web pages, read authoritative magazine and journal articles, take pertinent books out of the library, and perhaps conduct a survey or interviews. The process goes like this:

1. Look up material on the web, in research books, and so on.

2. Make one bibliography card per source.

3. Get your hands on the material. This includes downloading articles, bookmarking web pages, printing the material, and taking out library books, for instance.

4. Read the material.

5. Take notes on the material.

By locating all the material first, you make sure that there is enough information available to use as the basis for your research paper. If you cannot find the material, you might be looking in the wrong places or the material might not be available. This gives you time to review research methods, access different databases, or change your thesis statement, if necessary.

And no need to panic: No one expects you to find *all* the information you need at once. As you keep researching and taking notes, you'll go back to the library or back online and get more sources. Just be sure to make up a new bibliography card for each source you find.

Regardless of the different methods you use, you will get piles and piles of great stuff. And here's the problem: If you don't have a way to track the information you find, the stuff has a nasty way of getting lost. Scraps of paper noting addresses for websites and call numbers for books seem to vanish into thin air. This is not going to happen to you. Not on my watch!

I lose my keys all the time, sometimes I even lose my car in the mall parking lot, but I never ever lose track of material that I researched. That's because I have a great system for keeping track of research. And now I'll share it with you. My foolproof system is based on making *bibliography cards.*

Record: Make Bibliography Cards

As you find each source on your topic, make a bibliography card for it. The word *bibliography* comes from two roots: *biblio* and *graphy*. *Biblio* means "book"; *graphy* means "writing." A bibliography, then, is nothing more than a fancy way of saying "a list of books." For our purposes, we're going to define a bibliography as "a list of all the sources you find."

You will make bibliography cards to record publication and location information for each and every source you find. Use one card per source.

To do so, start by buying a pack of 3×5 index cards. These are your bibliography cards. Cards enable you to keep the most promising sources and discard the irrelevant ones at your convenience. In addition, bibliography cards can easily be arranged in alphabetical order when the time comes to type a Works Cited page for inclusion at the end of your paper.

> **You Could Look It Up**
>
> **Bibliography** cards note all the information you need to document a source.

There are several different bibliographic styles, ways of documenting sources. As you write your bibliography cards, follow the documentary style assigned by your instructor or preferred by the discipline in which you are writing.

♦ Use the *Modern Language Association* (MLA) style for research papers in the humanities, including literature, history, the arts, and religion.

♦ Use the *American Psychological Association* (APA) style for research papers in the social sciences, such as psychology and sociology.

Bibliography Cards for Electronic Sources

On each card, note as many items from the following list as are relevant and available for each source. Only rarely will you include all of the following information—or need to.

♦ Title of the site or literary work (novel, poem, short story, textbook, and so forth)

♦ Name of the author, editor, compiler, translator, or site maintainer (if available and relevant)

♦ Publication information for any print version

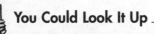

You Could Look It Up

Angle brackets (< >) around a text indicate that all the characters within the brackets must be treated as a single unit, without any space between them.

♦ Date of electronic posting or latest update, whichever is more recent

♦ Name of organization or institution sponsoring the website

♦ Date that you accessed the source

♦ URL, written in *angle brackets.* These brackets look like this: < >. They are located on the lower-right corner of your keyboard, above the comma and period.

Here are some sample cards in MLA format.

The following bibliography card records a website for an online book.

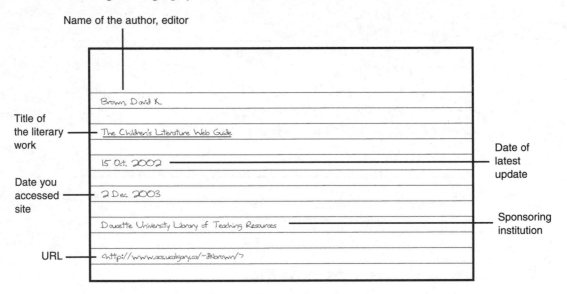

Name of the author, editor

Title of the literary work

Date you accessed site

URL

Brown, David K.

The Children's Literature Web Guide

15 Oct. 2002

2 Dec. 2003

Doucette University Library of Teaching Resources

<http://www.acs.ucalgary.ca/~dkbrown/>

Date of latest update

Sponsoring institution

A bibliography card for a website for an online book.

Ask the Librarian

If you are submitting your paper online, you can document sources in a new way—by using hypertext links. Electronic journals published on the web are already replacing traditional notes, Works Cited, and other supporting information with links to the documents being cited. The link appears in blue on the page and, when clicked, takes the reader directly to the source.

The following bibliography card records an article published in an online journal.

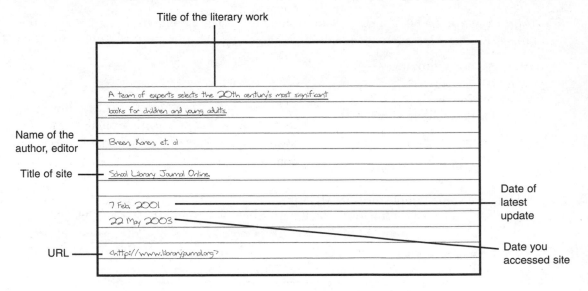

A bibliography card for an article published in an online journal.

The following bibliography card records an e-mail message.

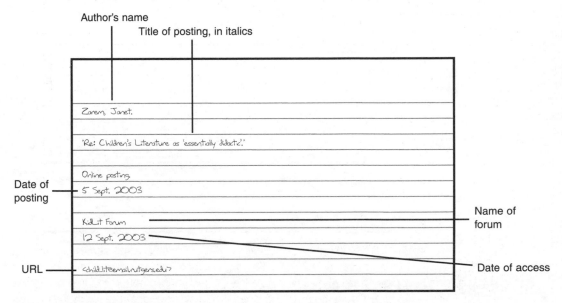

A bibliography card for an e-mail message.

Bibliography Cards for Books

On this type of bibliography card, note anything you are going to need to retrieve the book. Relevant information includes the following:

◆ Author/editor

◆ Title

◆ Place of publication

◆ Publisher

◆ Date of publication

◆ Call number

◆ For your own information, the library where you found the book. This last detail is very important, because it can save you a great deal of time and effort if you are using more than one library. (You will not note the library on your Works Cited page; this information is for your use only.)

Here's a model in MLA format.

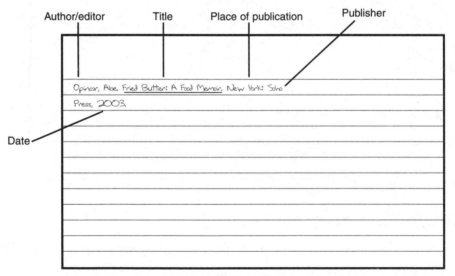

A model bibliography card for a book in MLA format.

Bibliography Cards for Periodicals

On the bibliography card, include the following information. You may also want to note whether the article contained pictures or illustrations that you may want to consult as you read the selection.

- ◆ Author
- ◆ Title of the article
- ◆ Title of the periodical
- ◆ Date of the article
- ◆ Volume number
- ◆ Page numbers
- ◆ Library (for your own use)

Study the following model card in MLA format.

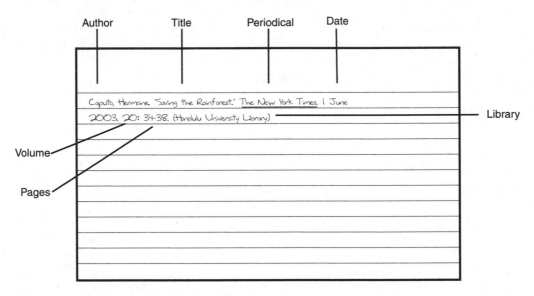

A bibliography card for a periodical.

Bibliography Cards for Interviews

On these cards, include as much of the following information as you can locate:

- ◆ The name of the person you interviewed
- ◆ The person's area of expertise
- ◆ The person's address and telephone number
- ◆ The date of the interview

Here's a model in the MLA format for you to use as you make your own cards.

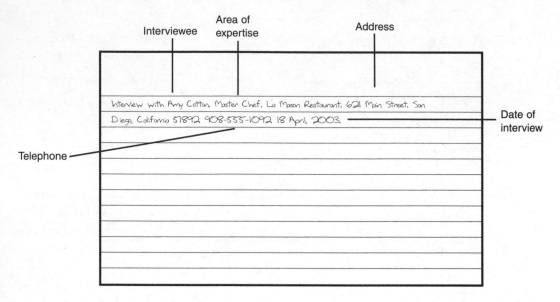

Interviewee | Area of expertise | Address

Interview with Amy Cotton. Master Chef. La Mason Restaurant. 621 Main Street. San
Diego, California 51892. 908-555-1092. 18 April, 2003.

Telephone

Date of interview

A bibliography card for an interview.

Ask the Librarian

Seems like there are a lot of picky little details on bibliography cards? Not to
worry. With the exception of an interview card, when you make a bibliography
card, you're just copying the information right from the citation you find online, in
a database, or a card catalog. You don't have to invent anything at all: The information should be right there for you to pick up.

Save Time!

I've just shown you how to copy information you find on a computer screen, in a
periodical, or in a book onto individual bibliography cards. This is the traditional way
to make bibliography cards and it works fine. My shortcuts, however, are faster and
easier. (That's why I call them "shortcuts.") I have two: cut-and-paste and keyboard
bibliography cards.

Cut-and-Paste Cards

You can easily copy the information from the screen to the card, but it's time-consuming. Further, there's a chance you might copy the information incorrectly and make a mistake. Instead of copying, follow these steps to make bibliography cards:

1. Look up sources on a computer.

2. Print the page listing the sources.

3. Cut the page apart, one source per strip of paper.

4. Staple, tape, or glue one source per card.

Voilà! You have bibliography cards. Of course, for this method to work, you must have a scissors and a stapler or tape. That's easy if you're working from home. However, if you plan to work from a public or school library, bring these office supplies with you. Librarians are not in the business of lending office supplies.

Keyboard Cards

Some people prefer to make their "bibliography cards" on a computer. I'm one of these people. To make a bibliography card on a computer, simply block-and-copy all the information onto the card rather than handwrite it. Always arrange the information on the page so it appears to be a 3×5 card. This makes it easy to sort the cards and work with them.

This method has several advantages. First, you can update, alphabetize, and correct your cards as you go along. Second, at the end of the project, you can rework this file to make it into your Works Cited list of sources.

However, be sure to back up your "bibliography cards" on floppy disks. In addition, print out hard copies as you work. This way, you won't lose your material if your hard drive crashes or the file develops a glitch.

Also be sure to store your bibliography cards in a safe place. If you are using traditional index cards, a file box is ideal. If you are keyboarding your cards, store them in a large manila envelope.

Working Bibliographies and Annotated Bibliographies

When you start your research, your instructor may ask you to prepare a *working bibliography* and/or an *annotated bibliography*.

You Could Look It Up

A working bibliography lists the sources you plan to use. An **annotated bibliography** kicks a working bibliography up a notch by including comments about the sources.

Don't be misled by the word *working*. A working bibliography doesn't mow your lawn or wash your dishes. Instead …

♦ A working bibliography lists the sources you plan to use. Your working bibliography differs from your Works Cited page in its scope: Your working bibliography is much larger. Your Works Cited page will include only those sources you have actually cited in your paper.

♦ An annotated bibliography is the same as a working bibliography except it includes comments about the sources.

To prepare a working bibliography, follow these two easy steps:

1. Be sure your bibliography cards are written in the documentation method required by your documentation system (MLA, APA, etc.).

2. Keyboard the entries on a sheet of paper following the correct form.

To prepare an annotated bibliography, follow these three simple steps:

1. Be sure your bibliography cards are written in the documentation method required by your documentation system (MLA, APA, etc.).

2. Keyboard the entries on a sheet of paper following the correct form.

3. Make notes about the sources as you read them. For example, you might note that some sources are difficult to find, hard to read, or especially useful. This enables your instructor to assess your progress. An annotated bibliography also helps you sort the material as you evaluate it for possible inclusion in your paper.

Refine: Narrow Your Search

Knowing a few tricks of the trade before you start to research can help you find what you need, save time, and prevent frustration.

1. Learn the lingo.

Nearly every research tool has an abbreviation—or two! *The Dictionary of Library Biography*, for example, is abbreviated as DLB; *Something About the Author* is called

SATA. You can learn the abbreviations for print sources by checking the introduction or index in the book itself. For online sources, check the Help screen.

2. Know your sources and search tools.

Although *Encyclopedia Britannica* and the *World Book Encyclopedia* are both encyclopedias, they're not interchangeable. (*Britannica* is written on a more sophisticated level than *World Book*, which means that each has a specific use for researchers.) Ditto with online versions of the same encyclopedias: In the online version, content may have been sacrificed for bells and whistles such as sound, visuals, and audio. You'll learn all about different reference sources in Chapter 8.

Web tools are all different from each other, too. For example, a growing number of meta-engines enable you to search several web indexes at the same time. The meta-engine submits your key words to other search engines, collects the results, and gives you a summary of the hits. Meta-engines include Webcrawler, Ask Jeeves!, Dogpile, Inference Find, Metacrawler, Savvy Search, Search.com, and Altavista. There are significant differences between each meta-engine (as with every search engine). I cover this in detail in Chapter 12.

Learn all about reference sources and search tools *before* you plunge into research. Even a little bit of knowledge goes a long way toward making your research easier and more productive. (Naturally, you'll have a great deal of knowledge because you have this book!)

Ask the Librarian

If you don't have a library card, get one now. It's easy to get and, in public libraries, it's free. The library card not only gives you the privilege of borrowing books, periodicals, and audiovisual materials, but also often allows you to access expensive and valuable databases off-site, from your office and home computer.

3. Know your library.

As you'll learn in detail in Chapter 6, libraries *are* the latest and the greatest. Familiarize yourself with your public library and a university library. As you'll learn later, they have very different collections because they have different missions. Thus, you will probably need both types of libraries to get all the research you need now as well as in the future.

Visit the libraries on a regular basis, walk around, and figure out where everything is located. Many libraries offer tours to help new patrons learn the stacks and become more comfortable finding what they need.

Use the following checklist of sources as you tour the library. Make sure you know where each source is located. Later, when you research, return to the list to help you use a range of sources.

❏ Almanacs

❏ Archival materials (rare books, charts, maps, etc.)

❏ Atlases

❏ Audiovisual materials

❏ Books

❏ Encyclopedias

❏ Government documents

❏ Indexes

❏ Magazines

❏ Newspapers

❏ Online sources

❏ Pamphlets

❏ Reviews of books, movies, plays, and TV shows

Ask the Librarian

Libraries try to meet the needs of handicapped patrons. For the visually impaired, libraries offer books written in large type and books on tape. For the hearing impaired, libraries offer TTD/TTY services, usually at the reference desk. Ask your librarians what special accommodations are available if you require these services.

All libraries offer some special services. Find out from the start what extra help is available. Many libraries will get books, newspapers, and magazines for you through interlibrary loans. There may be a charge for this service, and it does take time—often as much as two to four weeks. Ask your reference librarians (a.k.a. "media specialists") what special services the library offers, their cost (if any), and the time involved.

4. Cozy up to the reference librarians.

I'll teach you how to find nearly every reference source you need on your own, but you might hit a research roadblock. That's why we have reference librarians. Don't be afraid to ask these marvelous experts for help.

Reference librarians are experts on research methods and their job is to help you find what you need. In addition, they are very well educated. Most librarians in colleges and universities, for example, are required to have earned two Master's degrees, one in information-retrieval methods (library science) and one in a subject area (such as English, history, math, and so on).

Research: Search Smarter, Not Harder

You've already got your topic and thesis statement, so you know what material you need.

Sometimes it's really easy to find material because your topic is so obvious. For instance, if you're writing a paper on Godzilla, the easiest way to find information is to look under "Godzilla."

Other times, however, there's more than one way to look up a topic. Because your topic and research are apt to be sophisticated, you will likely find material located under many different categories. To find what you need, you must first figure out what to call your topic. To do so, you'll use *key words*, which are variations on a word, synonyms, and related words about a topic. They may be words or phrases.

> **You Could Look It Up**
>
> **Key words** are variations on a word, synonyms, and related words about a topic. They may be words or phrases.

Identify Key Words

Start by listing key words for your topic that you'll use to search for sources. A key word that is too narrow will not give you enough information, while one that is too broad will yield too much. Try these hints:

- Try variations of the words, such as *cowboy, cowboys.*

- Use synonyms for the word, such as *ranch hand, rancher, cattle farmer, cowgirl, cattle baron.*

- Study the results you get to help you focus your search.

- Look for key words in an encyclopedia. The key words are often written in the margins of an article as well as on the top of the page.

For example, key words for a research paper on Charlotte Perkins Gilman's *The Yellow Wall-Paper* might look like this:

- ◆ Gilman, Charlotte Perkins (author)
- ◆ *The Yellow Wall-Paper* (title)
- ◆ Mental illness (a topic in the story)
- ◆ Nineteenth-century medicine (another important topic)
- ◆ Postpartum depression (another important topic)
- ◆ Feminism (a movement that embraced this story)

Here's another example for a research paper on cowboys who settled the West and Pacific Northwest. *Cowboys*, *West*, and *Pacific Northwest* would all be too broad.

- ◆ Oregon Trail
- ◆ Dodge City
- ◆ Chisolm Trail
- ◆ Jesse James

Learning key words is such an important skill that it deserves a bit of practice. Brainstorm key words for the following topics. If you want, use an encyclopedia or computer to help you come up with any key words you might have overlooked.

1. The *Titanic*

_____   _____

_____   _____

_____   _____

2. Irish potato famine

_____   _____

_____   _____

_____   _____

3. Hemophilia

_____   _____

_____   _____

_____   _____

4. Overcrowding in national parks

_____   _____

_____   _____

_____   _____

5. Maglev trains

_____   _____

_____   _____

_____   _____

Use Boolean Logic

The computer engineers who wrote the software code for search engines set up specific, logical rules for their search engines. Called a *Boolean search*, it uses the terms *and, or, not,* and the symbols + and – to expand or restrict a search. A Boolean search is sweet because it's easy to use and makes sense. Here's how a Boolean search works:

- ◆ **and**   Link two key words with *and* to narrow your search to only those sources in which *both* terms appear. For example: <u>shopping and malls</u>

- ◆ **or**   Link two terms with *or* to get all sources that contain *either* term. For example: <u>shopping or malls</u>

- ◆ **not**   Link two key words with *not* to get all sources about the first term except those mentioning the second term. For example: <u>shopping not malls</u>

- ◆ **+ or –**   Some search engines use + for *and* and – for *not*. Place the symbols directly before the word. For example: +<u>shopping or –malls</u>

No matter how you search the Internet, there is help available electronically. Look for introductory screens, welcome messages, or files with names such as these:

- ◆ About
- ◆ FAQ (Frequently Asked Questions)
- ◆ Formulating a search with
- ◆ Readme
- ◆ ?

The Least You Need to Know

- ◆ As you find each source, make a bibliography card for it by recording publication and location information. Follow MLA or APA documentation format.

- ◆ You can save time by cutting-and-pasting printouts on bibliography cards or by blocking-and-copying text on your cards.

- ◆ If required, create a working bibliography and/or an annotated bibliography.

- ◆ Narrow your search by learning research abbreviations and special terms; becoming familiar with sources, search tools, and your library; and asking reference librarians for help when necessary.

- ◆ Use key words and Boolean logic to narrow your search.

Chapter 5

Take Note(s)!

In This Chapter

◆ Explore the note-taking process

◆ Practice summarizing research material

◆ Learn how to paraphrase research—and why!

◆ Document direct quotations from your sources

Taking good notes is a skill, and like any other skill, it can be taught and learned. Unlike many other skills, however, note taking is essential because it forces you to digest and evaluate what you read. As a result, taking good notes is key to using reference material effectively to support your thesis. Without this step, you won't have the opportunity to fully understand and judge all the material you have located. Then, you won't be able to use your research to the best advantage.

In this chapter, you will find out the easiest and most effective ways of taking notes, including techniques for summarizing, paraphrasing, and documenting direct quotations. So clear some space around the piles of fabulous research you've gathered, because it's time to distill everything you've gathered into a form you can use.

Start Evaluating Your Sources

Now that you've gathered all your sources (or the vast majority of them), it's time to take notes on the good material. *Good* is the key word here. How can you tell what you'll need for your paper and what will end up in the scrap heap? Follow these three steps:

1. Evaluate your sources.

2. Choose whether or not to include the source.

3. Decide what notes to write.

Let's look at the process in detail.

Lost in (Cyber)Space

Caution: Why not just spread out all your sources and start to draft ... without first taking notes? Because it doesn't work, that's why. (Take it from me; I've tried.) The act of note taking forces you to evaluate and distill the material before you integrate it.

1. Evaluate your sources.

Judging reference material is so important and so challenging that I devote two complete chapters to it: Chapters 13 and 14. These chapters show you how to winnow the treasures from the trash.

2. Choose whether or not to include the source.

Here's your mission: "I will use information that I found through research to help me advance my thesis." The research supports your point and helps you make new connections among ideas. No matter how many sources you use, their purpose remains the same: to help you support your thesis. Keep this in mind as you decide what to include. I know this is easier said than done, especially if you're a novice researcher.

3. Decide what notes to write.

On *note cards*, you record important information for your research paper. Fortunately, taking notes is a process of discovery as well as recording. By choosing what to write, you're refining your thinking about your thesis statement. You'll discover new ideas and new ways of thinking about the topic as you sift through the research material. You might end up with some notes that you don't need when it comes time to write your paper, but the lost time will be worth it because you'll end up with a more thoughtful and focused paper.

You Could Look It Up

Note cards record important information for your research paper in an easy-to-use manner.

The following chart will help you focus your thinking as you dive into the wonderful world of note taking.

What to Write	What Not to Write
Key ideas that support your thesis	Many minor details
Authoritative quotes	Untrustworthy quotes
Reliable facts	Unreliable facts
Current facts	Out-of-date information
Accepted opinions from reliable sources	Unorthodox opinions from dubious sources
Material that substantiates information you have already found	Material that doesn't seem to fit information you have already found
Sufficient evidence to make your point	Insufficient evidence to make your point

Pack rat alert! It's tempting to take notes on every single source. After all, you don't know what you need until you need it, right? Okay, I'll give you a point for that, but remember what you learned about time management in Chapter 3: You just don't have the time to take notes on everything. And you don't want to because it's not necessary.

Here's your way to make sure you can go back and find a source if you need it:

◆ Keep all your bibliography cards.

◆ Keep a printout of all your sources.

◆ Keep everything until you finish your paper.

Store everything in a folder, bag, or envelope to make sure that nothing inadvertently gets misplaced.

For *very, very* brief research papers, you can usually gather information without taking notes. In these cases, photocopy the sources, highlight key points, jot ideas in the margins, and start drafting. But with longer, more complex research papers, you'll have to make note cards to handle the flow of information efficiently. Figure on making note cards with any research paper more than a page or two long.

Five Steps to Great Notes

Here's the inside skinny: In most cases you won't be able to tell what's going to make the final cut and what won't. Even the most experienced researchers end up with far more note cards than they need. Not to worry: That's the nature of this beast.

The deeper you dig into your subject, however, the more perceptive you'll become about what you need to prove your point most convincingly. Follow my five-step process as you start taking notes. It will help you stay organized and focused.

1. Before you start reading, arrange your sources according to difficulty.

As you judge the difficulty of a work, look for dense type, footnotes/endnotes, and style. Lay all the sources out on the carpet like this: most difficult → average → least difficult.

Your stacks will probably look like this.

Most Difficult	Average	Least Difficult
Scholarly books	Newsstand magazines	Personal websites
Scholarly articles	Newspapers	Listservs
Serious books	University-sponsored websites	E-mails
Serious articles	Encyclopedias, interviews	
Reference books	Government documents	

2. Read the least difficult sources first.

Look for general, introductory material. Use this to lay the foundation for the more specialized and technical material you'll need to make you an expert in the field.

3. Look for facts, expert opinions, explanations, and examples that support your thesis or the other side.

Now focus on the facts: See what you can find that will help you make your case or refute the opposition. Pay special attention to strong information from people recognized for their expertise in the field.

Ask the Librarian

For a good overview of your topic and any major issues it contains, consider starting your research by reading some encyclopedia articles on your subject.

4. Note any controversies swirling around your topic.

Pay close attention to both sides of the issue: It's a great way to test the validity of your thesis.

5. Read in chunks.

Finish an entire paragraph, page, or chapter before you stop to take notes. This will help you get the "big picture" so you can locate the pertinent information.

Process and Product

You can write your notes by hand or keyboard them. Each method has its advantages and disadvantages. Writing notes longhand allows you to take notes in stolen minutes of spare time, when it might be too cumbersome to set up your laptop. Also, some people may be more comfortable handwriting than typing.

On the other hand, keyboarding notes makes it much faster and easier to write your final paper, because all your material is already entered. It also makes it a snap to correct simple spelling errors, because of the computer's spell-check feature. Finally, the notes are easier to read because they're typed.

As you have probably already guessed, I'm a huge fan of keyboarding rather than handwriting notes. I'm not alone: There's even special software for note taking, although it's just as easy to keyboard notes on your familiar word processing program.

Don't waste time writing out each and every word in your notes. Whether you are keyboarding or handwriting your notes, use abbreviations to save time and space. Here are some standard abbreviations:

> & = and
> + = and
> w/o= without
> @ = at

If you create your own abbreviations, be sure to keep a record of them in case you forget what they mean!

Write by your notes by hand if …

- ♦ You write faster than you can keyboard.

- ♦ You don't have access to a computer.

If you do decide to handwrite your notes, write them on 4×6 index cards. I've found through trial-and-error that this size works best. You don't want cards so small that you can't fit anything on them—or cards so large that you'll end up wasting most of the space.

Keyboard your notes if …

- ♦ You keyboard faster than you can handwrite.

- ♦ You have access to a computer.

If you do decide to keyboard your notes, be sure to back up all your files on disks. It's also a great idea to print as you go along. That way, you've got your notes in case your computer does something wicked to you.

How to Write Notes

There are three main ways to write notes: *write direct quotations, summarize,* and *paraphrase.* You can use the three methods of note taking together on a note card or you can use them individually. For example, a note card might contain a brief quote within a longer summary—as long as the entire card is on one subtopic and one subtopic only.

The following sections explain in detail how to write direct quotations, summaries, and paraphrases. Regardless of the methods you use, the overall techniques remain the same. Here are my 10 guidelines:

1. Label each card with a subtopic, in the upper-right or -left corner. Take your subtopics from your outline.

2. Include a reference citation showing the source of the information. Place this in the lower-right or -left corner.

3. Be consistent. Follow the same format on all your cards because it will help you keep the information straight.

4. Be sure to include a page number, if the source is print.

5. Be sure to include a date of access, if the source is online.

6. Write one piece of information per card.

7. Keep the note short. If you write too much, you'll be right back where you started—trying to separate the essential information from the nonessential information.

8. Be sure to mark direct quotes with quotation marks. This can help you avoid plagiarism later.

9. Add any personal comments you think are necessary. This will help you remember how you intend to use the note in your research paper.

10. Check and double-check your notes. Be sure you've spelled all names right and copied dates correctly. Check that you've spelled the easy words correctly, too; many errors creep in because writers overlook the obvious words.

To save time, instead of writing the source, use a code system. Here's my simple system: Number each bibliography card. Write the corresponding number on each note card that contains notes from that source.

Here's a model card template:

Subtopic:

Information: One piece of information goes here.

Source:

Comments:

Here's a model card filled in.

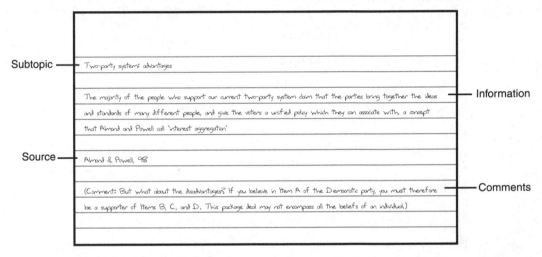

Subtopic —

Two-party system: advantages

The majority of the people who support our current two-party system claim that the parties bring together the ideas
and standards of many different people, and give the voters a unified policy which they can associate with, a concept
that Almond and Powell call "interest aggregation"

— Information

Source —

Almond & Powell, '98

(Comment: But what about the disadvantages? If you believe in Item A of the Democratic party, you must therefore
be a supporter of Items B, C, and D. This package deal may not encompass all the beliefs of an individual.)

— Comments

A model note card with comments.

Some sources will be better for your purposes than others. For example, you might get 10 note cards from 1 source, but only 1 card from another source. However, don't rely too heavily on any one source—no matter how good it looks. It's fairly common to find one source that seems to say it all, and just the way you like. But if you take too much from one source, you'll end up doing a book report, not a research paper. And worst-case scenario: What happens if the source turns out to be invalid or dated? Speaking as a professor of writing, the grade won't be pretty.

Direct Quotations: Straight from the Expert's Mouth

When you write a direct quotation, you copy the material exactly as it appears in the source. Show that a note is a direct quotation by surrounding it with quotation marks (" ").

In general, quote briefly when you take notes. Remember that long quotations are difficult to integrate into your paper. Besides, readers often find long quotations hard to follow and boring to read.

What should you quote?

◆ Quote key points, passages that sum up the main idea in a pithy way.

◆ Quote subtle ideas. Look for passages whose meaning would be watered down or lost if you summarized or paraphrased them.

◆ Quote expert opinions. Because they carry weight, expert opinions help you convince your readers that your point is correct or at least deserves serious consideration.

◆ Quote powerful writing. If the passage is memorable or famous, it will give your research paper authority.

Here's a sample.

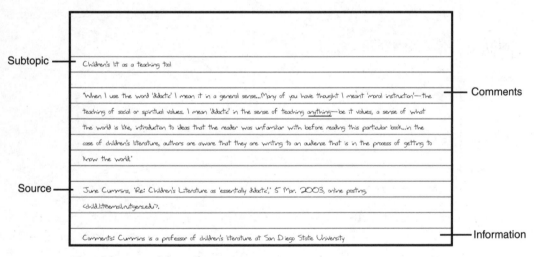

A model note card featuring a quote.

1. Use square brackets to add material.

If you need to add explanations or missing words, enclose the extra information in square brackets. The square brackets tell your readers that the additional information is not part of the original quote. Check out the following example. The word *Children* does not appear in the original quote. The writer adds it for clarity.

Example: Egoff reports that "[Children] have shown extraordinary good sense" in jettisoning sentimental books such as *Pollyanna* (Fenner, 61).

2. Use "sic" in square brackets to indicate that an author or typesetter has made a mistake.

Errors creep into even the most carefully prepared books. You might find a misspelling, a wrong date, or an error of fact, for example.

If there is an error in the source, copy the error. Write [sic] next to the mistake. Enclose the word *sic* in square *brackets.* The Latin word *sic* means "thus" and tells a reader, "It is thus in the original."

> *Example:* "Abraham Lincoln was assassinated in 1869 [*sic*]."

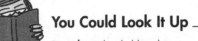

You Could Look It Up

Brackets look like this: [ ]. Parentheses look like this: ( ). They are not interchangeable marks of punctuation.

3. Use an ellipsis when you omit something.

An *ellipsis* is a set of three spaced dots (use the period key when you type them). An ellipsis is used to show that you have omitted something from a direct quotation. When an ellipsis takes the place of one or more sentences, use one dot to show the period and then write the ellipsis. This gives you a total of four dots. Following is an example of a quotation in which a sentence has been omitted:

> *Original quote:* "No titles should be required. Nor should children be asked to read books for extraliterary, utilitarian reasons—learning moral lessons, improving their personalities, improving reading skills, or preparing for some future job. We reject the notion of some authorities, notably Arbuthnot, that the major purposes of reading literature are to add to a child's life by satisfying his need to know, his need to love and be loved, his need to belong, and his need for change" (Anderson, 1972).

> *Edited quote:* "No titles should be required. ... We reject the notion of some authorities, notably Arbuthnot, that the major purposes of reading literature are to add to a child's life by satisfying his need

You Could Look It Up

An **ellipsis** is a set of three spaced dots (...) used to show that you have omitted something from a direct quotation.

to know, his need to love and be loved, his need to belong, and his need for change" (Anderson, 1972).

Of course, never deliberately edit a quote so that it says what you want it to say. Twisting the meaning of a quote is not using research ethically. This is covered in detail in Chapter 16.

4. Use single quotation marks for quotations within quotations.

Remember that quotation marks are used to enclose short works (such as poems, short stories, newspaper and magazine articles, and so on), to indicate a speaker's exact words, and to emphasize a word. When you have two sets of quotation marks, one within the other, change the inside set to single quotation marks.

Example: Children's author Jackie Ogburn puts it this way: "It's not that 'message' isn't a part of the work. It's just that it's usually the least *interesting* part" (emphasis hers).

Summaries: Short and Sweet

A *summary* is a smaller version of the original, reducing the passage to its essential meaning. A summary is always written in your own words. Be sure to summarize carefully so you don't distort the meaning of the original passage. In general, you should summarize when you want to …

◆ Extract the main idea in a passage.

◆ Use the research for background material in your own paper.

To write a summary, follow these steps:

1. Read the source all the way through. Make sure that you understand the document before you begin your summary.

You Could Look It Up

A **summary** is a relatively brief, objective condensation of a passage.

2. Identify the main idea and restate it in your own words. If you cannot identify the main idea, look for the topic sentence or thesis statement. It will usually be the first sentence in the passage.

3. Write a brief summary of each paragraph. Concentrate on the main ideas rather than the details.

4. Revise your summary so it is clear and logical. Eliminate unnecessary words and details.

Here's a sample to use as a model:

Original source: The Mayflower Compact

In the name of God, Amen. We, whose names are underwritten, the Loyal Subjects of our dread Sovereign Lord King James, by the Grace of God, of Great Britain, France, and Ireland, King, Defender of the Faith, & etc. Having undertaken for the Glory of God, and the advancement of the Christian Faith, and the Honour of our King and Country, a Voyage to plant the first Colony in the northern parts of Virginia; do by these Presents, solemnly and mutually in the Presence of God and one another, covenant and combine ourselves together in a civil body politick, for our better ordering and preservation, and furtherance of the ends aforesaid: and by virtue hereof do enact, constitute, and frame such just and equal laws, ordinances, acts, constitutions, and offices, from time to time, as shall be thought most meet and convenient of the general good of the Colony; unto which we promise all due submission and obedience. In witness whereof we have hereunto subscribed our names at Cape Cod, the eleventh of November, in the reign of our Sovereign Lord King James of England, France, and Ireland, the eighteenth, and of Scotland, the fifty-fourth. Anno Domini 1620.

Summary:

The Mayflower Compact

The Compact consolidated Mayflower passengers into a "civil body politic," which had the power to frame and enact laws appropriate to the general good of the planned settlement. The Compact established rule by the majority. Signed 11/11/1620 at Cape Cod.

Bradford, 76.

Comments: First constitution written in America; remained the colony's primary principle of government until the colony was absorbed by the Massachusetts Bay Colony in 1691.

Ask the Librarian

To remember that a summary is a shorter version of the original, remember that both *summary* and *shorter* start with "s."

Paraphrase: In Your Own Words

A *paraphrase* is a restatement of the writer's original words. As such, a paraphrase may be longer, shorter, or the same length as the original. A paraphrase often includes examples and explanations from the original quotation. It may also incorporate brief direct quotations.

You Could Look It Up

A **paraphrase** is a restatement in your own words of a passage. A paraphrase may be longer, shorter, or the same length as the original.

Paraphrasing is the most difficult form of note taking. As a result, it is where novice researchers are most likely to commit plagiarism—using someone else's words as their own. You can avoid this by putting quotes around words you copy directly and being very sure that you do indeed restate the material in your own words. Also, be very, very, very sure to give credit to your original source. See Chapter 17 to discover what to document and how to avoid plagiarism.

Paraphrase when …

◆ You want to keep all the points in the original passage.

◆ You want to communicate ideas in your own words, usually to make them clearer than the original.

Here's a sample to use as a model:

Original source:

For, in a society where we make money the standard of everything, it is necessary to practice many crafts which are quite vain and superfluous, ministering only to luxury and licentiousness. Suppose the host of those who now toil were distributed only over as few crafts as the few needs and conveniences demanded by nature. In the great abundance of commodities which must then arise, the prices set on them would be too low for the craftsmen to earn their livelihood by their work. But suppose all those fellows who are not busied with unprofitable crafts, as well as all the lazy and idle throng, any one of whom now consumes as much of the fruits of other men's labors as any two of the workingmen, were all set to work and indeed to useful work.

Paraphrase:

Abolish luxury and realign workers. Our nation judges people by the contents of their pocketbook, their outward show of luxury and status. As a result, we spend far too much time producing wasteful extravagances that contribute to our depravity. Instead, we should consider having these tradesmen work at producing what we really need, not what we merely want. While this realignment would give us the goods we need, the craftsmen wouldn't earn enough to support themselves. To correct this problem, we should reform our workforce by making unemployed people and lazy people work for a living.

More, 506

Comments: This excerpt from Sir Thomas More's *Utopia* suggests radical redistribution of labor. Strong tone.

The Least You Need to Know

◆ Before you take notes, evaluate your sources to decide whether or not to include each one.

◆ Sort all your material and begin reading from easiest to most difficult pieces.

◆ Keyboarding your notes is easier than writing them by hand.

◆ The three ways to take notes are direct quotations, summarizing, and paraphrasing. Summaries are shorter than the original; paraphrases rework the material in your own words.

◆ Combine the three methods on one note card or use them individually.

Chapter 6

It's the Latest, It's the Greatest—It's the Library!

In This Chapter

♦ Trace the history of libraries

♦ Explore public libraries

♦ Investigate academic libraries and school libraries

♦ Learn about private libraries

♦ Discover research libraries and specialized libraries

Libraries bring you the world.

Today, the United States boasts more than 124,000 libraries. In addition to public libraries in almost every community, there are thousands of libraries in schools, colleges, universities, hospitals, law firms, businesses, government offices, the armed forces, and more. Because many libraries offer free access to all, they bring opportunity to all.

In this chapter, you'll brush up on your library skills as you compare and contrast different kinds of libraries—public libraries, academic libraries, school libraries, private libraries, research libraries, and specialized libraries—to see what services they each provide. This brief survey into the riches of our library system will help you use libraries to their fullest.

Explore the History of Libraries

Far back in antiquity, people recognized the value of libraries. The oldest libraries were established by the Sumerians in the Middle East between 2000 and 3000 B.C.E. These libraries were pretty dull places by our standards: Instead of bestsellers, Barney tapes, and Beastie Boy CDs, the Sumerian libraries housed clay tablets inscribed with business and legal records. Even though the libraries were eventually destroyed by fires and earthquakes, a surprisingly large number of the clay tablets survived.

Ramses II created the first Egyptian library in 1250 B.C.E. Housing 20,000 papyrus scrolls, it was a nifty place to visit if you could read hieroglyphics. The title of "Greatest Library in the Ancient World," however, goes to the library established by the Greeks in Alexandria in the third century B.C.E.

The Library of Alexandria

Founded by Ptolemy I (c. 323–285 B.C.E), enriched by his son Ptolemy II Philadelphus, and his grandson Ptolemy III Euergetes, the *library* imported manuscripts from all parts of Asia and Greece, eventually amassing a collection of 700,000 papyrus rolls. Scholars flocked to the library from the entire Hellenistic world, resulting in the introduction of standard editing, systems of punctuation, and textual scholarship. As Alexandria's power was eclipsed, the library fell into neglect. In 270 C.E., much of it was demolished; about a century later, fire destroyed what little remained. Only a few of the scrolls survived, mainly those that had been widely copied and passed around.

You Could Look It Up

Although the word **library** is derived from the Latin *liber* ("book"), the term *library* now refers to collections of data in many other formats as well: video, audio, slides, photographs, magazines, journals, artwork, microforms, CDs, and DVDs.

Libraries in the Middle Ages

In the eighth and ninth centuries, Muslim scholars copied and preserved mathematical and scientific texts. Thanks to the Chinese method of paper making, the price of manuscripts dropped, so more libraries could afford more books. For example, by the tenth century, the library in Córdoba, Spain, had a library of 400,000 books.

In Western Europe, books were safeguarded in monasteries. In the "scriptorium," monks toiled at copying manuscripts of religious and classical works. Not surprisingly, common people never got their grubby paws on the pages. In fact, books were so valuable that in some places, they were chained to the shelves!

Johann Gutenberg's invention of the printing press in 1440 helped books become more common, but they were still costly luxuries. People could afford pamphlets and newspapers, but few families had more than a handful of books—if that. During the 1600s and 1700s, national libraries sprung up around Europe. For instance, the Royal Society of London, founded in 1660, set up a specialized collection for research; Sir Thomas Bodley established the library at the University of Oxford.

The First Public Libraries

In England, the government set up the first public library to educate the masses in 1850 in Manchester. In America, we have Ben Franklin to thank for the first library.

In 1731, Ben Franklin and some of his friends started the Library Company of Philadelphia, the first public lending library. People paid to join, but the cost was nominal. Suddenly, ordinary people like you and I had affordable access to books. Following the Land Grant Act of 1863, which provided for public funding of higher education, college and university libraries open to the public were established throughout the United States.

In the 1880s and 1890s, thanks to the largess of steel tycoon Andrew Carnegie, public libraries flourished in many cities. In all, Carnegie funded 1,681 public libraries! The door had opened to a new age of access for one and all. If knowledge is power (and it is), with the creation of free libraries, we now had power at our fingertips.

Libraries Are Forever

People said the invention of the airplane would destroy train travel. They were wrong.

People said the invention of television would destroy radio. They were wrong.

People said the invention of the Internet would sound the death knell for libraries. Wrong, wrong, wrong.

In a recent poll, 91 percent of the total respondents believed libraries will exist in the future, despite all the information available on the Internet. The same number of people believe libraries are changing and dynamic places with a variety of activities for the whole family. Nearly all the people polled agreed libraries are unique because they offer patrons access to nearly everything on the web or in print, as well as personal service and assistance in finding materials. More than 80 percent believe libraries and librarians play an essential role in our democracy and are needed now more than ever. [Source: March 2002 KRC Research and Consulting survey for the American Library Association]

From the Reference Desk
According to widely accepted library lore, circulation and the economy have an inverse relationship: When the economy goes down, library circulation rises and vice versa. According to this theory, in tough times, people tighten their belts and look for free entertainment. Libraries certainly fit the bill, offering free books, movies, tapes, and DVDs to borrow; free concerts, recitals, and shows to enjoy; and free programs to attend. A 2002 study conducted by the Illinois Library Research Center found that libraries do indeed see an upturn in usage during a downturn in the economy. The study found that circulation increased significantly (by 8 to 9 percent) beginning in March 2001, when the National Bureau of Economic Research identified the beginning of the latest recession.

Different kinds of libraries provide different services and have different holdings. Learning the similarities and differences among libraries will make your research easier and more productive. Libraries are categorized as follows:

- Public libraries
- Academic libraries
- School libraries
- Private libraries
- Research libraries
- Specialized libraries

Come with me as we let our fingers do the walking through each kind of library.

Today's Public Libraries

Public libraries are open to all. This means everyone has access to a public library. If you do not live in the area served by a particular library, you still have access to that public library. You may not be able to take items from the library, but you will still be given access to everything that *circulates* in the library's collection.

According to the American Library Association, you've got a lot of public libraries in which to do your research. Here's the breakdown:

- Public libraries (administrative units) – 9,074

- Central libraries* – 8,915

- Branch libraries – 7,383

- Buildings – 16,298

(*The number of central buildings is different from the number of public libraries because some public library systems have no central building and some have more than one.)

You Could Look It Up

Circulate is library lingo for "items that leave the building."

Card Me

America is a large continent so it's hard to generalize, but in most places, a public library card is free. It's one of the few free things in life that's actually worth far, far more than what you pay for it. You need the card to take items from the library, so if you don't already have a card, you'll want to get one today (right after you finish reading this chapter, of course).

To get a public library card, in most places you must prove residency. Usually, you need two forms of proof of residency, such as a gas or electric bill, a telephone bill, or a driver's license. You may be able to get the card at once, or you may be issued a temporary card while your permanent card is being processed.

When you apply for your card, make sure that it's coded for any special services that your library offers. These might include some or all of the following:

- **Direct access.** The right to access materials from any library in the system. Some libraries will even ship the books to your home library, free of charge. Others charge a nominal fee.

- **AV/video.** The right to take out movies, DVDs, books on tape, and so on.

- **Internet.** The right to access the Internet from the library.

Public libraries are financed primarily by town, city, or county governments. When the economy is flush, services tend to be free. When the economy is hurting, you may have to pay a nominal fee for special library services. For example, some public libraries might require patrons to pay the shipping costs for interlibrary loan items.

Attention college students! Many public libraries grant full or limited borrowing privileges to students attending college in the area. Because a public library has a different collection from most college and university libraries, you will want to avail yourself of a public library card in the community in which you are attending school.

More Than Research

So why do people use the public libraries? If you think it's mainly for educational purposes, thing again. According to a poll on the American Library Association's website, the stats for educational uses and entertainment uses were neck-in-neck: close to 50 percent.

Of those respondents who reported using the public library in person in the last year …

- ◆ 67 percent said they had taken out books.

- ◆ 47 percent had consulted a librarian.

- ◆ 47 percent used reference materials.

- ◆ 31 percent read newspapers or magazines.

- ◆ 26 percent connected to the Internet.

- ◆ 25 percent took out CDs or videos.

- ◆ 14 percent heard a speaker, saw a movie, or attended a special program.

[Source: March 2002 KRC Research and Consulting survey for the American Library Association]

Internet "filtering" is a hot topic in public libraries nowadays. On June 23, 2003, the Supreme Court upheld a lower court's ruling that mandates filtering software in the children's room. However, libraries that refuse to disable filters at the request of an adult patron or those that impose substantial burdens on a patron's ability to have the filter disabled risk a lawsuit. The library will be a defendant.

Academic Libraries and School Libraries

As you read earlier in this chapter, many libraries were established around universities, colleges, and schools. Although these libraries share many similarities, they also differ in significant ways.

The Ivory Tower

Colleges and universities maintain their own libraries. Some are small, no more than a few floors of a building, whereas others are magnificent mansions. Each academic library has its own patron access policy. As a result, unlike public libraries, these libraries may be closed to outsiders.

Open stack libraries allow free access to all, whereas *closed stack* libraries require you to present a valid student/faculty/staff ID just to walk through the doors. Sometimes, students may be allowed to use the library after they graduate, but may have to pay for the privilege. In addition, the library may be closed to visitors and alumni during peak use times such as exam weeks. Because these libraries usually obtain all or nearly all their money from the academic institution, their first loyalty is to their own people … the ones paying the bill.

Because many academic libraries are stunning showplaces well worth the visit (as well as spectacular research institutions), always call ahead to find out the library's policy on access for outside patrons.

You Could Look It Up

Open stack libraries allow patrons access to the materials; **closed stack** libraries do not. Thus, in a closed stack library, patrons cannot browse the stacks, much less remove materials themselves.

According to the American Library Association, there are 3,658 academic libraries in the United States, divided as follows:

Two-year colleges	1,438
Four-year and above	2,220

Of the nation's largest libraries (as calculated by the number of books in the collection), half of the top 10 are academic libraries, as the following chart shows.

Ranking	Institution	Volumes Held
2	Harvard University	14,437,361
3	Chicago Public Library	10,994,943
5	Yale University	10,492,812
8	University of Illinois—Urbana-Champaign	9,469,620
9	University of California—Berkeley	9,107,757

However, don't throw out that student ID number—ever! Even if you do not purchase an alumni library card after you graduate from college, many college and university libraries allow alumni to access their online databases off-site for free. When it comes to research, getting access to a college or university's databases off-site is the equivalent of winning the lottery: You've hit the mother lode. You'll learn all about off-site access in Chapter 12.

Libraries of different types are often linked through a number of interlibrary systems, through loan arrangements, and through other cooperative programs. For example, public libraries are often linked to major university libraries. This helps patrons get far more materials at less expense to each member library.

School Libraries

"School libraries" include elementary school, middle school, and high school libraries. You know the places, where Mrs. Dinkelmeyer read you *Goodnight, Moon*. Thanks to the Mrs. Dinkelmeyers of the world, we discovered the joys of libraries in first grade.

School libraries are not open to everyone. Just the opposite, in fact: With fears of child abduction rising, many schools have clamped down. Only bona fide students, teachers, and staff members are allowed access to the school building.

Currently, America has 93,861 school libraries, divided as follows:

Public schools	76,807
Private schools	17,054

Private Libraries

Private libraries are just what their name says: libraries open only to members. Some private libraries are open to anyone with the required membership fee, whereas others are restricted to people in specific areas of expertise.

For example, the Boston Athenæum is one of the oldest and most distinguished private libraries in the United States. It was founded in 1807 by members of the Anthology Society to combine "the advantages of a public library [and] containing the great works of learning and science in all languages." Established in 1827, the library was soon flourishing. For nearly 50 years the Athenæum was the unchallenged center of intellectual life in Boston, and by 1851 had become one of the five largest libraries in the United States. Today it holds more than half a million volumes, with particular strengths in Boston history, New England state and local history, biography, English and American literature, and the fine and decorative arts.

In addition to books and periodicals, the Athenæum offers art shows, lectures, exhibit openings, musical presentations, documentary films, reading discussions, and other cultural events.

Many private libraries offer tours. They're fine places to visit and you may want to join some!

Research Libraries and Specialized Libraries

Research libraries and specialized libraries are designed to serve specific professional needs. Many of these libraries are integral parts of organizations and businesses, whose staff members and clients require the library in the course of their work. The staff in a research or specialized library is usually trained in the appropriate subject area as well as in information retrieval.

Research Libraries

These hidden jewels mainly serve the needs of scholars. Supported by private endowments and contributions, research libraries house many rare and valuable materials. As a result, nothing circulates: The material must be used on the premises. Surprisingly, many of these research libraries are open to the public, so you can have a nice walkabout and look around. It's rare that nonscholars can access the material, but very often, manuscripts, pictures, and other artifacts are on open display for everyone to enjoy.

There's a research library for every interest—I could fill an entire book on research libraries alone. My personal favorite is the Folger Shakespeare Library in Washington, D.C. This research library holds the largest collection of Shakespearean material in the world, including 79 copies of the First Folio. It also has rare books and manuscripts of the Renaissance. Although the stacks are only open to scholars, the Folger offers spectacular arts programs and performances of Shakespeare's plays in its Elizabethan theater, which resembles an innyard theater in Shakespeare's day.

Specialized Libraries

According to the latest count, America boasts 9,170 specialized libraries. These include many different types of institutions. Among the most useful for research are the following:

- ◆ Government libraries
- ◆ Corporate libraries
- ◆ Medical libraries
- ◆ Law libraries
- ◆ Religious libraries

For example, the National Archives and Records Administration (NARA) coordinates many of our presidential libraries. Not every president has his own library, but a surprisingly large number of our past leaders do, starting with Hoover. (Materials for presidents before Herbert Hoover are held by private institutions.) Here are a few of my favorites:

- ◆ Herbert Hoover Library (West Branch, Iowa)
- ◆ Franklin D. Roosevelt Library (Hyde Park, New York)
- ◆ Harry S. Truman Library (Independence, Missouri)
- ◆ John Fitzgerald Kennedy Library (Boston, Massachusetts)
- ◆ Gerald Ford Library (Ann Arbor, Michigan)
- ◆ Jimmy Carter Library (Atlanta, Georgia)

I've done research at the Herbert Hoover Library and it's a honey of a place.

The government alone supports 1,326 specialized libraries, including 329 armed forces libraries. The Mother of All Specialized Libraries is the Library of Congress. It's specialized because it's the largest library in the world. The main building looks like Cinderella's castle—and it's just as magical because of the riches it holds. These include the following:

- ◆ 18 million books
- ◆ 2.5 million recordings
- ◆ 12 million photographs
- ◆ 4.5 million maps
- ◆ 54 million manuscripts

All told, the Library of Congress houses more than 120 million items on approximately 530 miles of bookshelves. The collection includes 24,616,867 volumes.

Created in 1800 to serve Congress, the Library of Congress was originally housed in the Capitol. After the British set the building on fire in 1814, burning all the books, Thomas Jefferson offered to sell the Library of Congress his personal library of 6,000 volumes. Congress bought Jefferson's collection and erected the impressive Italian Renaissance building bearing his name. As the collection grew, two more buildings were added: the John Adams in 1939 and the James Madison in 1980.

Lost in (Cyber)Space

The Library of Congress is *not* a lending library. This means that you can't take materials out.

The Library's mission is "to make its resources available and useful to the Congress and the American people and to sustain and preserve a universal collection of knowledge and creativity for future generations." This means that anyone can do research at the Library of Congress. It's open to the general public, so you can march right in to read and take notes to your heart's content. I strongly suggest that you call first to find out which building houses the materials you need and what hours that building is open. You can also e-mail the Library of Congress at www.loc.gov/.

If you want to conduct research in any specialized library, contact the library first to find out their requirements for access.

Choose the Best Library for Your Needs

So many libraries, so little time! What's a researcher to do? Shop smart, that's what.

Each type of library has a different focus and a different emphasis. Being able to distinguish among the different types of libraries and knowing what each one holds can help you save time and effort.

Use the following chart to help you focus your search.

Type of Library	Collection Focus
Public libraries	"Classic" literature, popular reading, bestsellers; reference books, self-help books, and self-help videos; popular magazines and newspapers; social services information; videos, tapes, CDs, DVDs; children's literature
Academic libraries	"Classic" literature, some popular reading; academic books, journals, videos, CDs, DVDs, tapes; reference materials, government documents; material that serves the needs of the specific institution

continues

continued

Type of Library	Collection Focus
School libraries	"Classic" literature, popular reading; reference books, newspapers, and magazines; videos, tapes, computer software, CDs, DVDs; children's literature
Private libraries	Material specific to the institution; may have original manuscripts, artwork
Research libraries	Material specific to the institution; may have original manuscripts, artwork
Specialized libraries	Material specific to the institution; may have original manuscripts, artwork

If you're not sure what type of library you have visited, ask the reference librarian. Ask him or her to describe the collection as well. Don't be afraid to ask the reference librarians for help: After all, that's their job!

The Least You Need to Know

- Libraries are as old as writing itself. As with their forebears, today's libraries are repositories of culture and learning.

- Public libraries are open to all and offer a wide variety of materials and cultural opportunities. Be sure to get a library card so you can take materials from the library.

- Academic libraries, sponsored by colleges and universities, have more scholarly works and may restrict access. School libraries, housed in elementary and secondary schools, are closed to outsiders.

- Private libraries, open only to members, offer specialized collections and cultural events.

- Research libraries mainly serve the needs of scholars; specialized libraries are supported by many agencies, including the government, corporations, hospitals, law offices, and religious institutions.

- The Library of Congress, located in Washington, D.C., is the largest library in the world. It is open to the public for research.

- Each type of library has a different focus and a different emphasis. Being able to distinguish among the different types of libraries and knowing what each one holds can help you save time and effort.

Part 2

Seek and Ye Shall Find

Answer this test question:

> What, in your opinion, is the most reasonable explanation for the fact that Moses led the Israelites all over the place for 40 years before they finally got to the Promised Land?
>
> A. He was being tested.
>
> B. He wanted them to really appreciate the Promised Land when they finally got there.
>
> C. He refused to ask for directions.

In this section of the book, you'll get all the directions you need for locating reference material. You'll learn how to find it all: general books, reference texts, periodicals, academic journals, media sources, and government documents. There's a complete section devoted to researching with electronic media, too.

Chapter 7

Find the Books You Need

In This Chapter

- ◆ Call numbers
- ◆ The Dewey Decimal catalog system
- ◆ The Library of Congress catalog system
- ◆ Superintendent of Documents (SuDocs) numbers
- ◆ Paper and online catalogs

Books are "user-friendly"—they're light, easy to use, and familiar. They can't crash as computers can, either. Best of all, because it takes time to write and publish a book, they tend to be reliable sources, but more on that in Part 3 of this book. In this chapter, you'll find out how to locate the books you need to complete your research.

First, you'll learn about call numbers, each book's unique ID number. Then I'll take you through the three different ways that materials are classified in a library: the Dewey Decimal catalog system, the Library of Congress catalog system, and the Superintendent of Documents (SuDocs) numbers. Once you understand these three systems, you'll find it a snap to locate the material you need—in any library in the country! Finally, we'll discuss how to use paper and online catalogs and the advantages and disadvantages of each.

Classification Systems

Libraries usually have a lot of books. How many is *a lot?*

♦ A small village library often has around 100,000–125,000 books on the shelves.

♦ A midsize community library can have about 250,000 volumes circulating.

♦ A university library can have more than a million volumes available.

And that doesn't count the books that are placed in storage because of lack of space, the books out at the bindery being repaired, and the books sitting under my bed right now because I haven't gotten around to returning them (shhh …).

You Could Look It Up

Libraries use different **classification systems** to track, shelve, and retrieve the materials in their collection.

The number of books in a library's collection raises a key issue: How can the books be arranged so people can find what they need quickly and easily? To solve this problem, *classification systems* were created. Classification systems track the volumes in a library's collection. They also allow us to locate the books we need to complete our research. Knowing how these classification systems work will make it a snap for you to find the books you need to complete your research.

Although I'm just focusing on books in this chapter, be aware that almost all materials in a library have a call number. Otherwise, how could we locate them?

Materials that carry a call number include everything in a library that can be borrowed, such as the following:

♦ Books

♦ Journals, newspapers, magazines

♦ Audiocassettes

♦ Videotapes

♦ DVDs, CDs, and books on tape

♦ Archive collections

♦ Microfilm

The Three Main Types of Classification Systems

Books are divided into two broad classes: fiction and nonfiction. Fiction may be cataloged under the author's last name or according to a number, depending on the classification system being used.

Nonfiction documents are classified in three different ways:

◆ The Dewey Decimal classification system

◆ The Library of Congress classification system

◆ The Superintendent of Documents (SuDocs) classification system (This classification system is used only for government documents.)

The systems use completely different sets of letters and numbers, as you'll discover in the next sections.

What Is a Call Number?

Each book has a *call number*. Think of the call number as the address of the book on the shelf. A call number can be found in three places:

◆ On a label on the book's spine

◆ Inside the book, usually on the reverse side of the title page

◆ In the card catalog

In libraries all over the world, call numbers serve three purposes:

1. **A unique identification number.** Every book has its own call number. No other book can have the same call number.

2. **A subject formula.** Books written about the same subject have similar call numbers, which means that these books are grouped together on the shelf. This makes it easier for you to browse the library's holdings on a specific subject.

3. **A location code.** The call number for each book also appears in the catalog entry. Thus, you can look up the book in the card catalog so you know where it is shelved in the library.

You Could Look It Up

A book's **call number** is its classification number. The Dewey Decimal system, the Library of Congress classification system, and the SuDocs system each use a different set of call numbers.

The same call number can be written from top to bottom or left to right. Both forms are equally correct. For example:

Top to Bottom	Left to Right
LB	LB2395 .C65 2003
2395	
.C65	
2003	

The Dewey Decimal Classification System

Melvil Dewey (1851–1931) had a thing for order. Dewey likely contributed more to the development of library science than any other person in America.

Born in New York, Dewey was still a student at Amherst College when he devised a decimal system for classifying and cataloging books. This may not sound as revolutionary as sliced bread or freedom fries, but before Dewey created the classification system that bears his name, many libraries filed books by color or size, a chaotic system at best.

Categories of Nonfiction Books

Dewey's classification system, published in 1876, classifies fiction under the author's last name and nonfiction books into 10 broad categories, as follows:

000–099	General works such as encyclopedias
100–199	Philosophy
200–299	Religion (including mythology)
300–399	Social sciences (including folklore, legends, government, manners, vocations)
400–499	Language (including dictionaries and grammar books)
500–599	Pure science (mathematics, astronomy, chemistry, nature study)
600–699	Technology (applied science, aviation, building, engineering, homemaking)
700–799	Arts (photography, drawing, painting, music, sports)
800–899	Literature (plays, poetry)
900–999	History (ancient, modern, geography, travel)

Each category is further divided. For example, the numbers 500–599 cover "pure" science, including mathematics. The math books are shelved from 510–519; geometry is listed under 513. There are finer and finer categories to make it a breeze to shelve and locate material.

Model Dewey Decimal Call Number

For example, Helen Gurley Brown's *Sex and the Single Girl* has the following Dewey Decimal call number: 301.412B. Here's what it means:

301.412   =   social sciences

B   =   first initial of author's last name

Dewey's system works so well that today it's used by most elementary schools, high schools, and small public libraries. The Dewey Decimal classification system is *not* used by most college and university libraries for their books, however.

Library of Congress Classification System

The Library of Congress classification system, in contrast, was designed for just one library—you guessed it, the Library of Congress. Because the Library of Congress classification system allows for finer distinctions than the Dewey Decimal classification system, it's been a big hit with large libraries. As a result, it's been adopted by nearly all big college and university libraries. Here's how it works.

Categories of Books

The Library of Congress classification system arranges materials by subjects. Fiction has a call number, not simply the author's last name. This classification system has 20 classes, as follows:

A   General works (encyclopedias, dictionaries, newspapers, magazines, yearbooks, almanacs, directories, museums)

B   Philosophy, psychology, religion

C   Auxiliary sciences of history

D   History and topography (except America)

E–F   American history

G	Geography, anthropology, folklore, manners, customs, recreation
H	Social sciences
J	Political sciences
K	Law
L	Education
M	Music
N	Fine arts
P	Language and literature
Q	Science
R	Medicine
S	Agriculture
T	Technology
U	Military science
V	Naval science
Z	Bibliography, library science, general information resources

As with the Dewey Decimal classification system, each category in the Library of Congress system is further divided into subclasses. For example, C (auxiliary sciences of history) includes the following subclasses:

- ◆ CB   History of civilization
- ◆ CC   Archaeology
- ◆ CD   Diplomatics, archives, seals
- ◆ CE   Technical chronology, calendars
- ◆ CJ   Numismatics (coins)
- ◆ CN   Inscriptions
- ◆ CR   Heraldry
- ◆ CS   Genealogy
- ◆ CT   Biography

Model Library of Congress Call Number

Each Library of Congress classification call number usually has four parts, as the following sample number shows:

line 1   PA

line 2   112

line 3   .G53

line 4   1998

Here's the code breaker:

line 1   This can be a single letter or a double letter. Read the first line in alphabetical order, as follows:

A B BE C ...L, LA, LB, LC, etc.

If a book's call number begins with a single letter that is the same as the first letter of a call number that begins with a double letter, then the book with the single letter is shelved first (to the left) on the shelf.

line 2   This is always a number from 1 to 9999. Read this as a whole number, as in:

1, 2, 3, … 100, 101, 102, … 2000, 2001, 2002, etc.

If the letters on the second line of the call number are the same, the book with the smaller number is shelved to the left of the book with the larger number.

line 3   This is always a decimal point, followed by a letter and a number. Read the letter alphabetically. Read the number as a decimal, as follows:

.C76 = 76   .H876 = 876

Books are shelved alphabetically according to the letter to the right of the decimal point. For example, a book with .G on the third line of its call number is shelved to the left of a book with .H. If two books have the same letter on the third line, then the book with the smaller decimal is shelved to the left of the book with the larger number. For example, .G53 is shelved to the left of .G532 because .53 is smaller than .532.

line 4   The fourth line of a Library of Congress call number is always a year of publication or a volume number. An earlier edition is shelved to the left of a later edition.

The following chart shows how call numbers are put in order according to the Library of Congress classification system.

(LA before LB) ↓	(2327 before 2328) ↓	(.34 before .344) ↓	
Book 1	**Book 2**	**Book 3**	**Book 4**
LA	LB	LB	LB
2301	2327	2328	2328
.M37	.M3	.C34	.C344
1999	1989	2003	

Because the Dewey Decimal system and the Library of Congress system group related topics together, you can often find unexpected but related avenues to follow as you research. You can use this to your advantage by browsing the shelves as you gather the books you looked up.

Mix 'n' Match Classification Systems

Some libraries classify all their materials according to the Dewey Decimal Classification system. Other libraries classify all their materials according to the Library of Congress classification system. Most libraries use the SuDocs system for their government documents. However, there is no rule that says that a library *must* use one or the other classification system. A library can use either classification system … or both.

Some major university libraries, for example, classify books under the Library of Congress system and magazines and journals under the Dewey Decimal system. Other large libraries may classify books for young people, curriculum materials, and archival materials according to the Dewey Decimal system, whereas books, magazines, journals, and media are classified under Library of Congress numbers.

Other libraries may have begun with a Dewey Decimal system, but as they grew switched over to Library of Congress system. The switch may not be complete, and so the materials are classified under both systems in a totally haphazard manner. Or, the library may have received some donated books from another library that are still tagged with call numbers from the other classification system.

What to do? Check the library's home page or speak with a reference librarian to see which classification system(s) is being used. And remember: Because you know all three methods of classification, you're at home in any library!

Location Prefixes

Both the Dewey Decimal classification system and the Library of Congress classification system use some *location prefixes*. Because these are prefixes, they come *before* the call number.

Location prefixes mean that the book is shelved in a special place and may have some loan restrictions. You may not be able to take the book out of the library, for instance. Here are some common location prefixes and their meanings.

You Could Look It Up

Location prefixes are a letter or series of letters before the call number that show a book is shelved in a special area of the library or has restricted borrowing privileges.

Prefix	Meaning	Restrictions
J, Juv	Juvenile (children's books)	None
YP	Young people (children's)	None
R, Ref	Reference	Does not circulate
O	Oversized	None

Libraries are free to invent any location prefix they choose, so if you see one that's not listed on this chart, just ask what it means.

Government Document Classification System

Collections of U.S. government documents are usually shelved according to a classification system developed by the U.S. superintendent of documents. If stars and germs can be named after their discoverers, why not library classification systems? Thus, the classification system developed by the U.S. superintendent of documents is called the Superintendent of Documents classification system, abbreviated *SuDocs*.

You Could Look It Up

Government documents are classified under their **SuDocs** classification numbers.

Following are some of the most commonly used SuDocs prefixes and their meanings.

Prefix	Meaning
A	Agriculture Department
C3.	Census Bureau

continues

continued

Prefix	Meaning
D	Defense Department
E	Energy Department
ED	Education Department
GA	General Accounting Office
GS	General Services Administration
HE	Health and Human Services Department
I	Interior Department
I 19.	U.S. Geological Survey
J	Justice Department
Ju	Judiciary
L	Labor Department
LC	Library of Congress
NAS	National Aeronautics and Space Administration
S	State Department
SI	Smithsonian Institution
T22.	Internal Revenue Service (Treasury Department)
W,Y	Congress
Y4.	Congressional Committees

Here's a sample SuDocs number explained:

C 61.34:999

C = the issuing agency; in this case, the Commerce Department

61. = subordinate bureau; in this case, the International Trade Administration

34: = number of the specific publication; in this case, U.S. Industrial Outlook

999 = year of publication; in this case, 1999

Systems Failure

Library call numbers don't work like the Celsius and Fahrenheit temperature systems, so there's no magical formula you can use to convert the call numbers in one system to the call numbers in the other system. You simply have to become familiar with each classification system.

The following examples illustrate my point. Notice that the numbers are not linked to each other in any way because the classification systems are totally self-contained. This is especially noticeable when it comes to fiction, which is shelved according to the author's last name in the Dewey Decimal system but according to a call number in the Library of Congress classification system.

	Call Number	
Nonfiction Book	**Dewey Decimal**	**Library of Congress**
American Renaissance	810.9M	PS201.M3
	Call Number	
Fiction Books	**Dewey Decimal**	**Library of Congress**
The Sea-Wolf	London	PS3523.046 S43
Under Western Eyes	Conrad	PR6005.04U9

To save yourself hours of extra work, try these five handy hints as you gather books for your research paper:

1. Read through this chapter several times so you fully understand the three different classification systems.

2. Choose one library system for the books you need for each research assignment—either a university or public library system—and stick with it. Because you are working within a system, you will have many different libraries from which to choose. If possible, try to avoid switching from university to public libraries in midstream for your books, and vice versa.

3. Learn your library. Know which classification system(s) are used there and where different types of books (fiction, nonfiction, reference, oversized, juvenile, etc.) are located.

4. Come prepared. Have paper and pen or your laptop with you when you research in a library.

5. Work carefully. Write a formal bibliography card for each book you find, as you learned in Chapter 4. Be sure to copy down the call number *exactly* as it appears in the card catalog. Otherwise, it will be difficult—if not impossible—to find the book. Don't scribble information on paper scraps or your hand! (Been there, done that, and learned the hard way that it doesn't work!)

Using Card Catalogs

Back in B.C. (before computers), library card catalogs were a series of paper cards arranged in drawers. There was one card for each book. You flipped through the cards to find what you want. Great for paper cuts, but not so great for research. Why?

♦ Lazy patrons ripped out the cards rather than copying down the numbers. No card = no record of the book.

♦ Cards had to be prepared by hand, so there was often a significant lag time between the acquisition of a book and its placement on the shelves.

♦ Cards got soiled and became difficult to read.

♦ Cards often fell out of the drawers.

Although some libraries still use paper catalogs, most libraries have moved to computerized online card catalogs. Researchers around the country greeted this innovation with shouts of joy. Why?

♦ No one can rip out cards because everything is displayed on a computer screen. If the library owns it, there's a record of it.

♦ Click a few keys and the book is entered into the system. As a result, books are shelved much faster.

♦ Cards can't get soiled. They are always easy to read because they're onscreen.

♦ Cards can't fall out of the drawers because there aren't any cards.

Online card catalogs have a number of other significant advantages over paper catalogs. Here are some of the most important ones:

♦ **Keyword search.** An online catalog offers an especially useful way to search not offered by a paper catalog: a keyword search. You simply enter a keyword, as you learned in Chapter 4. You no longer have to browse through the shelves to find related books on a topic.

♦ **Full collections.** In addition to books, online card catalogs also list everything in a library's collection: magazines, newspapers, journals, electronic resources, videos, and more. Thus, you can access the library's entire collection from one terminal rather than having to check a series of print indexes.

♦ **Off-site access.** Increasingly, online card catalogs can be accessed off-site, 24/7. You simply dial in from your home computer to find out if a book (or other resource) is part of the library's collection. You can also find out whether the book is available from other member libraries, has been taken out, or has been placed on reserve, for example. Later, when you visit the library, you know what books are and are not available.

Search Methods

Whether you use an online card catalog or a paper catalogue, there are three different ways that you can locate material in books:

1. Subject search

2. Title search

3. Author search

Your topic determines how you search for a book. Because most research papers deal with topics and issues, you'll likely be searching by subject. Nonetheless, you'll probably have to check titles and authors as well. Consider all three ways to find information as you look through the card catalog.

> ### From the Reference Desk
>
> As early as the thirteenth century, people in China and Europe wore eyeglasses. With the invention of the printing press, everyday people had access to books, newspapers, and journals. Even though most people still couldn't read, eyeglasses became a status symbol. Why? Because wearing them showed the person was smart!

Reading an Online Catalog Entry

Some online catalogs list a brief entry and/or a full one. You may have to click on the brief entry to gain access to the full one. Here is a sample full entry:

Title	*The Complete Idiot's Guide to Writing Well* by Laurie Rozakis, Ph.D.
Author	Rozakis, Laurie, 1952–
Publisher	New York, Penguin/Putnam, 2000
Subject	English language and rhetoric writing instruction letter writing grammar and usage style publishing

continues

continued

Material	448 p., ill., 23 cm. Includes index
Notes	Includes sample term papers and index
	Also available as an e-book
LC Call No.	PE1413.R852000
ISBN	0-02-863694-5

Some of the entries are live links, so if you click on them, you can get additional information. For example, if you click on my name in the previous entry, you would go to a list of all the other books I have written that the library has in its collection. If you clicked on the subject entry, you would see a list of other books on the subject of writing.

I know this chapter could be titled "Everything You Need to Know About Classification Systems ... and Much, Much More," but relax. When you start researching books (and other material) in a library, all the information you learned here will fall into place. I promise.

The Least You Need to Know

- Three different classification systems track the volumes in a library's collection. The systems use completely different sets of letters and numbers, referred to as a call number.

- The Dewey Decimal classification system classifies fiction under the author's last name and nonfiction books into 10 broad categories. This system is used by most elementary schools, high schools, and small public libraries.

- The Library of Congress classification system classifies all books under 20 categories by subject. This system is used by nearly all big college and university libraries.

- Location prefixes mean that the book is shelved in a special place and may have some loan restrictions.

- The Superintendent of Documents (SuDocs) classification system is used only for government documents.

- Each classification system is discrete, so you have to become familiar with each one.

- Although online card catalogs have significant advantages over paper catalogs, all can be searched according to subject, title, and author.

Chapter 8

Research with Reference Books

In This Chapter

- ◆ Almanacs
- ◆ Atlases
- ◆ Dictionaries
- ◆ Encyclopedias
- ◆ Other reference books

When you research, you look for two kinds of information: opinions and facts. *Opinions* are beliefs and theories. You may or may not agree with the opinions you find. *Facts* are statements that can be proven by observation or empirical evidence. Facts are truth, not theory. Facts are reality, not speculation. You need to use facts to decide which opinions are valid. Then you use facts to back up the opinions you support.

Reference books are a great place to get the facts you need. That's because reference books specialize in facts. Happily for researchers, reference books are easy to locate and use. And there are so many different ones, you're sure to find several on the topic that you are researching.

In this chapter, we'll survey the most useful reference books, starting with almanacs and atlases, moving on to dictionaries and encyclopedias, and concluding with a survey of other types of reference books.

Almanacs: All-in-One General Reference Texts

◆ Fish and visitors smell in three days.

◆ Never leave till tomorrow that which you can do today.

◆ Early to bed and early to rise makes a man healthy, wealthy, and wise.

Most of us know the almanac from Benjamin Franklin's famous *Poor Richard's Almanac*, a collection of wit and wisdom published every year from 1733 to 1758. As with most almanacs of the time, Franklin's almanac contained practical information about the calendar, the sun, the moon, and the weather. It also contained a treasure chest of homespun sayings and observations, many of which are still used today—as is the case with the three aphorisms that begin this section.

You Could Look It Up

An **almanac** is a book published yearly that contains useful and interesting facts about the seasons, U.S. states, countries of the world, sports, and so on. Unfortunately, publishers have ditched the memorable sayings.

Today's *almanacs* are annual publications containing calendars, statistics, and useful and interesting facts about U.S. states, countries of the world, sports, and so on. Unfortunately, publishers have ditched the memorable sayings, but we *do* still get all the useful facts. The *Information, Please* almanac states that its purpose is to "answer virtually all the questions the general reader might ask." This makes almanacs a must-have book for all researchers. If you buy just one book every year, make it an almanac.

Almanacs have the following four advantages for researchers:

1. **Timely.** They are updated every year.

2. **Authoritative.** Facts are carefully checked.

3. **Comprehensive.** Information is complete.

4. **Easy to use.** They feature charts, graphs, and other visuals that fit a lot of information in a small space.

What's in an Almanac?

So what can you find in an almanac? Here are some samples from *The World Almanac and Book of Facts 2003* (New York: World Almanac Books, 2003).

- ◆ Top 10 news stories of 2002

- ◆ Essays on important issues in the news

- ◆ The year in review (including a chronology of the past year's events, notable Supreme Court decisions, last year's Nobel Prize winners, major actions of Congress, notable quotes from the previous year, offbeat news stories, historical anniversaries, obituaries of famous people, miscellaneous facts)

- ◆ United States government (president's administration, cabinets of the United States, Congress, U.S. Judiciary, state government, vital statistics, health, economics, agriculture, employment, taxes, energy, environment, meteorology, disasters)

- ◆ Photographs of key events of the past year

- ◆ National defense

- ◆ Aerospace

- ◆ Trade and transportation

- ◆ Telecommunications

- ◆ Education

- ◆ Arts and media

- ◆ Awards, medals, prizes

- ◆ Crimes in the United States

- ◆ U.S. states

- ◆ U.S. population statistics

- ◆ World history, historical figures

- ◆ Flags and maps

- ◆ U.S. history (U.S. presidents, U.S. facts, buildings, bridges, tunnels)

- ◆ Languages

- ◆ Religions

- Calendar and astronomy

- Science and technology

- Weights and measures

- Consumer information (postal information, associations and societies, Social Security, travel and tourism)

- Nations of the world

- Sports

As you can tell, information in an almanac is *not* arranged alphabetically. Nearly all almanacs have a brief table of contents, but the index in the back of the book is more complete. Using an almanac is a snap. Here's how to do it:

1. Decide on a topic.

2. Look in the index at the back of the book to find the topic.

3. Turn to the page(s) indicated.

Trustworthy Almanacs

Almanacs are not only chock-a-block with great facts; they're also among the least expensive books you can buy. They average under $10! (My latest almanac cost $7.49 at a wholesale club; the most I've ever spent for an almanac is $9.99 at a bookstore.) An almanac unquestionably gives you the most bang for your research buck.

Buy any almanac that fires your jets. Following are three different ones that I have sitting on my shelf right now. All are excellent research sources.

- *The World Almanac and Book of Facts*

- *The New York Times Almanac*

- *Information, Please Almanac*

From the Reference Desk

The word *almanac* comes from the Spanish and Arabic *al manākh,* which roughly translates to "a calendar of the heavens." Almanacs in various forms date from ancient days and were probably the first publications in most countries. Ancient almanacs were carved on wooden sticks and stone slabs; medieval almanacs were recorded on parchment. *Kalendarium Novum,* the earliest existing printed almanac, dates from 1576 and was printed in red for lucky days and black for regular days!

Atlases: Your Source for Maps

An *atlas* is a collection of maps or charts bound in a volume. An atlas may cover the entire world or just a specific country; the maps might show political borders, land forms, historical or cultural features, or all of the above. You don't have to be an explorer to need an atlas: They're great for researchers as well. That's because a good atlas often contains the following information in addition to maps:

◆ An index of place names

◆ Population statistics

◆ Other factual information on geography, climate, agriculture, diseases, language, astronomy, and so forth

You Could Look It Up

An **atlas** is a book of maps or charts.

So how did the atlas get its name? Title pages of old atlases had a picture of the mythological Greek figure of Atlas holding the earth on his shoulders.

Dictionaries: More Than Just Words

When asked why he robbed banks, the famous bank robber Willie Sutton replied, "Because that's where the money is." When people ask why you're researching words in a dictionary, you can answer, "Because that's where the words are."

A *dictionary* is an alphabetical reference list of the words in the language. There are two main kinds of dictionaries: abridged and unabridged.

◆ An *abridged dictionary* contains only the most common words that people use every day. The dictionary you carry around in your briefcase or backpack is an abridged dictionary.

◆ An *unabridged dictionary* contains all the words in English. These dictionaries come in many volumes, like a set of encyclopedias. You'd need a hand truck to carry one around.

You Could Look It Up

A **dictionary** is an alphabetical reference list of the words in the language. **Abridged dictionaries** are one-volume books that contain the most common words; **unabridged dictionaries** are multivolume books that contain all the words in a language. Everyday dictionaries are abridged.

Dictionaries are chock-a-block with words listed in alphabetical order. A dictionary entry includes the following:

- Pronunciation guides

- Word definitions

- Word histories

- Spelling

- Parts of speech

- Irregular forms of the word

- Etymology (the derivation and development of words)

An entry may also contain synonyms and antonyms of the word; prefixes, suffixes, and other elements in word formation; and abbreviations. Thus, dictionaries help researchers in scores of ways, from providing definitions, pronunciations, and spelling to furnishing a word's history. Knowing how a word is pronounced can save you embarrassment if you're doing an oral report or business presentation, too.

Types of Dictionaries

All dictionaries are *not* the same. Different types of dictionaries fit different needs. For example, dictionaries have been written just for scholars, people who research the history of language. The most famous scholarly dictionary is the *Oxford English Dictionary*. An unabridged dictionary, the *OED* (as it's abbreviated) contains more than 500,000 entries. Don't rush right out to buy one to stash in your bookcase, however, because the OED now contains about 60 million words in 20 volumes. If shelf space is an issue and you simply can't live without an OED, however, online and CD-ROM versions are available. You can carry these without getting a hernia.

General dictionaries have been created just for adults, college students, high school students, and elementary school students, too. The best-selling general dictionaries include the following:

- *American Heritage Dictionary of the English Language, Fourth Edition*, 2002

- *Merriam-Webster Collegiate Dictionary, Eleventh Edition*

- *Merriam-Webster Dictionary*

- *Merriam-Webster's Pocket Dictionary*

- *The Random House College Dictionary*

- *The Shorter Oxford English Dictionary*

- *Webster's II New Riverside Pocket Dictionary*

- *Webster's 3rd New International Dictionary*

Most of these dictionaries, as well as others like them, are available in electronic versions.

Then we have special dictionaries, which are often very different from the ones described above. More than 32,000 dictionaries are listed on Amazon.com! Many of these are special dictionaries tailored to specific research needs. For example:

- *Dictionary of American Regional English.* This dictionary contains terms used around the country, like *soda* versus *pop* for the sugary carbonated drinks I consume by the caseload.

- *Dictionary of Foreign Phrases and Abbreviations.* This dictionary contains non-English words used in English.

- *Dictionary of Finance and Investment Terms.* This dictionary contains specialized terms for money.

- *The Official Scrabble Players Dictionary (Third Edition).* Merriam-Webster publishes this handy guide for Scrabble fans looking for ways to score 64 points with a "Z."

- *The Oxford Spanish Dictionary.* Many dictionaries, like this one, contain words in foreign languages.

- *Surfin'Ary: A Dictionary of Surfing Terms and Surfspeak.* This dictionary contains surfing words. (Hey, you never know when you'll have to research waves and surfer dudes.)

- *Brewer's Dictionary of Phrase and Fable.* This famous work contains nearly 20,000 entries that reveal the etymologies, trace the origins, and otherwise catalog words with a tale to tell.

- *Slayer Slang: A Buffy the Vampire Slayer Lexicon.* This volume proves that there *is* a book for every researcher ….

- *Milady's Skin Care and Cosmetic Ingredients Dictionary.* Want to research what's in your lipstick—and what all those big words on the side of the tube means? Here's the source.

- *Newton's Telecom Dictionary (Nineteenth Edition).* Covering telecommunications, networking, information technology, and computing, this is a dictionary of telecommuting terms.

Using a Dictionary

Because English has so many different spellings for the same sound, finding an unfamiliar word when you don't know how to spell it can be a pain. You can solve this problem by becoming familiar with different spelling patterns for the sounds of English words.

When you're trying to find a word in the dictionary, always begin by making an educated guess as to its spelling. The odds are in your favor. However, the more spelling patterns you know for a sound, the better your chances for finding the word fast. You can find a pronunciation chart in the beginning of any dictionary. When you've narrowed down your search and you're flipping through the pages, use the *guide words*, located on the upper corners of the pages, to guide your search. Then follow strict alphabetical order.

The following diagram shows how to read a sample entry. I've tried to make the experience as sweet as possible by using the word *candy* ....

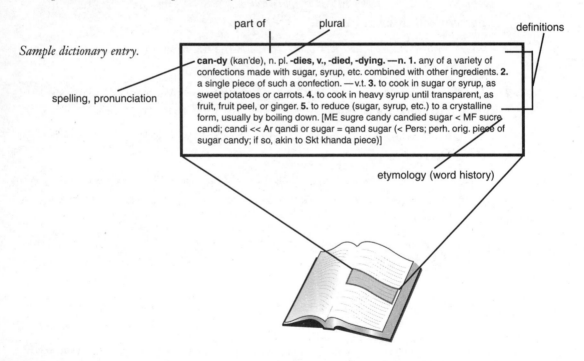

Sample dictionary entry.

Encyclopedias: The Big Daddy of Reference Books

Let's start with the spelling: Is it encyclopedia or encyclopaedia? Not to worry: Both spellings are correct.

No matter how you spell it, encyclopedias are a great way to get a general overview of your research subject or background information on your subject. As a result, reading an encyclopedia article helps you put the entire issue into perspective and see the "big picture."

The encyclopedia is *the* classic reference tool, the gold standard, the Real Thing. That's because a standard encyclopedia is always there for you and can fulfill nearly all your needs. You can tell this from the word itself: *encyclopedia* comes from the Greek *enkyklopaideia*, which meant "a complete system of learning, an all-around education."

You Could Look It Up

An **encyclopedia** is a collection of articles on many topics.

To give you a complete education, encyclopedias contain many articles on different subjects. Some of these entries might be just a brief paragraph, while others might be pages long. Both kinds of entries are useful, each in their own way. The following chart sums it up.

Brief Encyclopedia Entries	Long Encyclopedia Entries
Provide a quick overview	Give in-depth information
Are succinct	Are detailed
	Include a reference list

The information in a new encyclopedia will be at least some months old and might be years old. If you need very up-to-date information, an encyclopedia probably isn't a good source of information. Check the date the encyclopedia was published to give you an idea if the information is recent enough to be useful. But don't be so quick to toss out that volume in favor of a web page!

For example, an article on ancient Rome in an old encyclopedia might be better than a recent article on ancient Rome from a web page, because ancient Rome hasn't changed since the old article was written. The encyclopedia article has been carefully edited, revised, and vetted, too. The recent article hasn't had as much careful polish. Nonetheless, it's always a good idea to use the most up-to-date encyclopedias you can locate.

So What's in an Encyclopedia?

Encyclopedias may include some or all of the following features:

♦ Biographies of famous people

♦ Bibliographies (lists of reference works on the topic)

♦ Detailed articles

♦ Lists of abbreviations

♦ Lists of foreign expressions

♦ Sidebars

♦ Visuals such as pictures, illustrations, and maps

From the Reference Desk

The first fragments of an encyclopedia that have survived through the ages were written by Speusippus, one of Plato's nephews, around 339 B.C.E. Speusippus took a cultural approach, summarizing the lectures his uncle and Aristotle delivered at the Lyceum. The Romans, in contrast, tried to fit in all knowledge. Their first known encyclopedia came out in 183 B.C.E. Meanwhile, in the East, the Chinese have created encyclopedias for about 2,000 years, but their volumes were a combination of literature and the dictionary. The first Chinese encyclopedia, *Emperor's Mirror,* was written around 220 C.E. The Chinese can take credit for what is probably the world's largest encyclopedia, the *Great Handbook,* published in the fifteenth century. Only a few of the nearly 23,000 chapters survive.

Today, encyclopedias come in one volume or many volumes. Whether one volume or a set, information is arranged in alphabetical order by subject.

All-Purpose Encyclopedias

As with dictionaries, encyclopedias come in two flavors: general and specific. Here are some of the best-known general encyclopedias:

♦ *Encyclopedia Britannica.* The oldest and largest encyclopedia in English. *Britannica* has been continuously published since 1768, when its first edition was published in Scotland.

♦ *Columbia Encyclopedia (Sixth Edition),* 2001. This encyclopedia contains more than 50,000 articles, 40,000 bibliographic citations, and 80,000 cross-references.

♦ *World Book. World Book* is an excellent encyclopedia for students because it is written on an easier reading level than *Britannica.*

♦ *Compton's Encyclopedia.* Similar to *World Book* in its level of difficulty.

◆ *Funk and Wagnalls.* Small and easy to handle, this encyclopedia is very good for a quick read and general overview.

◆ *Encarta.* Available on CD-ROM and online, Encarta is published by Microsoft and includes an interactive world atlas, almanac, book of quotations, and English dictionary along with the encyclopedia. The deluxe version includes 7 CDs housing more than 73 million words, 25,000 photos and illustrations, and 300 video clips.

Encyclopedias on Specific Subjects

Special encyclopedias are devoted to a single subject. Encyclopedias exist on just about every topic you can imagine: wildlife, sports, rules for sports, insects, science, technology, fashion, African Americans, the environment, UFOs—you get the idea. Special encyclopedias are especially useful if you are …

◆ Trying to narrow your topic.

◆ Researching a definite topic.

◆ Looking for a very specific fact.

To find an encyclopedia on a specific subject, do a key word search using the name of your subject and the word *encyclopedia.* Here are some well-known encyclopedias on specific subjects:

◆ *The Encyclopedia of World History (Sixth Edition),* 2001

◆ *The Encyclopedia of the U.S. Presidency*

◆ *Encyclopedia of the Dog*

◆ *The Columbia Gazetteer of North America*

CAUTION

Lost in (Cyber)Space

If your teacher or professor says, "Don't use an encyclopedia," chances are he or she means "Don't use *only* an encyclopedia" or "Don't cite an encyclopedia as a source." Whether or not you are permitted to use an encyclopedia as a reference source, encyclopedias can help you put your topic in perspective, get a dependable overview, and find the key words to use in your search.

Print vs. Online Encyclopedias

Today's encyclopedias are available in print and online versions. You would expect the online and CD-ROM encyclopedias to match their print counterparts, but this is not the case. The print versions have two-dimensional photographs and illustrations, whereas the online and CD-ROM versions also feature video and audio clips. In addition, some CD-ROM versions sacrifice print content for visuals, so pages of text might have gotten axed to allow space on the CD for the video clips. Thus, the print and online/CD-ROM versions are *not* interchangeable.

So should you use the print version or the online version? (Or both?) Here are some factors to consider:

♦ The print versions are almost always shelved as reference books, kept on a separate set of bookshelves, and are not for loan. This means they are always there when you need them.

♦ If you use the book version, you can take notes on the information you need or photocopy the parts of the article you want.

Ask the Librarian

Some online encyclopedias charge a fee for access from your home computer. Accessing these online encyclopedias from a library portal, however, is free to you because the library has already paid the fee. Remember: Increasingly, you can access a library's databases off-site.

♦ If you use the online or CD-ROM version, you can print the page or save it to your hard drive or a floppy disk.

So which will it be: print or online encyclopedias? Personally, when it comes to encyclopedias, I'm a print gal all the way. I find the books much easier and faster to use. Online and CD-ROM encyclopedias have so many hypertext links that I spend hours browsing around. The pages are pretty and it's fun to bounce around, but when I need to verify a fact fast, I hit the book rather than the button.

Other Reference Books

In addition to specific books on your topic, here are some general reference sources to consider:

♦ **Bibliographies.** You'll save time if you find a bibliography, a list of books, articles, and other documents on a specific subject area. Well-known bibliographies include the following:

♦ *Guide to the Literature of Art History*

♦ *Communication: A Guide to Information Sources*

♦ *Science and Engineering Literature*

♦ *Social Work: A Bibliography*

◆ *Books in Print.* This annual listing of books currently in print or slated for print can tell you whether a book is still being issued by the publisher. If so, the library can order a copy of the book or you can buy one yourself at a book store.

◆ *Guide to Reference Books.* Published by the American Library Association, this useful guide has five main categories: general reference works; humanities; social and behavioral sciences; history and area studies; and science, technology, and medicine.

◆ *Who's Who in America.* Are you researching a famous person? If so, check *Who's Who* because it includes biographical entries on approximately 75,000 Americans and people linked to America. *Who Was Who* covers famous dead people.

◆ **Books of quotations.** Arguably the title of "most famous book of quotations" goes to *Bartlett's Familiar Quotations*, but many other books of quotations are available, including *The Columbia World of Quotations* and *Simpson's Contemporary Quotations*. There are also many excellent websites for quotations.

◆ *Dictionary of Literary Biography.* One of my favorite series, DLB (as it's abbreviated) features biographies of famous authors.

◆ **Factbooks.** Factbooks are a gold mine for researchers. *Facts on File* and *The World Factbook* (the U.S. government's complete geographical handbook) are both superb.

◆ **Telephone books.** Lots of good stuff in those white pages (individual people), yellow pages (businesses), and blue pages (government information).

◆ **Roget's *II: The New Thesaurus.*** Stuck for a word? If so, you want a thesaurus, a book of synonyms and antonyms. *Roget's* is the most famous name in thesauri, but many other volumes are available.

Ask the Librarian

Bartleby.com is a superb site for reference materials.

◆ **Speeches.** Need some speeches? Among your many sources are *Inaugural Addresses of the Presidents of the United States* and *The World's Famous Orations*.

The Least You Need to Know

♦ Almanacs (issued annually) are superb all-in-one general reference texts, providing calendars, statistics, and useful and interesting facts about U.S. states, countries of the world, sports, and so on.

♦ Use atlases to get reliable maps or charts for research.

♦ Dictionaries include pronunciation guides, word definitions, word histories, spelling, parts of speech, irregular forms of words, and etymology.

♦ Encyclopedias, available in print, on CD, and online, are a great way to get a general overview of your research subject or background information on your subject. *Encyclopedia Britannica*, *World Book*, and *Encarta* are standard encyclopedias.

♦ There are heaps of useful reference books, including bibliographies, biographical sources (such as *Who's Who in America*), books of quotations, and factbooks.

Chapter 9

Research with Periodicals

In This Chapter

- ◆ Define periodicals: newspapers, magazines, academic journals
- ◆ See how periodicals are classified
- ◆ Explore different types of articles
- ◆ Weigh the advantages and disadvantages of using periodicals and books
- ◆ Access periodicals through print indexes and computerized databases

Do you want late-breaking news? Do you need timely information, fresh off the presses (or close to it)? The odds are good that you will indeed need up-to-the-minute facts for many of the topics that you research. Newspapers, magazines, and journals are an excellent source for current information because they are produced quickly but have still been edited.

In this chapter, we'll explore different types of periodical literature—newspapers, magazines, and academic journals—and their advantages and disadvantages for researchers. Then I'll show you how to use these sources to find the facts and opinions you need.

What Are Periodicals?

Periodicals include all material that is published on a regular schedule, such as weekly, biweekly, monthly, bimonthly, four times a year, and so on. Newspapers, magazines, and academic journals are classified as periodicals.

> **You Could Look It Up**
>
> **Periodicals** is the general term for newspapers, magazines, academic journals, and any other material published on a regular schedule.

Periodicals include many different types of publications, but the most common ones are newspapers, magazines, and academic journals. These three types of periodicals can be classified many different ways. Knowing how periodicals are categorized will help you locate and evaluate them. Here are some of the most common methods.

Newspapers

Newspapers are often classified in three different ways: publication schedule, types, and size.

- **Publication schedule.** Daily, weekly, monthly, and so forth. For example, daily newspapers include *The Daily News*, *The Wall Street Journal*, and *Newsday*. *USA Today* is issued six times a week: every day Monday through Friday, with one issue for Saturday and Sunday. *The Farmingdale Observer* and *The Massapequa Post* are issued weekly, as are the various *Pennysavers* delivered to your home.

- **Types.** Newspapers can also be classified by their types: U.S. newspapers, international newspapers, tabloid newspapers, newswire services, syndicated newspaper columns, and so on.

> **You Could Look It Up**
>
> **Tabloids** are newspapers measuring about 11×15 inches and known for their lavish photographs and sensational content.

- **Size.** Newspapers are also categorized according to their size. *Tabloids*, for example, are newspapers whose pages are approximately 11×15 inches, about half the size of a standard newspaper page. Usually, the tabloids (or "tabs," as they are often called) concentrate on sensational news such as illicit love affairs, political scandals, and the various misbehaviors of public figures. They are heavily illustrated with sensational photographs, too. The tabloids are rarely considered a reliable source for quality research.

Magazines

Magazines, like newspapers, can be classified in different ways. These methods are similar to the ways that newspapers are categorized.

◆ **Publication schedule.** Weekly, monthly, quarterly, and so on. For example, newsmagazines such as *Time, U.S. News and World Report*, and *Newsweek* come out weekly, as does *TV Guide* and the showbiz mag *Daily Variety*. Other magazines such as *Atlantic, Harpers*, and *Ladies Home Journal* come out monthly. Scholarly magazines, such as *Foreign Affairs*, usually come out quarterly.

◆ **Subject matter.** Magazines can also be classified by their subject matter: literary, travel, leisure, hobbies, health, children, and so on. There is a magazine on every possible topic under the sun (and likely over the moon, too!).

◆ **Publishing venue.** The majority of magazines are still published on paper, but several publishers are experimenting with online publication only. *Salon* and *Slate* are issued only online; at this time, there is no print version of these magazines.

Academic Journals

Academic journals are different from newspapers and magazines because of their tone and content. These journals have a serious, scholarly tone. The content is very narrow, depending on the audience. Guess what topics the following academic journals deal with:

◆ *San Diego Law Review*

◆ *The American Transcendental Quarterly: A Journal of Nineteenth Century New England Writers*

◆ *Scandinavian Journal of Economics*

◆ *A Pedagogical Journal in Russian*

◆ *Scottish Journal of Political Economy*

In addition, the articles are carefully reviewed by a panel of experts who check facts and verify information. This is called "peer review"—the authors have their articles reviewed by their peers or equals in their subject area. When a journal uses this review process before publishing articles, the journal is called a *refereed journal*. What does this mean for you as a researcher? It means that the journal has been carefully and responsibly edited. As a result, academic journals tend to be the most reliable periodical literature for scholars and researchers.

You Could Look It Up

Refereed journals have undergone a peer review process, the articles carefully checked for content. This results in a dependable scholarly research source.

Because most academic journals are published quarterly and size is rarely a significant feature, these periodicals are most often classified by subject matter.

Knowing how periodicals are classified can help you locate them in the library. Local daily newspapers and weekly newsmagazines, for example, are often displayed on racks for people to read. In university libraries, scholarly journals may be displayed as prominently because they are used often. Public libraries, in contrast, would rarely display scholarly journals.

Different Types of Articles

Aside from general articles about a subject, a number of other types of articles are published in periodicals. Among the most important for researchers are articles written by experts, obituaries, and articles written as part of a series. Let's look at these now.

◆ **Articles written by experts.** Often, authorities on a specific subject publish articles on their specialty. This is especially common in scholarly journals, whose articles are written almost exclusively by the top honchos in their respective fields. This makes the articles a "must-read" for their quality information and careful fact-checking.

◆ **Obituaries.** Obituaries, death notices, often provide a good overview of a person's life, especially if the person is famous. Obituaries are most often found in newspapers and magazines, although they can also appear in scholarly journals.

From the Reference Desk

Although newspapers are the most common source for a series of articles today, some magazines publish complete books, one chapter at a time or in their entirety. In the nineteenth century, authors such as Charles Dickens routinely serialized their novels in periodicals, issuing a chapter each month or so. Likely the most famous such publication in modern times occurred in 1946, when *The New Yorker* (a well-respected literary magazine) published John Hersey's book *Hiroshima* in its entirety. *Hiroshima* is Hersey's now classic account of the aftermath of the August 6, 1945 bombing of Hiroshima that resulted in the Japanese surrender and the end of World War II. While the ashes of Hiroshima were still warm, Hersey interviewed the survivors. His trip resulted in this world-famous document, the most significant piece of journalism in modern times.

◆ **Series of stories.** Series of stories trace how key events unfold. For example, you might research the sequence of events in a war, the 9/11 attack, or the *Challenger* tragedy. Reading the entire series helps you analyze changing points of view and see how opinion and facts affected the interpretation of historical reality. Series are most often published in newspapers.

Weighing Different Print Sources

While newspapers, magazines, and journals are all classified as periodicals, they have different uses for research. The following section describes the distinctions.

Use newspapers when you want …

◆ Immediate news, photographs, and opinions (through editorials and letters to the editor).

◆ A summary or overview of a current event.

◆ Pictures of the event.

Use magazines when you want …

◆ Up-to-date general information about a subject.

◆ Pictures of the event.

◆ More detailed analysis than is available in newspapers.

Use academic journals when you want …

◆ Very detailed information about a subject written by experts.

◆ Research, theories, the results of studies and experiments, and analysis.

◆ Longer articles.

Books vs. Periodicals

Now, I'm not claiming that newspapers, magazines, and scholarly journals can solve your problems by giving you a brighter smile, firmer abs, and a better credit rating (although they may, based on the information they provide).

But research time being short, should you concentrate on finding relevant periodicals, relevant books, or a combination of both?

Your primary considerations are always as follows:

◆ **Topic.** The more contemporary your topic, the more likely you are to need periodicals rather than books.

◆ **Audience.** Academic audiences demand carefully vetted scholarly research, so you will likely use academic journals in these instances. On the other hand, a general readership is usually more comfortable with the average reading level found in newspapers and magazines.

◆ **Time constraints.** When time is a big factor, it is usually easier to locate and use periodicals because the articles are shorter and easier to absorb.

Let's look at the upside and downside of each print source in more detail.

Pros and Cons of Periodicals

The following chart summarizes the primary advantages and disadvantages of using periodicals.

Advantages	Disadvantages
They possess an immediacy and freshness that books lack.	Because they are produced fast, they may contain errors.
They often include pictures, diagrams, and other visuals that can help you understand a topic more fully.	Content may be sacrificed for visuals; visuals may be misleading.
They may include quotations that will help you make your point in your research paper.	They often do not contain sufficient information, unlike books.
They may lead you to an expert you may want to interview later.	They may be written by staff writers rather than experts.

Pros and Cons of Books

I love books. But even me, a book lover extraordinaire, must admit that books have drawbacks.

As you learned in Chapters 7 and 8, books are often an excellent source of material for your research paper. However, books have a number of important drawbacks when it comes to research.

- **Books may not be up-to-date.** It usually takes about a year to write, edit, and publish a book. Academic books can take far, far longer to create and issue. As a result, the information a book contains may be dated by the time the book appears on the library shelf. This is especially true with fast-changing topics such as medical issues and current events.

  For some topics, the age of a source may not be a pivotal factor, but for other topics, it's crucial. In addition, responsible researchers (like you) always want to balance classic books with contemporary sources to get the best of the old and the new. Periodicals and academic journals are more timely than books because they are published much more quickly than books.

- **Books are pricey.** An "average" paperback can easily cost $12; a textbook usually tops $100. Increasingly, books are so costly that many libraries are cutting back on their purchases, putting their funds instead into online sources, where they get far more bang for their budgeted bucks.

  In addition, books get lost, maimed, and otherwise damaged. This also makes them less attractive to cash-starved libraries. As a result, you may not be able to get the books you need easily. This can delay your research. Periodicals and academic journals can be less expensive than books, especially when they are published online and not in print. Thus, libraries order more of them so they're easier for patrons to get.

- **Books can be cumbersome to use.** I stubbornly maintain that print dictionaries and encyclopedias are easier to use than online versions, but even I can't make a case that all books are easier to use than all online sources.

  It can take a long time to sift through a book to find the information you need. You may have to do a lot of reading to find the nugget you need. Periodicals and academic journals are often easier to use than books simply because they are shorter.

But on the other hand, books have many significant advantages.

- **Books are more scrupulously written than most periodicals.** Because they are written more slowly, books are more thoughtfully checked for errors than newspapers and magazines.

- **Books are often written by experts.** Many scholars write for scholarly journals, but articles in newspapers and magazines are usually written by staffers who lack any particular expertise.

◆ **Books may be easier to use than magazines.** Increasingly, magazines are sac-rificing content for style: Many modern mags sport bizarre graphics, heavily retouched or even falsified pictures, and sound bites of information. Books are often easier to read simply because the typeface is easier to scan.

Only you can decide the percentage of books and periodicals to use in each research paper you write. I suggest that you find all relevant and important print sources and then decide what to use. The odds are excellent that you're going to be using articles from magazines, newspapers, and journals as well as books to find information for your research paper.

Locating Articles

Back in the good old days, periodicals were indexed in print. To get an article, you first you had to look in an index such as the big green *Readers' Guide to Periodical Literature*, jot down the bibliographic citation, ask a clerk to retrieve the magazine, and then read it. If the periodical was on microfilm or microfiche, you had to jimmy the film into a machine to read.

You followed the same procedure if you wanted to find newspaper articles: You checked a newspaper index, such as the *New York Times Index*, a thick red book. The same was true for scholarly articles. Because print indexes were usually issued annu-ally, they listed the publications for a single year. To investigate what had been pub-lished over a number of years, you had to search several volumes. Some libraries still index their periodicals in print indexes.

In today's technological age, many libraries use *computerized databases* in place of print indexes. Some databases include only periodicals; others include books, media, tele-phone numbers, and much more. No matter what information is indexed, each entry provides the title, author, publication information, and sometimes an abstract (a summary). You read the entire article or an abstract from the screen and print it or e-mail it to your home computer. This is a wonderful thing because it's easy, fast, and fun.

You Could Look It Up

A computerized data-base is a bibliographic computer file of reference sources.

Full Text and Abstracts: How Much Is Enough?

Some computerized databases provide a *full-text article*. This means you get the entire article: all the words, pictures, and bibliographic information. Everything that is printed on the page appears on the screen and can be downloaded.

Other articles, in contrast, are only brief summaries. Called *abstracts*, these may be no more than a paragraph long. If you want the complete article, you will have to access the microfilm, thread it through the reader, and read the article that way.

Both full-text and abstracts have their uses, as the following chart shows.

Use full-text ...	Use abstracts ...
When it's likely that you will need the entire article.	To get an overview of the topic.
When it is easily available.	To preview the article and decide if you really need it.

Read the citation carefully to see whether the article is a full-text article or an abstract. In nearly all cases, the database will indicate a date when full-text articles were first entered.

You Could Look It Up

A **full-text article** is complete; an **abstract** is a brief summary.

Locating Periodicals Through Databases

Every library has different periodical databases. Be sure the index you're searching includes sources on your topic. For example, in the Humanities index you probably wouldn't find any articles on stock mutual funds. For this topic, you should check the Business index. If you're using the wrong index, you might mistakenly assume that the library doesn't have any material on your topic.

Here are some of the databases that many libraries have purchased for your use. There are many more; this is a representative sampling of especially reliable sources.

These databases are often much more complete than the ones you can access through your regular Internet provider, so start your research by using the library's databases on-site or accessing them off-site from your home computer.

- ◆ EBSCO Host. This database of databases includes the following databases:

  - ◆ MasterFILE Premier provides full text for nearly 2,000 general-reference publications, with full-text information dating back to 1975. MasterFILE Premier also includes about 300 full-text reference books, nearly 100,000 biographies, 75,000 primary source documents, and an image collection of more than 100,000 maps, flags, and photos. The database is updated daily.

  - ◆ Business Source Elite provides full-text articles for more than 1,100 scholarly business journals, including full-text for more than 450 peer-reviewed business publications. The database is updated daily.

- ◆ Primary Search provides full-text for more than 60 popular magazines for elementary school research. The database is updated daily.

- ◆ Middle Search Plus provides full-text articles for more than 150 popular magazines for middle and junior high school research. The database is updated daily.

◆ EBSCO Animals provides in-depth information on a variety of topics relating to animals. The index includes full-text articles.

◆ MagillOnLiterature provides editorially reviewed critical analyses for standard works of literature.

◆ MEDLINE provides authoritative medical information. Created by the National Library of Medicine, MEDLINE allows users to search abstracts from more than 4,600 current biomedical journals.

◆ ERIC (Educational Resource Information Center) provides more than 3,000 educational-related digests and scholarly journals.

◆ Health Source—Consumer Edition includes the full text for nearly 200 journals as well as abstracts for about 200 general health, nutrition, and professional health-care publications.

◆ Newspaper Source provides full-text for more than 180 regional U.S. newspapers, international newspapers, and wire services. It also includes abstracts for national newspapers.

◆ TOPICsearch allows researchers to explore social, scientific, political, and economic issues. It contains more than 64,000 full-text articles from more than 3,000 sources, including more than 1,500 full-text periodicals.

◆ EBSCO Host Español. The Spanish version of EBSCO.

◆ Infotrac/General Reference Center. This database lists more than 1,000 business, technological, and general-interest periodicals, as well as *The New York Times* and the *Wall Street Journal.* Many are full-text.

◆ ProQuest. This database includes full-text and images for many periodicals, including *The New York Times.*

◆ Electric Library—Elibrary. A superb database of databases.

◆ Gale Databases. Includes many databases, such as these:

  - ◆ Customer Newspapers

  - ◆ National Newspaper Index

  - ◆ Informe

- MILCS. This is a database of all the holdings of academic and public libraries in specific regions.

- PubMed Central. This database provides free access to full-text articles of life-science research articles.

Ask the Librarian

Use the same search strategy with online databases as you do with a print index: Use key words, title, author, or any combination of these.

- OCLC First Search. This database lists all the periodicals, media, and books in the United States and Canada. It has many indexes.

- LEXIS/NEXIS. This database affords access to thousands of full-text articles.

The March of Progress

While more and more libraries are replacing their print indexes with online databases, many libraries still maintain their print indexes. In addition, the online databases may not go back far enough for the sources you need. This is especially true if you are doing historical or literary research. As a result, to do a complete search for materials, you must use everything that pertains to your topic. This means you will often be using both print and online indexes.

The Least You Need to Know

- Periodicals include all material that is published on a regular schedule, including newspapers, magazines, and academic journals.

- Periodicals are classified in several ways, including publication schedule, types, size, and subject matter.

- Consider topic, audience, and time constraints when deciding what proportion of books and periodicals to use, since each source has its advantages and disadvantages.

- Online articles are available in full-text (complete) or abstracts (brief summaries).

- Use computer databases if available to locate and download articles; otherwise, use print indexes.

- Databases available through your library (both on-site and off-site) are often much more complete than the ones you can access through your regular Internet provider, so start your research by using the library's databases.

Chapter 10

Research with Interviews, Media Sources, and Surveys

In This Chapter

◆ Conduct interviews

◆ Use media sources

◆ Study a sample research paper

Although you'll probably conduct most of your research in the library, remember that there's a lot of great research to be done *outside* the library and offline. For instance, consider the possibility of conducting original research. You can do this by interviewing knowledgeable people and devising and distributing questionnaires. Media—including CDs, DVDs, and videos—is also an excellent source of research.

In this chapter, I'll take you step by step through this aspect of the research process.

Straight from the Expert's Mouth: Interviews

Interviews are personal meetings with individuals or groups. An interview can be as casual as a quick Q&A at a picnic, but more often interviews are formal meetings in a businesslike setting. They can be conducted via telephone, e-mail, snail mail, or person to person.

Interviews allow you to …

◆ Conduct primary research.

◆ Acquire potentially valuable information unavailable in print and online sources.

◆ Gather quotations from people who have direct knowledge of a particular subject.

◆ Add authority, credibility, and immediacy to your research paper.

You Could Look It Up

Interviews are meetings arranged to obtain information by questioning a person or group of people.

Entire books have been written on how to conduct an effective interview. Fortunately, whether you want a 10-second sound bite or a 10-hour oral history, the process is the same.

Top Ten Interview Tips

Following are my top 10 hints for conducting a great research interview.

1. Choose subjects carefully.

Try to select a person who has both the ability and the desire to provide the information you want, because one without the other is a waste of your time. For instance, while I was researching information for my doctoral dissertation on the influence of political events on the literature of the 1930s through the 1950s, I interviewed a famous magazine editor about his involvement in the politics of the 1930s and 1940s. An old family friend, he promised to reveal key information I needed. Although he had long been cleared of any involvement in the Red Scare of the 1950s, he was still unwilling to discuss that time. Instead, he stonewalled me by steering the conversation to his children. Result? I had a very frustrating afternoon and left empty-handed.

Because you can never be sure that an interview subject will give you the facts you need, try to arrange for backup people to interview.

And don't be afraid to go to the top. If you want to interview a well-known person, make the effort. The person can always turn you down, but you'll never know until you try, right?

2. Call and confirm a face-to-face interview.

Always telephone the day before a personal interview to make sure that plans have not changed. People take sick, get called out of the office on business, and get dragged into important meetings. This isn't personal; it's just reality.

Increasingly, people are conducting business via e-mail, but a phone call is still a more reliable way to confirm an interview. When it comes to e-mail, servers crash and not everyone checks e-mail as often as we would like.

3. Arrive early for a personal interview.

Allow yourself ample time to find the location, set up any equipment you need, and get your bearings. This gives you a strong advantage because you will be more relaxed and can concentrate on the subject of the interview more completely.

If you are conducting an e-mail or telephone interview, make sure the line is clear.

4. Research and prepare questions well in advance of the interview.

Do your homework. If you are lucky enough to interview someone famous, it may take weeks of research before you're ready to ask the first question. And even if you are interviewing an everyday Jane or Joe, it is only professional to know about the person's background, including his or her accomplishments, education, and other relevant facts.

Research will give you names, dates, events, places, and data that you can add to your interview. You'll ask better, more productive questions if you know what you're talking about. If you ask appropriate questions, the subject will usually respect you—and then you can get to the meat and potatoes of the interview faster.

Doing your background legwork is also a sign of respect for the person you are interviewing. It shows that you honor their time and cooperation and you're not merely using them for a fishing expedition.

As you write your questions, keep these hints in mind:

- Focus all your questions on your research project. Avoid going off on tangents.
- Keep your questions simple but open-ended. Try to avoid questions that result in "yes" and "no" answers.
- Structure your questions so that you can ask one at a time. (During the interview, be sure to give your subject time to answer each question before moving on.)
- Write polite and courteous questions. Remember that the subject is doing *you* the favor.
- Your last two questions should be: "Who else should I talk to?" and "What have I missed?"

Some researchers submit the questions to their subject ahead of time as a courtesy. The more complex your topic, the more likely this technique will be successful for you.

5. Always ask permission *beforehand* to tape-record or videotape an interview.

Whether or not to tape/video an interview is a hot debate topic because each side has its supporters and its critics. Of course, if you're doing an oral history, you must tape/video because that's the basis of this type of research. The following chart summarizes the pros and cons of this issue.

Advantages of Taping	Disadvantages of Taping
Provides a complete and accurate record.	May stifle spontaneity by intimidating the subject.
Can protect you against lawsuits for misquoting.	Can take you days to transcribe the tape.
Frees you to listen more carefully because you're not taking notes.	May not work in a public setting because of excess background noise.

If you do decide to tape/video an interview, obtain a signed release for the right to use the subject's remarks on the record.

6. Test recording devices and have a backup ready.

Stuff breaks. One of the corollaries of Murphy's Law states that a tape recorder/video recorder will break just when you need it the most. (Okay, I made that up, but we all know it's true.) Follow the guidelines below to make sure that you don't fall victim to Murphy's Law:

Ask the Librarian

Never turn the tape recorder off until the subject walks away. As the interview winds down, people often relax and let down their guard. You frequently get the best stuff at the very end of the meeting.

- Be sure your equipment is working. If possible, set everything up in the interview location and test it *before* your subject arrives.

- Use a high-quality tape recorder to avoid distortion.

- Before you start the interview, make sure the tape is rewound and at its starting point.

- Always carry a backup tape, recorder, and a set of new batteries.

7. Be polite and professional.

Treat the meeting as you would a job interview. Follow these guidelines:

◆ Get plenty of sleep the night before so you're fresh as a daisy.

◆ Under no circumstances drink alcohol before or during the interview—even if your subject does. It's not a bad idea to go easy on the caffeine, too, if it makes you jittery.

◆ Dress in a professional manner. If in doubt, wear a suit or other standard, accepted outfit. Nix on the heavy cologne, make-up, and jewelry. Ditch all chewing gum. Of course, never smoke.

◆ Be nice to everyone you meet: the security guard, the receptionist, people you meet in the hall.

◆ Thank the subject at the end of the interview, even if he or she has not been helpful.

8. Transcribe notes immediately after the interview.

Whether or not you have recorded the interview, write up your notes as soon as possible. Many researchers sit in the car and begin writing immediately after the interview. This way, they can recall nuances, body language, and other nonverbal hints that often reveal additional information.

9. Contact the subject with follow-up questions and clarifications, if needed.

You don't want to be a pain, but neither do you want to make a mistake based on a misunderstanding. Straighten out any issues as soon as you can, while the interview is still fresh in everyone's mind. If necessary, go over your notes with the subject to make sure everything is accurate. As long as you emphasize that you want to be accurate, the subject will usually be more than happy to cooperate.

10. Write a note thanking the person for his or her time.

In the old days, the note had to be handwritten, but today, e-mail notes are considered acceptable, especially for busy executives.

Should You Conduct an E-mail Interview?

E-mail interviews have several strong advantages:

◆ The interview doesn't require travel, so it saves time and money.

◆ It eliminates the tension that comes from making a "cold call" to a stranger. Many people are so intimidated by calling and meeting strangers that they refuse to do face-to-face interviews.

- The subject sends you the answers, so you know they're as accurate as your source can make them—or is willing to make them.

There are disadvantages as well:

- It's usually easier to deflect e-mail than telephone calls, so you may never get through to the person at all.

- Emotions don't come across on a computer screen, so you may find it much more difficult to get a read on your subject.

- People can be more cautious and thoughtful through e-mail than in person, so you may not get the answers you need.

If you decide to conduct e-mail interviews, you'll find the following suggestions helpful:

- Keep your questions short and to the point. You'll get a faster and better response.

- If you need to contact many people, send each one an individual e-mail rather than a mass mailing. Mass mailings look like *spam* and are often deleted without being read.

You Could Look It Up

Spam is junk e-mail.

- Always make it clear why you are contacting the person and how you intend to use the research you gather.

- Follow the rules for a personal interview. Even though e-mail is an informal medium, be formal and polite. Be sure to check your spelling and grammar carefully, too.

Authenticate Experts

Interview only respected people in the field. Don't waste your time with cranks and people with private agendas to further. Great advice, but how can you tell whether someone really is an expert without appearing to pry into their life? Try the following hints:

- Ask the person for his or her resumé or curriculum vitae (abbreviated CV, the academic equivalent of a resumé). You can then not only verify that the person has the expertise you need, but also copy the relevant credentials into your research paper to establish the person's qualifications. If the person doesn't have a resumé or CV, carefully consider why he or she would be considered a reliable expert source.

◆ Look up the person in a well-respected reference book. You learned all about reference books in Chapter 8. Choose the book that matches the person's field. For example, I'm listed in the multivolume series *Something About the Author*.

◆ Check the person's publication record. For books, check amazon.com or barnesandnoble.com. For scholarly articles, check the appropriate indexes for the subject area.

> **CAUTION**
>
> **Lost in (Cyber)Space**
>
> Don't rely on a personal web page to authenticate a person's credentials. A person is free to post whatever he or she chooses on a personal web page: the truth, nontruth, or statements that massage the truth.

Use Media Sources

In addition to interviews, you may be able to use a variety of media sources for your research paper. These include but are not limited to the following:

◆ Audiocassettes

◆ Cartoons

◆ CDs

◆ DVDs

◆ Illustrations

◆ Maps

◆ Movies

◆ Paintings and other fine art

◆ Photographs

◆ Slides

◆ Videotapes

You know the old saying, "A picture is worth a thousand words." It's often true. Watching a documentary film can help you get a better understanding of a historical time. For example, watching a documentary of the Great Depression of the 1930s or the polio terror of the 1950s can help you understand the panic that people felt. Seeing it yourself rather than having it described to you gives the experience a real immediacy. Videos can also give you a quick overview of a subject.

Audiovisual materials can often be borrowed from your library as you would books, magazines, and other print sources. Many libraries have large collections of media. The New York Public Library, for example, has a magnificent collection of photographs that circulate. When I wrote *The Complete Idiot's Guide to Shakespeare*, I found wonderful old movie stills in the New York Public Library. Excellent online sites for pictures and photographs include www.corbis.com, www.magnumphotos.com, and www.mepl.co.uk/index2.shtml.

Sample Research Paper

The following research paper, written by Jessica Swantek while she was an undergraduate student at the College of William and Mary, makes extensive use of interviews and media sources. In an interview with me, Jessica said:

> My curiosity about clogging and step dancing began when I read an article about the Irish dancing show *Riverdance*. The author stated that Irish step dancing had a major influence on Appalachian clogging, a form of American folk dancing. I'd never heard of clogging before, and my knowledge of step dancing was limited as well. The article led to my decision to choose step dancing and clogging as the topic of my term paper.
>
> I wanted to find out more about each one, compare and contrast them, and examine each dance's place in contemporary America, especially with regard to issues such as cultural identity and authenticity.
>
> Two clog dancers provided me with insight that I couldn't get from books. What follows is a chronological account of the history of Irish step dancing and Appalachian clogging, and a discussion of the two dances as they exist today.

As you read the paper, see how Jessica uses this research to support her thesis.

Irish Step Dancing and Appalachian Clogging: The Roots of American Dance

Jessica Swantek

Although Appalachian clogging is often considered a traditional American form of dance, it actually has its roots in Irish step dancing. Irish step dancing had its beginnings in the early 1700s during the turmoil of British oppression. The

Irish wanted to learn upscale dances like those done in France and England. To accommodate their demands, dance masters invented Irish step dancing by adapting the French and English dances to fit with traditional Irish music (Harrison <http://www.inx.net/~mardidom/rcidance.htm>).

This led to the distinctive foot percussion seen in Irish step dancing, known as *battering*. The new dance style was named "step dancing," because each dance sequence executed within eight bars of music was called a step (Richens and Haurin).

A dance master would travel within a county, staying in each village for about six weeks and teaching step dancing to boys. A local family provided room and board, and it was considered an honor to have a prominent dance master stay in one's home.

Ever since St. Patrick introduced Christianity to Ireland in the fifth century, the Catholic Church played a very important role in the lives of the Irish. By the mid-1700s the Church had condemned dancing, so this expression of Irish culture was practiced with some secrecy. Step dance was taught in kitchens, barns, and other fairly private indoor locations. Sometimes a stage was as small as a tabletop or a half door. Because of the lack of adequate dancing space, early step dancing was rather stationary in style. Step dancers tried their best to stay in one place while doing quick footwork (Richens and Haurin).

For most dancers, competition eventually became the primary reason for learning to step dance. The winner of a competition was the dancer who knew the most steps, not necessarily the one who performed them the best (Richens and Haurin).

There were several different step dances that the dance masters taught, all of which are still done today. The *jig* is perhaps the most recognizably Irish dance that is still in existence. It is performed to music played in a 6/8 time signature. The *reel* originated in Scotland, but was perfected by Irish dance masters. It is a relatively fast dance in 4/4 time. The hornpipe evolved from an English dance in the mid-1700s. It is done in 4/4 time, and has a distinct triple rhythm in the music: one-and-a-two-and-a-three-and-a-four-and-a. *Set dances* are performed to a specific tune that remains set over time. It has two parts, the lead around, which is danced as an introduction during the first 8 to 16 measures, and the set, which usually begins at the twelfth to sixteenth measure. Set dances are done in jig or hornpipe time, and greater interpretation of the dance is expected in comparison with other step dances (Richens and Haurin).

The First Irish-American Immigrants

The first substantial number of early Irish settlers arrived in the mid-1700s. Most of these immigrants eventually settled during the eighteenth century in the Appalachian mountain region, in what is now Pennsylvania, Virginia, West Virginia, and North and South Carolina. According to the first U.S. census of 1790, America had a 12 percent Scotch-Irish population (*Gale Encyclopedia of Multicultural America* 62).

The Irish, like most other immigrant groups, brought their music and dance with them to America, and incorporated it into their new lives. Irish settlers contributed largely to the making of folk music of America (Cullinane 125).

Irish fiddle tunes influenced American country music, while their ballads had an impact on American folk songs (*Gale* 62). Similarly, Irish dance had an effect on new kinds of American dancing that were soon to come about.

The Creation of Appalachian Clogging

The first official record of a dance master in the United States was recorded in 1789. Based in Philadelphia, he taught reels, jigs, and hornpipes. Irish step dancing, especially the heavy jig and hornpipe, was sometimes referred to as "clog dancing," so it follows logically that when a new form of dance, influenced by Irish step dancing, came into being, it would be called *clogging* (Cullinane 125).

Clogging was influenced not only by the step dancing from Ireland, but also by dances brought to America by other settlers from the British Isles, as well as Native American traditional dances, and solo buck and wing dances of the African American slaves (Mangin <http://www.access. digex. net/~jmangin/clogging.htm>).

Clogging began as a very social dance, a far cry from the competitive nature of Irish step dancing. The inhabitants of the Appalachians were part of a rural society, and they worked hard during the day, many in the coal mines or on the farm. After sundown, for special occasions or just for enjoyment, families and neighbors would gather together in a barn or on a porch to play music and dance (Charlton 23).

Traditional clogging has been described as the most energetic form of step dance, and is characterized by a relaxed upper body and fast-moving, percussive footwork ("Stepdance/Clogging in Nova Scotia" <http://fox.nstn. ca/~blee/dans/stepindex.html>).

It is a mobile, informal dance whose steps have become somewhat standardized only within the past century. Distinct steps and their names used to vary from region to region, and West Virginia is one of the last places to retain those differences (Charlton 23). The two most basic steps, which are the foundation for most other clogging steps, are called the shuffle and the buck, and are very similar, if not exactly the same, as some dance steps seen in modern tap dancing.

Subsequent Irish Immigrants: The First Great Wave

The First Great Wave of Immigration to America lasted from 1841 until 1890. Included in the approximately eight million foreigners who immigrated to the United States were three million Irish and British (*Encyclopedia of Multiculturalism* 291).

The Irish moved primarily to large American cities like Boston, New York, and Philadelphia. They often lived in isolated ethnic communities, such as the Hell's Kitchen area of New York City (*American Immigrant Cultures* 76).

The Evolution of Modern Irish Step Dancing

In 1893 the Gaelic League was founded, which encouraged the revival of Irish culture (Richens and Haurin). This finally brought Irish dancing out into the open, and began a chain of events that would result in the worldwide awareness and recognition of step dancing. The 1921 treaty that established the Irish Free State in the south and Northern Ireland as two separate countries also helped to stir up enthusiasm for the outward expression of Irish culture (*American Immigrant Cultures* 76).

In 1929, the Irish Dancing Commission was founded to standardize Irish dance by establishing universal rules regarding teaching, judging, and competitions. The commission established a 100-mark judging system. The points were distributed evenly among four categories: timing, deportment/style, construction of steps, and execution/method (Richens and Haurin).

Starting near the turn of the twentieth century, women began to step dance. They had most likely been doing so privately for quite some time, but it was considered indecent by the Church for women to dance, so any such displays in public were previously unacceptable. However, the gender dynamic had completely reversed itself by the 1930s. Because of the influx of female dancers, a new, more feminine dance was invented specifically for women, called a "slip jig." Danced to music in 9/8 time, a slip jig's steps consist of graceful skipping, hopping, and toe pointing. Soft shoes were introduced around 1924 for use during slip jigs. They are soft leather shoes with flexible soles, much like Western ballet shoes, and they lace up the front and tie around the dancer's ankle (Richens and Haurin).

The prevalence of female dancers also led to the unique posturing of Irish step dancing that is its trademark today. Parish priests felt that women dancing with loose arms were far too provocative, so in order to increase their self-control, Irish step dancers must dance with their torso rigid, arms firmly at their sides, and faces expressionless (Richens and Haurin).

Clogging Evolves

Around the onset of World War II, a new style of synchronized clogging emerged, called "pitter pat." The older clogging style was referred to as "traditional style or mountain style." Pitter pat is more static than mountain style clogging, and teams often assemble themselves in a line formation on stage. The clogging steps are executed more quickly than in mountain style clogging, and modern dance steps as well as arm and hand movements are used. Pitter pat has become the most popular clogging style, and teams can be found all across the United States ("Brooke's Clogging Page" <http://www.geocities.com/Nashville/Opry/2891>).

Clogging and Step Dancing in Present-Day America

In 1964, the Irish Dance Teachers Association was founded, and there are currently more than 300 certified Irish dance instructors in North America. The North American Feis Commission was founded in 1968 to regulate competitions in the United States and Canada, and an annual North American championship competition started in 1969. The step dancing competition scene is remarkably organized, in part due to the assistance of these new organizations.

I learned from step dancer Brooke Earnhardt that many organizations hold independent clogging competitions, such as the Showstoppers National Talent Competition, the National Clogging and Hoe-down Championships, and the Clogging Champions of America Competition. However, none of these organizations is affiliated with one another or overseen by a higher establishment. As a result, there is no set teaching or judging criteria. Some judges look for precision, some judge the choreography, some watch for the dancers' ability to stay with the music, and some pay attention to the costumes. Usually a group will be rated numerically, though the number range varies from one competition to the next, on some combination of the above categories.

Identity/Community

So who are these dancers? Is Irish step dancing still just the dance of the Irish? Is clogging only done by white descendents of settlers from the British Isles? I asked Brooke and Katie Mullen about their family backgrounds in order to see if there was a predictable pattern. Interestingly, while both dancers fit the historic description of their respective dances—Katie is 100 percent Irish and Brooke has Scottish and English ancestors—both denied that their heritage had anything to do with their choice of dance. Also, neither Brooke nor Katie had any history of family members who were involved in their dance, so they were both first generation dancers, so to speak. Apparently for Brooke and Katie, any ethnic link was purely coincidental. I concluded that in order to accurately and more completely explore this issue, I'd need to ask more than one person from each dancing community. It would be an interesting topic for further research.

Media Attention

Irish step dancing has obviously received a lot of media attention lately, largely due to the huge commercial successes of the step dancing shows *Riverdance* and *Lord of the Dance.* Interest in Appalachian dance was somewhat revived along with the folk movement in the late 1970s. The Green Grass Cloggers often performed publicly to live music, and apparently had quite a following (Mangin <http://www.access.digex.net/~jmangin/clogging.htm>).

Perhaps at the height of clogging's visibility, the Leather 'N' Lace Cloggers, a precision team from Leicester, North Carolina, performed at the opening ceremonies of the 1996 Summer Olympics in Atlanta before an audience of thousands; their performance was broadcast via television to millions worldwide (Mangin <http://www.access.digex. net/~jmangin/clogging.htm>). So while clogging may not have the fame that step dancing currently enjoys, it seems to be quietly holding its own.

Appalachian clogging and Irish step dancing are two dynamic, thriving dance forms. It will be interesting to see what the future holds for step dancing and clogging. Both dances have proven to stand the test of time, and almost certainly will be around in some form for the enjoyment of many generations to come.

Works Cited

"Banjo." *The New Grove Dictionary of Musical Instruments*, vol. 1. 1984 ed.

Charlton, Angela. "Cloggers Shuffle and Skip to Save Appalachian Tradition." *The Associated Press.* June 1997.

Cullinane, Dr. John. *Aspects of the History of Irish Dancing in North America.* Cork City, Ireland: Dr. John P. Cullinane, 1997.

Earnhardt, Brooke. "Brooke's Clogging Page." <http://www.geocities.com/ Nashville/Opry/2891> (9 October 1998).

Earnhardt, Brooke. E-mail to the author. 9 November 1998.

"Fiddle." *The New Grove Dictionary of Musical Instruments*, vol. 1. 1984 ed.

Harrison, Bill. "A Brief Overview of Irish Dance." 27 December 1997. <http://www.inx.net/~mardidom/rcidance.htm> (16 October 1998).

"Introduction." *Gale Encyclopedia of Multicultural America*, vol. 1. 1995 ed.

"Ireland." *Compton's Interactive Encyclopedia*. 1998 ed.

"Irish." *American Immigrant Cultures: Builders of a Nation*, vol.1. 1997 ed.

"Irish Americans." *Gale Encyclopedia of Multicultural America*, vol. 2. 1995 ed.

"Irish Americans." *Encyclopedia of Multiculturalism*, vol. 4. 1994 ed.

The Irish Emigrant, Ltd. "The IE Glossary." January 1997. <http://www.emigrant. ie/emigrant/glossary.html> (18 November 1998).

The JVC/Smithsonian Folkways Video Anthology of Music and Dance of the Americas, vol.1: Canada and the United States. Dir. Hiroaki Ohta. Prod. Stephen McArthur and Multicultural Media. Victor Company of Japan, Ltd., 1995.

The JVC/Smithsonian Folkways Video Anthology of Music and Dance of the Americas, vol. 2: the United States. Dir. Hiroaki Ohta. Prod. Stephen McArthur and Multicultural Media. Victor Company of Japan, Ltd., 1995.

Mangin, Julie. "The Clogging Page." 9 October 1998. http://www.access. digex. net/~jmangin/clogging.htm (14 October 1998).

Matthews, Gail. "Movement and Dance: Nonverbal Clues About Culture and Worldview." *The Emergence of Folklore in Everyday Life: a Fieldguide and Sourcebook*. Ed. George H. Schoemaker. Bloomington, Indiana: Trickster Press, 1992. 101 –105.

The JVC Video *Anthology of World Music and Dance*, vol. 20: Europe I. Dir. Nakagawa Kunihiko. Prod. Ichikawa Katsumori. Victor Company of Japan, Ltd.

Live Performance: October 10, 1998 at Hofstra University's John Cranford Adams Playhouse. Scotch/Irish-Canadian performers, the Leahy family, musicians & step dancers.

Mullen, Katie. E-mail to the author. 10 November 1998.

Richens, Ann, and Don Haurin. "Irish Step Dancing: A Brief History." February 1996. <HYPERLINK http://tigger.cc.uic.edu/~aerobin/irhist.html http://tigger.cc.uic.edu/~aerobin/irhist.htm> (17 October 1998).

Riverdance. Dir. John McColgan. With Jean Butler and Colin Dunne. Composer Bill Whelan. Columbia Tristar, 1997.

"Stepdance/Clogging in Nova Scotia." <http://fox.nstn.ca/~blee/ dans/stepindex. html> (17 October 1998)

Times Ain't Like They Used to Be: Early Rural and Popular American Music, 1828–1935. Prod: Sherwin Dunner and Richard Nevins. Yazoo Video of Shanachie Entertainment Corp., 1992.

The Least You Need to Know

♦ Interviews allow you to conduct primary research that adds authority, credibility, and immediacy to your research paper.

♦ Follow the guidelines in this chapter to help you conduct effective interviews. Interview only people respected in their field.

♦ Consider using media sources such as CDs, DVDs, and movies.

♦ Study models of successful research papers to learn how writers combine their findings with their own ideas.

Chapter 11

You're Not Done Yet: Explore Other Research Sources

In This Chapter

- ◆ Search government documents
- ◆ Access archives
- ◆ Locate articles and clippings in the vertical file
- ◆ Take a survey
- ◆ Explore other research sources

Who's the largest publisher in the United States? It's the government! The government publishes tons of pamphlets, reports, catalogs, and newsletters on most issues of national concern. In this chapter, I'll take you step by step through the research potential of government documents, special collections, the vertical file, and other great research sources.

Government Documents: Uncle Sam Helps *You*

A veteran congressman was asked what he had learned in the rough-and-tumble political arena. "Well," he said, "I found it wasn't so much whether you won or lost, but how you placed the blame."

There's a lot we can blame on our government, but there's one thing they have unquestionably gotten right: high-quality publications. Government documents are often excellent research sources because they tend to be factual and unbiased. They're usually loaded with reliable statistics, too, and often include helpful charts, diagrams, and other visuals.

Further, U.S. government publications are available in an astonishingly wide variety of forms and topics. Government documents are issued as articles, pamphlets, books, web pages, illustrations, maps, and much more.

Here's just a sampling of the topics covered in the wealth of government documents:

- Agriculture output and trends
- Career and job outlooks, including jobs with the federal government
- Child care, cooking, and home-management skills
- Economics
- Education
- Government officials
- Health
- National parks
- Population statistics
- Supreme Court decisions
- Taxation
- Weather patterns, including storms

So How Do I Obtain Government Documents?

You can locate government documents in three ways:

1. Get them from the library.
2. Access them online.
3. Purchase them.

Read on to find out how you can get your hands on this great research material easily.

Access Government Documents in a Library

Because the federal government publishes so many documents, not all libraries can receive them. A library can be designated a *Federal Depository Library* or a *Partial Federal Depository Library*. The first type of library gets all government documents; the second, only the ones relevant to the library's collection and patron needs. Thus, a business library might receive only federal documents concerning tax laws and those on economic trends, whereas the library at an agricultural college might get the documents on farming issues only.

Government documents are often shelved in a separate section of the library. Some libraries even have dedicated computer terminals set aside to make it easier for you to search these collections. Remember that government documents are catalogued according to the Super-intendent of Documents (SuDocs) numbers (see Chapter 7).

> **You Could Look It Up**
>
> **Federal Depository Libraries** have been designated as recipients of federal documents. **Partial Federal Depository Libraries** receive only some of the documents, depending on their needs and storage capabilities.

Here are some standard print indexes for government documents.

◆ *Monthly Catalogue of the United States Government Publications.* This is an up-to-date listing of all government documents. The items are arranged in alphabetical order.

◆ *American Statistics Index.* This index catalogs all the statistical documents produced by the government. Here's a place to look if you need numbers.

◆ *The Congressional Information Service (CIS).* As you no doubt surmised by the title, this index covers all papers written by Congress. Because Congress is famously long-winded, there's a lot of stuff here: texts of hearings and reports, for instance. Pour a cuppa java and get comfortable with this index because it's big.

Access Government Documents Online

Various federal agencies maintain websites to make it easy for government employees, everyday citizens, and scholars to research their publications. Two standard sites are GPO Access and FedWorld. Both are very useful for experienced as well as novice researchers.

GPO Access (www.gpoaccess.gov/index.html)

This site is maintained by the U.S. Government Printing Office (abbreviated GPO), the same wonderful folks who created the SuDocs classification system that you learned about in Chapter 7. This site includes many useful links. Here are several that you can access from the home page:

- ◆ **A–Z Resource List.** A comprehensive list of all the official federal documents available on GPO Access. Make this your starting point as you explore the site.

- ◆ **Locate a Federal Depository Library.** This link helps you find a library in your neighborhood that has the federal documents you need.

- ◆ **Legislative Resources.** Find all congressional bills, congressional records, laws, and so on through this link.

- ◆ **Executive Resources.** This site contains presidential materials.

- ◆ **Judicial Resources.** This is the Supreme Court website.

- ◆ **U.S. Government Online Bookstore.** Here's where you can purchase any government documents you need.

- ◆ **GPO Access User Support Team.** This site offers personal help for using GPO Access.

FedWorld (www.fedworld.gov/)

A program of the U.S. Department of Commerce, FedWorld.gov is a database for many different online sources for government documents. My three favorite ones include these:

- ◆ **FirstGov.** This is an index of 30 million government web pages.

- ◆ **www.ntis.gov.** This is a resource of scientific and technical publications from all government agencies.

- ◆ **www.scitech.resources.gov/.** This is a good source for government, science, and technology web resource sites.

Purchase Government Documents

You can also order government documents that your library may not carry. You buy them from the government directly. I often order government docs to help me research some of my more retro hobbies, such as canning vegetables, making jams, and gardening. These pamphlets are very helpful and astonishingly inexpensive—usually a dollar or less. Your tax dollars at work, folks. You can easily buy government documents from the U.S. Government Online Bookstore, listed earlier in this chapter.

The Freedom of Information Act

Some highly sensitive government documents may be restricted for decades before they are finally declassified. Usually, these documents concern intelligence activities (think spies and all that cloak-and-dagger James Bond stuff). If a government document is not freely available, you may be able to access it through the Freedom of Information Act.

The Freedom of Information Act applies only to federal agencies and does not create a right of access to records held by Congress, the courts, or by state or local government agencies. For further information, access the U.S. Department of Justice Freedom of Information Act website at www.usdoj./gov/04foia/.

Special Collections

Many libraries and individuals have restricted collections. These archives may include some or all of the following materials:

- Artwork
- Diaries and journals
- Items of local interest
- Letters
- Manuscripts
- Maps
- Photographs
- Rare books

These collections often contain a magnificent—and often unexpected—assortment of treasures. For example, the Walt Whitman House in Melville, New York, boasts Whitman memorabilia; Hofstra University has original manuscripts written by the novelist Joseph Conrad. The Bethpage Restoration houses a delightful collection of household objects, tools, and other everyday objects from the 1800s. The actor

Patrick Stewart of *Star Trek* fame has long been helping a group of Trekkies raise funds for an archive of *Star Trek* memorabilia: sets, props, costumes, scripts, and so on. At last look, the material was stored on Long Island, New York. As you can tell, special collections and archives can often yield fascinating avenues for original research. So how do you find a collection that can help you?

Finding the Collection

In addition to the obvious places—museums, historic houses, historical societies, and libraries—check print indexes in your library to find archives. You'll also want to talk to a reference librarian or two, because they often know about local archives and gateway sites.

In addition, peruse the following representative sampling of online sources of archival indexes.

◆ **www.nara.gov.** This is the National Archives and Record Administration home page.

◆ **www.nara.gov/nara/mail.html.** This is the U.S. National Archives basic search page. This links to the regional offices.

◆ **lcweb.loc.gov/spcoll/cdmanu.html.** This is the site of the special collections in the Library of Congress: Manuscript Division.

◆ **lcweb.loc.gov/coll/nucmc/nucmc.html.** This is the Library of Congress's online version of the National Union Catalog of Manuscripts. The site also has links to its own manuscript collection.

◆ **www.pro.gov.uk.** Great Britain's Historical Manuscript Commission has a search engine that covers most of the country's manuscript holdings outside the Public Record Office. You can also check www.hmc.gov.uk.

◆ **www.archives.ca.** This is the home page for the National Archives of Canada.

◆ **www.archivenet.gov.au.** This is Australia's gateway page for the archives of Australia. It lists the country's major archives. You can also check www.naa.gov.au.

Accessing the Collection

Archives are usually stored in a special room or section of the library, and you'll very likely need permission to access them. To avoid a wasted trip, start with a query letter. Ask what materials the archives hold and how you can access them. If you want just a few documents, such as letters or journal entries, the archives may send copies of them to you for free. Or, they may mail or fax you an order form with instructions for obtaining the material easily.

But if you want to examine a lot of material, you'll likely need to visit the collection in person. To gain access, you often need academic credentials. This means you need a letter from university contacts (such as professors or administration) who can verify your need to know. This is the case with the Berg Collection in the New York Public Library, for instance.

While people who work in archives usually want to help researchers, increasing budget cuts have resulted in staff shortages and reduced hours. As a result, the *archivist* may brush you off or not even answer your letter. Don't be discouraged. Even if you can't get access in person to one particular collection, you may be able to find equally useful materials in another archive.

When you arrive at the building, you will have to sign in and present identification, so be sure to have your driver's license or other photo ID ready. Also have your letters of admission/authentication handy. You will have to check your coat and bags, but you should be able to take a laptop into the reading room. In many cases, you cannot take pens or markers into the reading room, so be sure to have some pencils with you.

I know that these rules can be very frustrating, but be patient and cooperative: Remember that the security process helps safeguard often irreplaceable documents and visuals.

> **You Could Look It Up**
>
> An **archivist** is a specialized librarian, knowledgeable about a special era, collection, or historical figure.

Examining the Documents

You will be allowed to examine the documents in two ways: either in their original form or on microfilm. The original is always preferable because of the thrill of handling something real and the possibility of finding something not recorded on microfilm. If you're fortunate enough to be allowed to handle the originals, be careful! Read on to find out why.

Chemicals have brought us such great inventions as plastic storage containers that burp and tomatoes that bounce. But chemicals have been a nasty thing for paper. Before

> **Ask the Librarian**
>
> If you can examine original documents, be sure to check the back as well as the front. Who knows what notes you may find there?

chemicals were introduced into the papermaking process, paper could exist for hundreds of years without turning brown. You can find books from the 1600s with snow-white pages, whereas many books from the 1940s are brown and crumbly.

Handle *all* documents with extreme care. Here are a few hints:

◆ Be sure that your hands are clean and free from lotions. Any dirt or oil on your hands can stain the paper.

◆ To prevent further damage, turn the pages slowly and don't bend back the binding.

◆ Keep all paper documents away from direct sunlight, if possible.

After you complete your work, be sure to send anyone who helped you a thank-you note. In addition to showing your appreciation, these notes may become part of a person's permanent folder and be used as part of the evaluation process for raises and promotions.

The Vertical File: Home to Clippings and Pamphlets

Articles that libraries have clipped from newspapers and magazines are another reference source to consider. So are pamphlets, little booklets published by private organizations as well as government agencies. These smaller documents can be a good source of information, especially from the days before computers were widespread. They're often a great source of local history and legend.

Because clippings and pamphlets are usually too small to place on the shelves, they are stored in the *vertical file*. This is just what the name implies: a filing cabinet with pamphlets arranged in files. *The Vertical File Index: A Subject and Title Index to Selected Pamphlet Material* lists many of the available titles. In addition, you can simply browse in the vertical file under your topic.

You Could Look It Up

Pamphlets are stored in a **vertical file,** a filing cabinet, or series of filing cabinets.

Today, many vertical files have been converted to microfilm or digital form.

Take a Survey

Surveys can help you assess how a large group feels about your topic or a significant aspect of it. On the basis of the responses, you can draw some conclusions. Such generalizations are usually made in quantitative terms: "Fewer than one third of the respondents support the reintroduction of girdles," for example.

If you decide to create a survey, follow these guidelines:

1. Be sure to get a large enough sampling to make your results fair and unbiased.

2. Don't ask loaded questions that lead people toward a specific response.

3. To get honest answers to your questions, it is essential to guarantee your respondents' anonymity. Written surveys are best for this purpose.

4. Make the form simple and easy. Few people are willing to take the time to fill out a long, complex form. Ask about 5 questions, certainly no more than 10.

5. Carefully tabulate your results. Check your math. If you're like me, check it again.

You Could Look It Up

A **survey** is a sampling of opinions used to approximate what a complete collection and analysis might reveal.

Lost in (Cyber)Space

Expect a low response rate and late answers from any survey, so plan accordingly. Your best friends will likely respond quickly but acquaintances and strangers feel no such responsibility.

In addition, many topics have been extensively discussed by experts on respected television news programs and documentaries. Contact television stations to obtain transcripts of the programs. You might also be able to videotape the programs or borrow copies of the programs that have already been recorded.

Other Great Sources

You're limited in your research only by your imagination and determination. You can often glean valuable facts from the most unlikely sources, so think creatively when you choose sources. Below are a few other sources that might fit the bill for your research projects:

♦ **Annual reports.** Publicly traded companies issue reports every year to their stockholders. The report summarizes the company's financial information and accomplishments for the year. Annual reports are also read by employees, stockbrokers, potential investors, and job applicants.

Primarily, an annual report aims to convince stockholders that the company is a good investment and a good corporate citizen. Annual reports are often helpful as much for what they don't reveal as what they do, so carefully "read between the lines" to make inferences about a company. Annual reports are available in many libraries and may be posted online at the company's website.

- **Civic, social, military, and religious organizations.** Many civic groups such as the Lions, Rotary, Veterans of Foreign Wars, and Hadassah are a rich source of research. They can often provide information not available elsewhere because they hold the history of their group and community. These groups may open their archives, allow interviews, and be able to point you to other sources, for example.

- **Travel.** Your travel can range from something elaborate such as riding a camel in Egypt for a book on "the ships of the desert" to something simple, such as dropping into some local financial institutions for information on banking. Here are a few examples from my own research forays:

  - Far from home, I went to the restored Globe Theatre in England to find the material I needed for my book *The Complete Idiot's Guide to Shakespeare.*

  - Closer to home, I spent a week trekking around flea markets for *The Complete Idiot's Guide to Buying and Selling Collectibles.* (Bought some great stuff, too!)

  - Closest to home, I visited several houses of worship and sat through the religious services to gather information for my *Complete Idiot's Guide to Interfaith Relationships.*

In each case, I was able to gather information in person that I couldn't get from books, phone interviews, or the Internet.

Keep all these sources in mind as you explore the tremendous resources available to you.

The Least You Need to Know

- The U.S. government publishes research material available in a wide variety of forms and topics. The material can be accessed online or through print indexes.

- If a government document is not freely available, you may be able to access it through the Freedom of Information Act.

- Many libraries and some individuals have special collections and archives. You can access these materials online, in person, or in print.

- Articles and clippings are stored in the vertical file, an actual cabinet, or on microfilm.

- Surveys can help you assess how a large group feels about your topic or a significant aspect of it.

- Other potentially valuable research sources include annual reports from companies; civic, social, military, and religious organizations; and first-hand visits that may entail travel.

Research with Electronic Media

In This Chapter

- ◆ Define the "Internet"
- ◆ Find out how to jump aboard the Internet
- ◆ Explore Internet terms
- ◆ Learn how to use search engines to research on the Internet
- ◆ Discover "netiquette": Internet manners
- ◆ Observe Internet ethics

Radio existed nearly 40 years before 50 million people tuned in. It took television 13 years to reach 50 million viewers. It took 16 years before 50 million people used personal computers. *But it took only 4 years for 50 million people to use the Internet.*

Researchers love the Internet, because it allows them to access information from around the world—including text, graphics, sound, and video—without ever getting up from their comfy chairs. If you're linked to the Internet, you can view masterpieces from the Louvre Museum in France, take an aerial tour of Bali, or dissect a virtual frog. You can search databases at the Library of Congress, interview someone via e-mail across the globe, and read electronic newsletters—without ever leaving your home. This makes the Internet an invaluable source of information as you prepare your research papers.

In this chapter, you'll discover how to use the Internet to gather reference material. If you're already an Internet maven, I'll bet I can teach you some new methods to save you time and help you gather better material.

What Is the Internet?

The Internet is an expanding global information computer network composed of three elements:

◆ People

◆ Hardware (computers)

◆ Software (computer programs)

Each regional network is linked to other regional networks around the world to create a network of networks. The Internet dates back to the 1960s, when scientists used it to collaborate on research papers. It's not owned or funded by any one organization, institution, or government. The Internet is directed by the Internet Society (ISOC), a group of volunteers. There's no president or CEO.

The *World Wide Web* is made of documents called web pages, which can combine text, pictures, and sound. The "home page" is the entry point for access to a collection of pages. Specific words, pictures, or icons (special places to click) act as links to other pages. It doesn't matter where the other pages are located—even if they're on the other side of the world, the computer programs will retrieve them for you.

You Could Look It Up

The **World Wide Web** (abbreviated WWW) is a network of pathways through the Internet that connects "pages" of material—whatever can be sent electronically.

"Wait a minute, Rozakis," you mutter, "there has to be a catch." Actually, there is. The web isn't like a library where information is arranged within an accepted set of rules. It's more like a really big garage sale, where similar items are *usually* grouped together—but not always. Further, websites come and go without warning. Even if they stay put, the good ones are updated often so the material changes.

So how can you search the web for information to use in your research paper? There are several different ways, each of them surprisingly easy and enjoyable. Read on to learn how to surf the information superhighway. (To "surf" is to navigate the Internet; a "surfer" is an enthusiastic Internet user.)

Getting Access to the Internet

An *Internet service provider* (ISP) is a company that provides access to the Internet. The best-known ISPs are the commercial online services such as America Online, CompuServe, Prodigy, Earthlink, Microsoft Network, Juno, and MSN. However, many national companies such as AT&T and MCI as well as regional and local companies provide Internet access. ISPs usually charge a monthly subscription rate and offer unlimited access to e-mail.

Check with your public library, too, because many libraries offer free Internet access. Some libraries even offer free Internet access from your own home, through their service provider. Professional organizations such as IEEE (an engineering group) also provide Internet access for little or no fee.

You Could Look It Up

An **Internet service provider** is a company that provides access to the Internet. Their name is abbreviated ISP.

What's Your Address?

Internet mail uses a hierarchical system of names to make sense of the millions of computers served. The name of each computer (or "domain") contains at least two words or abbreviations and at most five, separated by periods, with the top of the hierarchy at the right. Here's the Internet address of the president of the United States:

president@whitehouse.gov

Here's what it means:

◆ **president**   This is the recipient's personal mailbox.

◆ **whitehouse**   This is the organization, company, and so on.

◆ **.gov**   This shows the type of organization. Here, it's the government.

To send or receive e-mail, you need an address of your own and your recipient's address. You establish your e-mail address when you sign on with an Internet service provider. You can get your recipient's e-mail address by asking the person for it or by looking in an e-mail phonebook. There are many different ones available. *E-Mail*

Addresses of the Rich and Famous (Addison-Wesley, 1997), for example, lists media darlings, the world's movers and shakers, and other famous people.

The Password Is Swordfish

You'll need a password to access your e-mail account. Think of something clever and obscure, but also easy for you to remember. Your password should *never* be the same as your e-mail address. Neither should it be anything easy to research, such as your maiden name. Hackers are wise to these gambits. (Hackers are people who use their computer knowledge for illicit purposes, such as gaining access to computer systems without permission and tampering with programs and data.)

To make your exploration of the Internet easier and more rewarding, let's start with the language and conventions of the medium. That sounds a lot harder than it is, but don't worry: There are just a few terms and rules to learn.

Internet Terms and Symbols

All research mediums have their own lingo. Because the Internet is a new medium, new terms are created every day. Some of these words and symbols have become standard, whereas others change.

Top Twenty-Five Internet Words and Signs

I'll give you only the standard terms and symbols, but be aware that there's nothing stopping any Internet user (and that includes *you*) from creating his or her own terms. Who knows? They may soon become standard!

1. < >

Angle brackets around text indicate that all the characters within the brackets must be treated as a single unit. In most cases, angle brackets are used to enclose a web address to prevent misreading. It looks like this: <www.google.com>.

2. *

The asterisk is used in searches as a wildcard. If you are searching for all words that begin with a particular letter or letters, you use the asterisk to denote the unspecified portion of your search. For example, if you keyboard brain*, you'll get hits for brain, brains, brainchild, braindead, brainfever, brainless, brainstorm, brainteaser, braintrust, brainwash, brain wave, and so on.

3. @ (the "at" sign)

The @ sign (a symbol located above the 2 on your keyboard) separates the username from the domain name in an e-mail address. The sign shows that you are "at" a particular electronic address. For example, here's one of my e-mail addresses:

laurie.rozakis@farmingdale.edu

Read the address like this: "Laurie Rozakis is at Farmingdale, an educational institution."

4. . (the dot)

This is the period symbol. However, it's called a "dot" when used in an Internet address and is used to separate parts of an address and the URL. Thus, laurie.rozakis is read "Laurie dot Rozakis."

5. / (forward slash)

This symbol is used to separate parts of URLs, as in

http://www.farmingdale.edu.

(Don't confuse the forward slash with the backward slash (\) used in DOS.)

6. asynchronous communication

This is the term for e-mails and other electronic communications that are posted and read at different times. For example, if a friend sends you an e-mail at 10 A.M. on Tuesday, you might open and read it a few hours later.

In contrast, we have real-time communication, in which people converse at the same time with one another. IMs (instant messages) take place in real-time communication.

Ask the Librarian

Attention students: If you are sending your professor an e-mail with an attachment, be sure to include a subject line in the space provided that explains who you are, what you are sending, and why. Too many students have cutsie e-mail addresses like "cutiepie" or "surfdude," so professors don't have a clue who they are online and what they're sending. Most savvy people delete all attached files they can't recognize.

7. attachment

An attachment is a file sent along with an e-mail message. *Never* open an attachment if you do not know the sender and are not expecting to receive the file; it might contain a computer virus that can wipe out your hard drive.

8. bookmark

To bookmark a web page is to save it to your "Favorite Places" list. You simply click an icon (such as a heart) to bookmark a page. Bookmark good online research sites so you can easily return to them later.

9. browser

A browser is a computer program used for navigating the Internet. Examples of browsers include Netscape Navigator, HotJava, and Microsoft Internet Explorer.

10. cookie

This is a short file that stores information about your visit to a specific website. For example, if you buy some books online, the seller may ask your browser to record your preferences. If you return to the same site, the seller's computer can read the cookie and remember your preferences.

11. cyber-

Cyber- is a prefix for anything created electronically and accessible online. The prefix cyber- has attached itself to many words, such as cyberstore (online store), cyberspace (the Internet), and cyberstalking (people who lurk in chat rooms and prey on visitors there).

12. domain name

This is the group of symbols and letters that form the address of a website or e-mail service. There are two parts to a domain name: the server and suffix. The suffix shows the type of organization, such as the following:

- .com (commercial)
- .edu (educational institution)
- .gov (government)
- .mil (military)
- .org (organization)

These are read "dot com," "dot org," and so on. As you will learn in Part 3 of this book, reading the suffix of an e-mail address can help you evaluate the reliability of a site.

13. download

To download is to transfer information electronically from one computer to another. You can download a text file or a picture, for example.

14. FAQ

This is an abbreviation for frequently asked questions. FAQs are posted on most sites and provide a great way to familiarize yourself with the site's features.

15. gopher

No, it's not a furry creature hiding in a Kansas cornfield. When used in computer lingo, a gopher is a program for accessing Internet information. You can recognize a gopher because its address begins with gopher:// instead of http://. Gophers are a great way to research big collections of texts, such as specialized databases.

16. home page

This is usually the first page you see when you access a website.

17. hypertext

A collection of documents coded in HTML (Hypertext Markup Language), a computer code. Think of it as a universal translator, so Macs can communicate with PCs and so on.

18. MOO

Pronounced just as the cows do it, this term is an abbreviation for multi-user domain, object-oriented. It's an electronic coffeehouse in which people can chat at the same time. Classes, seminars, and buddies meet at a specific time to talk about a set topic.

19. MUD

Pronounced like the boggy soil, this term is an abbreviation for "multi-user domain." Like a MOO, it's an electronic space set aside for a specific purpose; here, for role-playing games.

20. spam

Spam refers to junk e-mail, not a canned meat product. The term can be a noun ("Boy, did I get a lot of spam today about home mortgages") as well as a verb ("Stop spamming me already!").

21. thread

A thread is a series of e-mail postings on a specific topic. Threads often occur in newsgroups, a group of people who meet online to post their ideas on the Usenet network. Each Usenet group has a specific topic.

22. URL

This abbreviation for Uniform Resource Locator is the address for each web page. It's pronounced "You-R-L."

23. username

This is the information that lets you access your e-mail (when you add your password).

24. virtual

This is a synonym for online.

25. virus

A computer program created to wreak havoc on other computers, software as well as hardware. Like people viruses, computer viruses spread fast and infect things.

E-mail Abbreviations

Yesterday I e-mailed a close friend to set up a lunch date. She said something funny and I responded *LOL*. She thought I meant "lots of luck" and took offense. Actually, I meant "laughing out loud," and I meant it as a compliment. Hmmm, I said to myself. Someone has not spent enough quality time glued to the computer sending e-mail.

So you're not misunderstood, here are the abbreviations and acronyms used in informal e-mail. You may come across these abbreviations when you correspond with a research source via e-mail. To date, these abbreviations are not considered acceptable in business or other formal correspondence and research.

Commonly Used Online Abbreviations

Abbreviation	Meaning
afaik	as far as I know
afk	away from keyboard
atm	at the moment
b	be
b4	before
bbiaf	be back in a few minutes
brb	be right back
btw	by the way
c	see
cul	see you later
f2f	face to face
focl	falling off the chair laughing
fwd	forward(ed)
hhoj	Ha! Ha! Only joking!
imho	in my humble opinion
irl	in real life
lol	laughing out loud
oic	Oh, I see!
r	are
rotfl	rolling on the floor with laughter
ttyl	talk to you later
u	you
y	why

E-mail Smileys

Smileys (also known as "emoticons") are cute little symbols that have become common in e-mail communication. Here are some of the most well-known ones. Read them sideways, left to right.

:-)	happy face	;-)	winky face
:-(	sad face	:-D	laughing face
:-X	lips are sealed	%-)	bleary eyed

Smileys are fun when it comes to personal e-mail, but they are inappropriate for professional e-mail, such as sending requests to interview people.

From the Reference Desk

Did you know that …

♦ About one third of all Americans send messages over the Internet. (*1999 World Almanac*)

♦ E-mail is currently the most popular and widely used resource on the Internet. (*1999 World Almanac*)

♦ Americans now send 2.2 billion e-mail messages a day, compared with 292 million pieces of first-class mail. (*U.S. News and World Report*, 2003)

♦ Traffic on the Internet doubles every 100 days. (UUNET, Internet backbone)

♦ Around the world, about 100 million people use the Internet. (*1999 World Almanac*)

♦ It is estimated that by the year 2005, about one billion people will be connected to the Internet. That's a lot of e-mail. (*1999 World Almanac*)

Researching on the Internet

Be sure to give yourself plenty of time to use the Internet because it may take you a while to find the information you want. Even experienced Internet users need time to find the authoritative, reliable sources they need. Further, searching on the Internet can be addictive, like spoon after spoon of peanut butter. Start with search engines.

Search Engines

Search engines, which work with key words, help you locate websites. You type in a key word and the search engine automatically looks through its giant databases for matches.

The more precise the phrase, the better your chances of finding the information you need. Here are some of the most popular search engines and their Internet addresses.

- **AltaVista**   www.altavista.digital.com

- **Cyberhound**   www.thomson.com/cyberhound/

- **Excite**   www.excite.com

- **Google**   www.google.com

- **GoTo.com**   www.goto.com

- **HotBot**   www.hotbot.com

- **InfoSeek Guide**   guide.infoseek.com

- **Lycos**   lycos.cs.cmu.edu/

- **Net Search**   home.netscape.com/escapes/search/index.html

- **WebCrawler**   webcrawler.com

- **Yahoo!**   www.yahoo.com

Other search engines are limited to a specific field. You can find a list of these search engines at Easy Searcher, located on the web at www.easysearcher.com.

Some search engines, such as Yahoo!, also let you search the web by categories. For example, here's the opening subject list on the Yahoo! screen:

Arts and humanities	News and media
Business and economy	Recreation and sports
Computers and Internet	Reference
Education	Regional
Entertainment	Science
Government	Social science
Health	Society and culture

You Could Look It Up

Search engines are programs that work with your browser to find information on the web. After you type a key word or phrase into your browser's dialog box, a search tool looks for web pages that have your key word(s). You get the results, called "hits." Meta-engines are a group of search engines all in one.

Click on any of these categories and you get loads of subcategories. Most provide links to current news, programs, and online chat rooms, too.

Meta-Engines

Meta-engines let you search several web indexes at the same time. The meta-engine sends your key word(s) to a group of search engines, collects the results, and gives you a summary of the hits. For example, Metacrawler checks nine different search engines at the same time, including Yahoo!, Altavista, and Excite.

Here are some of the best meta-engines and their addresses:

- **All-in-One Search Page**   www.allonesearch.com
- **Ask Jeeves!**   www.ask.com
- **Dogpile**   www.dogpile.com
- **Inference Find**   www.inference.com/ifind/
- **Metacrawler**   www.go2net.com
- **Savvy Search**   www.savvysearch.com
- **Search.com**   www.search.com

It's crucial that you type the address *exactly* as it appears. If you're even one letter, symbol, or space off, you won't reach the site. If you're not getting anywhere with your search, check your typing for spelling and accuracy.

Because not all search engines, meta-engines, and specialized search engines lead to the same sources, you should use more than one. *Bookmarks* or *hot lists* (accompanying each search engine) help you mark sources you want to return to.

WAIS and Newsgroups

Pronounced "ways" and standing for "Wide Area Information Service," WAIS enables you to search for key words in the actual text of documents. This increases the likelihood that a document you've identified has information on your topic. You can use WAIS to search web documents.

Newsgroups are composed of people interested in a specific topic who share information electronically. You can communicate with them through a listserv, an electronic mailing list for subscribers interested in a specific topic, or through Usenet, special-interest newsgroups open to the public.

These sources allow you to keep up with the most recent developments in your area of research and may also point you to useful information and resources you might not have found on your own.

Databases

As I've mentioned in previous chapters, libraries often have databases that nonmembers cannot use online without paying a fee. Clearly, going to the library to use these databases (or using them off-site through the library's portal, if your library offers this service) can save you a bundle. Best of all, the information on these databases has been vetted, so you know you're getting higher-quality research material.

Here's a representative sampling.

Area	Database
Associations	Associations Unlimited—Gale
Biography	Biography Resource Center—Gale
Business	General Reference Center Gold—Gale
	Business & Company Resource Center—Gale
	Reference USA (Business USA)
	Asian Business on ProQuest
Education	Gale's Literary Index
	Gateway to Educational Materials
Health/Medical	CancerNet
	Health Care
History/	History Resource Center: US Gale
Politics	National Newspaper Index—Gale
Magazines	Dialog@CARL
	Electric Library

Useful Sites

Following are some useful places to visit on the web as you begin your research. (Note: Every care has been taken to make this list timely and correct. But just as people move, so do websites. Since this book was published, the website may have moved. In that case, there will be a forward link. If not, use a "key word" search to find the new site.)

- ◆ **Guide to the web**   www.hcc.hawaii.edu/guide/www.guide.html

- ◆ **Internet resources**   www.ncsa.uiuc.edu/SDG/Software/Mosaic/MetaIndex.html

Ask the Librarian

Here are a few of my favorite sites: www.nytimes.com (*New York Times*), www.cnn.com (CNN Interactive), and www.savers.org/wash_times (*Washington Times*). For a big, fat list of online newspapers, hit www.yahoo.com/News_andMedia/Newspapers.

You Could Look It Up

Netiquette is the system of appropriate behavior that governs the Internet.

♦ **Library of Congress** www.lcweb.loc.gov

♦ **List of web servers** www.info.cern.ch/hypertext/DataSources/WWW/Servers.html

♦ **Newspaper links** www.spub.ksu.edu/other/journal.html

♦ **Nova—Links** www.nova.edu/Inter-Links

♦ **Sports** www.atm.ch.cam.ac.uk/sports/sports.html

♦ **U.S. federal agencies** www.lib.lsu.edu/gov/fedgov.html and www.fedworld.gov

♦ **Virtual tourist world map** www.wings.buffalo.edu/world

♦ **Who's who on the Internet** www.web.city.ac.ik/citylive/pages.html

Now, let's explore the culture of cyberspace and the system of manners that governs it.

Johnny B Good: "Netiquette"

E-mail has its own system of manners that has come to be called *netiquette—network etiquette*. It's the code of appropriate online conduct that netizens (Internet citizens) observe in virtual communities. Follow these three simple guidelines to make it easier for you to navigate your way through cyberspace:

1. **Don't flame.** A flame is a personal attack on someone. Flaming involves capital letters as well as invective. Using all capital letters, LIKE THIS, is considered the web equivalent of shouting. It's rude, so avoid it.

2. **Don't spam.** Spamming is sending the same message to hundreds or thousands of e-mail addresses in the hope of hitting a few interested people. Spam is even worse than junk snail mail, because you can throw away junk mail unread, but you often have to read spam to find out that it's junk. Spam clutters your mailbox, wastes time, and annoys people.

3. **Respect others' time.** Remember that your readers value their time. When you send e-mail, you're taking up other people's time. It's your responsibility to ensure that the time they spend reading your mail isn't wasted.

Internet Ethics

As you learned earlier, the Internet is open to all. That means every user is free to access and read any material published on the Internet. But when you *download* and *use* that information, you may have to ask permission, just as you would with a book, magazine, newspaper, video, or any other print or media source.

Material that has been copyrighted may include a notice to that effect. Look for the word *copyright* and the © symbol. This notice shows that the user must get permission from the copyright holder to use the material. Usually, all you need to do on a research paper is give full credit to the source. This process is explained in full in Chapters 17, 18, and 19.

And remember, if you don't give proper credit, you are committing plagiarism, literary theft. Today, teachers and professors can detect plagiarism easily by using specially designed software programs. In addition, many graphics posted on the web have digital watermarks that make it even easier to trace their origin.

To be on the safe side, always assume that all material on the Internet is copyrighted. Thus, give proper credit to all your sources.

The Least You Need to Know

- ◆ The Internet is a global information computer network made up of people, computers, and computer programs.

- ◆ The World Wide Web is made of documents called web pages, which can combine text, pictures, and sound.

- ◆ An Internet service provider is a company that provides access to the Internet.

- ◆ Search engines, which work with key words, help you locate websites. Meta-engines are a group of search engines all in one.

- ◆ Netiquette is the system of appropriate behavior that governs the Internet. Don't flame or spam. Respect others' time.

- ◆ Give full credit for all material you download and use in your research papers.

Part 3

Evaluate Your Research

Children's books you'll never see:

- ◆ The Pop-Up Book of Human Anatomy
- ◆ Why Can't Mr. Fork and Ms. Electrical Outlet Be Friends?
- ◆ The Boy Who Died from Eating All His Vegetables

We make judgments every day. Some people have to decide which books not to publish; other people have to decide which facts and opinions not to include in their research papers. That's your job now. In this part of the book, you'll learn how to evaluate your research on the basis of quality, bias, appropriateness, and reliability, paying special attention to evaluating electronic sources.

All Sources Are *Not* the Same

In This Chapter

◆ Compare free databases with subscription-only databases

◆ Survey subscription-only databases

◆ Learn how to access library databases off-site

◆ Refine search methods

In Chapter 12, we touched on the differences between the databases you can access free from conventional search engines such as google.com, yahoo.com, and altavista.com, and those available only through a library. In this chapter, we'll delve into the difference in depth.

First, I'll explain why you *really* want to do your research in subscription-only databases rather than through the free ones. I'll give you a list of superb sources so you know where to start your research, too. Next, I'll show you how to access these databases quickly and easily. (And they're all free to you as a library patron!)

By the end of this chapter, I'll have you convinced that accessing subscription-only databases is the *best* way to spend your research time!

You've Shopped the Rest, Now Shop the Best

You know this wise old adage: Your dinner is only as good as your ingredients. No matter how much sauce you heap on old fish, it's still old fish. In the same way, if you're using shoddy reference sources, you're going to end up with a shoddy research paper.

Remember, no one polices the Internet. This means that anyone can post just about anything on the web. Wading through all the rubbish to find the nugget of information you need is exhausting, time-consuming, and totally unnecessary. That's because someone has already done all the work for you. Those "someones" are the people who sell proprietary databases.

Companies such as Grolier, Gale, and the *New York Times* prepare their own databases of newspaper articles, magazine articles, and journals. Some companies, such as Gale, include information from many sources. Other companies, such as the *Times*, include only their own newspaper articles.

The Best Databases for Research

Databases of periodical literature available through library portals will give you the highest-quality magazine, newspaper, and journal articles. It's that simple. Why?

Because the articles have been *vetted*. This means that someone has sifted through the articles and chosen the most authoritative, best-written, and reliable ones to include. This is research gold, with the dross removed.

Naturally, these databases are not free because the company that compiled them has to recoup its research investment. Libraries purchase these databases and make them available to its patrons free of charge. Thus, because these databases are very costly, you can't access them through free search engines such as google.com and askjeeves.com. You must access them through the library portals.

You Could Look It Up

Vetted material has been read and reviewed for inclusion. Databases that are vetted are composed of carefully selected high-quality articles and information.

Keep the following in mind:

♦ Some proprietary databases are available for use only in the library.

♦ Other proprietary databases are available for use off-site. This means that you can access these databases from home, from an Internet café, from your office, or from anywhere you can get access to the web.

- Still other proprietary databases are available both for use in the library and off-site.

- The list changes often, so check with the reference librarian about the status of databases.

For example:

- Need a reliable article on psychology for your term paper? The subscription-only database Science Direct offers access to 900 full-text scientific journals, as well as abstracts and indexes covering 30 million records. Subjects covered include engineering and technology, aerospace, biotechnology, chemistry, psychology, and more. The articles in scientific journals are far more reliable research sources than the websites 12-year-olds post about their experiments with baking soda and vinegar.

Ask the Librarian

Libraries pay for subscription-only databases but offer them to their patrons free of charge. You do not pay to access a library's database.

- Have to find a poem for a literature research paper? Roth Publishing has subscription-only literature databases such as PoemFinder, StoryFinder, and EssayFinder that make locating quality literature a snap.

- Must have a reliable biography of a public figure for your research paper? Check the Biography and Genealogy Master index from Gale. Check Who's Who, too. All are great sources, and all are available from a library's database.

Easily Available Library Databases

In Chapter 12, I gave you a brief survey of the library's exclusive subscription-only databases. Below is a far more extensive list. Your library is likely to have many of these databases as well as others that are equally good. As I've mentioned before, the list changes often, so check frequently with a librarian to see which new databases have been added.

Area	Database
Art	Grove's Dictionary of Art
Associations	Associations Unlimited—Gale
Biography	Biography Resource Center—Gale
	Biography and Genealogy Master Index—Gale

continues

continued

Area	Database
Business	General Reference Center Gold—Gale
	Business & Company Resource Center—Gale
	General Business File ASAP—Gale
	Reference USA (Business USA)
	Business Source Elite—ESBCO
	Asian Business on ProQuest
Dictionaries	NetLibrary
Reference	Associations Unlimited—Gale
	ERIC—EBSCO (Education Index)
	America the Beautiful—Grolier
	AccessPage
Education	ERIC—NOVEL
	ERIC DIGESTS—NOVEL
	Gale's Literary Index
	Gateway to Educational Materials—NOVEL
Encyclopedia	Technology
	Grolier Suite—Grolier
	Funk & Wagnalls New World Encyclopedia
Health/Medical	Student Resource Center—Health Module—Gale
	CancerNet
	Health Source—Consumer Edition—EBSCO
	Health and Wellness Resource Center—Gale
	Health and Wellness Resource Center and Alternative Health Module—Gale
	Health Finder (reliable consumer health and human services information)—NOVEL
	Health Reference Center—Academic—NOVEL
	Medline—EBSCO
	Medline Workbench—NOVEL
	Medline Plus—NOVEL
	PubMed Central (life science research articles)
	Research Index: NECI Scientific Literature Digital Library—NOVEL
	Scorecard (environmental information service)
History/Politics	History Resource Center: US Gale
	National Newspaper Index—Gale
	General Reference Center Gold—Gale
	ProQuest—New York Times Consulta

Area	Database
Indexes	Biography and Genealogy Master Index—Gale
	National Newspaper Index—Gale
Literature/Poetry	Literature Resource Center—Gale
	Novelist—Gale
	PoemFinder—Roth Publishing
	StoryFinder—Roth Publishing
	EssayFinder—Roth
	Magill on Literature—EBSCO
Magazines/Journals	Dialog@CARL
	Electric Library—Elibrary
	Infotrac/General Reference Center Gold—Gale
	EBSCOhost/Masterfile Premier—EBSCO
	ProQuest—New York Times
Music	Grove's Dictionary of Music and Musicians
Newspapers	General Reference Center Gold—Gale
	ProQuest—New York Times
	National Newspaper Index—Gale
	Newspaper Source—EBSCO
Student	Student Resource Center—Bronze—Gale
	Opposing Viewpoints Resource Center—Gale
	Primary Search—EBSCO
	Middle Search Plus—EBSCO
	EBSCO Animals—EBSCO
	TOPIC Search—EBSCO
	Lands and People—Grolier
	Access Science
	Infotrac Junior Edition—Gale
Study Guides	Learning Express Library

As this list indicates, there's no shortage of subscription-only databases. If your head is spinning and you don't know where to begin, start with the following databases for general high-quality information:

◆ Electric Library—ELibrary

◆ Infotrac/General Reference Center Gold—Gale

◆ EBSCOhost/Masterfile Premier—EBSCO

How to Access Library Databases Off-Site

In the old days, you could access these costly restricted databases only by doing your research in a library on a library terminal. Today, however, most university, high school, and public libraries offer some off-site access. This means that you can access some (but not all) of these spectacular databases from home. To do so, follow these four easy steps.

Step 1: Go to your library's home page.

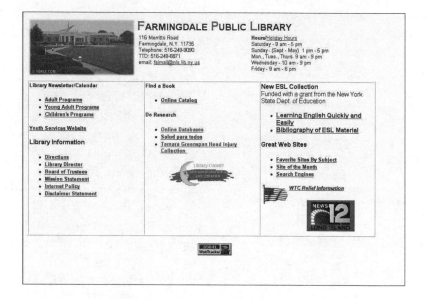

Step 2: Click "Online Databases."

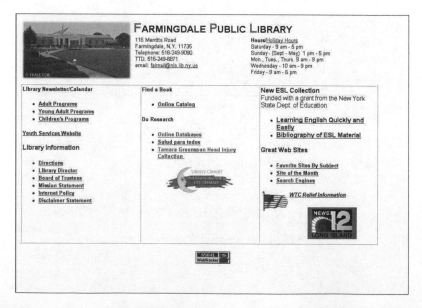

Farmingdale Public Library **Databases at Home** (NYState Library - NOVEL databases at the bottom of the page)	
Art	Grove's Dictionary of Art
Associations	Associations Unlimited - Gale
Biography	Biography Resource Center - Gale Biography and Genealogy Master Index - Gale
Business/Financial	General Reference Center Gold - Gale Business and Company Resource Center - Gale General Business File ASAP - Gale Reference USA (Business USA) Business Source Elite - EBSCO
Careers/Jobs/Employment	Career Cruising
Directories/Reference	Net Library (1st time users must register at Reference desk at library) Associations Unlimited - Gale ERIC - EBSCO America the Beautiful, Grolier Access Page Get a Grolier Username and Password
Education	ERIC - NOVEL ERIC DIGESTS - NOVEL Gale's Literacy Index - NOVEL Gateway to Educational Materials - NOVEL
Encyclopedia	Access Science - McGraw Hill Encyclopedia of Science & Technology Grolier Suite - Grolier Get a Grolier Username and Password Funk & Wagnalls New World Encyclopedia Nueva enciclopedia Cumbre en linea - Grolier Get a Grolier Username and Password
Health/Medical	Student Resource Center - Health Module - Gale Medline - EBSCO Health Source - Consumer Edition - EBSCO Salud para Todos - Gale Health & Wellness Resource Center and Alternative Health Module - Gale Health and Wellness Resource Center - Gale Health Reference Center-Academic - NOVEL
History/Politics/Current Events	General Reference Center Gold - Gale History Resource Center: US - Gale ProQuest - New York Times National Newspaper Index - Gale Consulta

Step 3: Click the database you want. Here's a sample of the page you will see.

Step 4: Enter your library bar code number. It is printed on your library card. This will open the database.

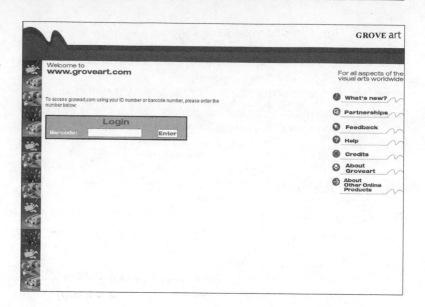

Your own library's home page and databases will look different, of course, but the basic process remains the same.

Finding the Articles You Need

You search these databases just as you would any database. You can use the following methods, depending on the specific database. Always start by reading the FAQs (frequently asked questions) to get your bearings on a new database.

- **Exact word search.** This is the same as any keyword search you've used in a web's search engine. Just type in the precise word(s) or term(s) that you want.

- **Title search.** This search enables you to retrieve journals and articles by title.

- **Author search.** Enter the author's last name and first name, or just the last name.

- **Concept search.** This option generates a list of words that appear close to the terms you actually typed and will retrieve documents containing these close terms even if the documents don't contain your exact key words.

- **"Fuzzy."** Some databases have an option that lets you check that you've spelled the keyword correctly. This option displays a list of possible correct spellings.

Ask the Librarian

Scan the Library of Congress Guide to Subject Headings for help finding synonyms and key words.

◆ **Boolean operators.** Here's where you use *and, or,* and *not* to limit or expand your search. For instance, you could keyboard "chocolate and health" or "chocolate and heart disease."

◆ **Truncation.** Some search engines that power these databases enable you to truncate (shorten) a word by cutting it down to its root. Then you add an asterisk (*). For example, "tech*" retrieves techie, technical, technician, etc.

Using the Articles

After you have access to the database, you can survey the articles. Depending on the amount of time you have and your learning style, you can deal with material in several ways:

1. Read the article on the screen (and take notes). Obviously, this method is very time-consuming. Further, you won't have a copy of the article if you need to refer to it again.

2. Print the article (and take notes). This method gives you a hard copy, but if you're working in the library, you'll likely have to pay for each sheet of paper you print. Most libraries charge 5¢ to 10¢ per page, so the cost can really add up fast.

   If you are researching in the library and you want a hard copy, try this hint: E-mail the articles to yourself. That way, at home you can print what you want.

3. Save the article to your floppy disk (and take notes). You can then work off the disk, printing only as necessary.

> **CAUTION**
>
> **Lost in (Cyber)Space**
>
> To access a library's databases off-site, you must have an up-to-date library card. If you owe any money on fines, cough it up and clear your card!

The Proof Is in the Pudding

"But it's so easy to access one of the commercial databases," you moan. "Why do I have to bother with a library database?" Indeed, you can easily access a commercial database from home and you might have to go to the library to access a subscription database. Further, if you access a library page off-site, you must have a valid library card. But it's all worth the tiny little bit of extra effort. Well worth it.

Check out the following examples. They'll prove my point in a New York minute.

Here's the assignment: Write a research paper in which you argue that chocolate has significant health benefits.

You first check google.com by using the keyword "chocolate." Here's the first page of the millions of web pages that follow.

Google page.

Every source but one is commercial, which means that you've got a lot of ads and almost no scholarship. The only source that shows any possibility of being useful is "Hershey Foods Corporation," shown from the fragment "and learn …." But it's a long shot.

Now we go to the place we should have tried first: Elibrary. Here's the top of the first page.

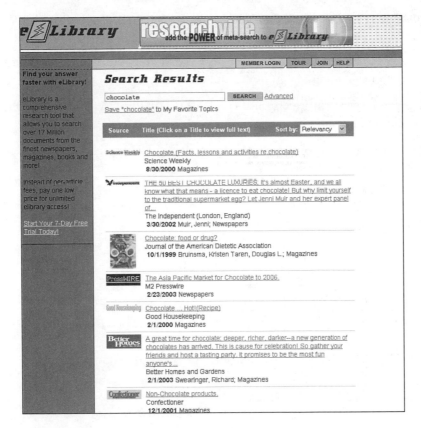

Elibrary page.

The icon for *Science Weekly* tells you immediately that you've hit potentially useful, reliable sources.

Now, I'm not bashing commercial databases. They're great places to get prices for parasailing in Panama. But for scholarly research, you need to access quality databases, the subscription-only databases available through libraries.

In this chapter, I've covered only newspaper, magazine, and scholarly journals available through library subscription-only databases, but be aware that many libraries have also put their catalogs on the web. The Mother of All Libraries, the Library of Congress, has its catalog on the web. You can access these huge library databases directly. However, you can't get the book through the web; to retrieve the actual book, you still have to get to the library, take the book from the shelf, and check it out.

The Least You Need to Know

- ◆ Databases of periodical literature available through libraries will give you the highest-quality newspaper, magazine, and journal articles because the articles have been chosen for reliability.

- ◆ You can access some of these databases from your home, others only from the library, and still others from home and on-site.

- ◆ For general research, Electric Library—Elibrary, Infotrac, and EBSCOhost are good places to start.

- ◆ Don't waste your valuable research time surfing commercial databases; go straight to library subscription-only databases.

Chapter 14

Junk or Jewel? How to Evaluate Your Findings

- ◆ Check the authority, origin, and timeliness of a reference source
- ◆ Find a source's bias and purpose
- ◆ Discover if a source is appropriate to your topic
- ◆ Check that the source fits your audience (readers) and purpose, too

We make evaluations on a daily basis; some are valid, whereas others may be a bit hasty. Nonetheless, in life and in writing, sometimes you have to be ruthless in your judgments. In this chapter, you learn to evaluate and track the material you use in your research paper to make sure you select only reliable sources.

An Embarrassment of Riches

Evaluating sources is nothing new; writers have always had to assess the reference material they find. But courtesy of the new electronic search techniques and burgeoning Internet resources, the task has taken on a new urgency.

In the good old days, a writer only needed to consider the quality of books, magazines, and journal articles; now, printed matter is just the

Lost in (Cyber)Space

Never assume that a source is valid without closely evaluating it yourself. This is the single greatest problem students have when they write research papers: evaluating materials.

beginning of the information available to the researcher. Further, in the past, editors, publishers, and librarians chose much of the material we could expect to find. Today, however, most online sources haven't been evaluated at all, so it's all in our hands. Besides, you can access just about everything online from the comfort of your own home. As a result, much of what you see won't even make it to the library's shelves.

One of the great strengths of a free press—both print and online—is its ability to print anything that does not libel its subject. As far as researchers are concerned, however, that very freedom presents its own problems. *Just because a source appears in print, in the media, or online does not mean that it is valid.* As a result, you must carefully evaluate every source you find before you use it. This means that you must read critically and carefully.

Before you decide to use *any* source, you have to judge its reliability, credibility, and appropriateness. Here's how to do it.

As you gather your sources, give them all the once-over—and more than once. Use the following criteria as you determine whether a source is valid for inclusion in your research paper:

1. Authority

2. Source

3. Timeliness

4. Bias

5. Purpose

6. Appropriateness

Let's look at each criteria in detail.

Who's the Boss?: Authority

Don't believe that all sources are created equal, because it's just not so: Some sources are more equal than others. That's because they were prepared with greater care by experts in the field and have been reviewed by scholars, teachers, and others we respect for their knowledge of the subject.

Don't be afraid to make value judgments about the source materials you find. Some sources *are* more reliable than others. As a result, they carry greater authority and will help you make your point in your research paper. You can use the following checklist to weigh the authority of the material you're contemplating using:

1. Is the author named?

Unless you're working with an encyclopedia article or an editorial, the author should be credited in a byline. (Increasingly, authors of encyclopedia articles are credited.) Be suspicious of sources that do not have the author's name. Ask yourself, "Why wouldn't the author be named?" Likely, the author is not a recognized expert or may even want to keep his or her identity secret because of a bias. Or, the author may not know much about the topic at all.

2. Are the author's credentials included?

Look for an academic degree, an e-mail address at a college or university, a byline in a reputable newspaper, and/or a list of publications. If this information is not included, it's a tip-off that the author does not have the appropriate credentials.

> **Ask the Librarian**
>
> There are a growing number of review tools for online materials. Among the best are Webcrawler's Best of the Net, Lycos Top 5%, and Gale's Cyberhound Guide.

3. Based on this information, can you conclude that the writer is qualified to write on this subject?

For example, is the person an expert or an eyewitness to the events described in the source? If not, why would you waste your time reading the article?

4. Does the person have a good reputation in this field?

Seek out publications by authors who are well-respected as scholars in the field. Stay away from cranks and zealots with an agenda. You can check a person's reputation in reference sources such as *Who's Who* or *Something About the Author.* Look on the web to find articles about the writers, interviews with them, and reviews of their other publications. Check out the person's web page and see what other publications they have listed, too.

5. Was the source well reviewed by other recognized authorities in the field?

Major scholarly books and publications are reviewed in well-respected magazines, journals, and newspapers. If the book wasn't reviewed, it is minor at best, untrustworthy at worst.

6. Is the source complete, or have certain facts been cut for their controversial nature or for space limitations?

Be very wary of sources that have been cut. What information or visual was cut … and why?

Lost in (Cyber)Space

Warning: The writer's education and academic degrees must match the field in which he or she is claiming expertise. Having a medical degree in brain surgery, for example, doesn't give someone the credentials to write about rocket science—or any other subject outside his or her field.

7. Does the author document his or her claims with other source materials?

If not, stay away from the source because it is not credible. If the writer's claims can't be backed up, don't trust the writer's assertions.

8. Are these sources credible?

Be especially suspicious of sources that claim to have the "secret" or "inside track" on a subject. If you can't find the same information in other sources, the material doesn't hold up to scrutiny. Give it the boot.

Now think about the source of the source.

What's Behind Curtain #3?: Source

As you evaluate the materials you locate, consider where the source comes from, its sponsoring agency, publisher, and so on. For example, *portable sources*, such as encyclopedias on CD-ROMs, are like printed books—they have credited writers and publishers. In addition, they change only when a new version is issued. As a result, you can determine their value as you would a book.

Online sources, in contrast, may be published anonymously, so you can't evaluate the writer(s). Also, they can be updated and revised without notification, which means there could be a lot of fingers in that pie. Most frustrating of all, the website may vanish without warning. This makes it difficult to evaluate its reliability as well as its origin. It's tough to work with something invisible.

Ask yourself these questions as you consider the source of a reference piece:

◆ Can I find the source of this reference piece? If not, it gets the heave-ho.

◆ Is the source reputable? The best sources are well-known; they appear on lists of "recommended" books or sites.

◆ Does the piece come from a place known for its authority, such as a reputable publisher or sponsored website? If the answer is yes, you've likely got a keeper. If the answer is no, throw the source overboard—or consider it with a leery eye.

It's All Relative: Timeliness

As we learned from Albert Einstein years ago, time is relative. If you're writing a research paper on a very current topic, the date of book publication or online posting is crucial, because you're going to need some contemporary data. But you're also likely to include some traditional, "classic" reference materials to give your paper the weight and authority it needs.

As a general rule of thumb, go for a mix of time-honored and recent reference materials. This helps balance your outlook, tempering the current with the classic.

To find reference materials that have withstood the test of time, ask academic librarians or follow the discussion in an academic MOO or listserv. You'll hear the same titles and authors coming up over and over.

Timeliness is a crucial issue with websites, because cyberspace is cluttered with piles of outdated sites. Sometimes people post information and move on to something new. The site hangs out there, forgotten and woefully outdated. Always check the dates on any websites to find out when the material was posted and last updated.

Find the Hidden Agenda: Bias

Every source is biased, because every source has a point of view. Bias is not necessarily bad, as long as you recognize it as such and take it into account as you evaluate and use the source. For example, an article on hunting published in *Field and Stream* is likely to have a very different slant than an article on the same subject published in *Vegetarian Times*.

Bias in reference sources can take many forms. Here are some of the most common forms of bias:

1. Writers make *bogus claims.*

A claim can be considered *bogus*, or false, when the speaker promises more than he or she can deliver. For example, the writer may speak vaguely of "many important experiments," or "recent clinical studies" to prove a point. Effective research sources use specific support—not just vague references to unidentified studies and sources. You can't evaluate "many important experiments," or "recent clinical studies" unless you know how they were undertaken, by whom, and where the results were published.

2. Writers use *loaded terms.*

A term becomes *loaded* when it is asked to carry more emotional weight than its context can legitimately support. As a result, it becomes slanted or biased. These sources are often not reliable. Words with strong connotations (emotional responses) often show bias. For example, a writer may refer to the governor's "regime" rather than "administration." "Regime" is a loaded term because it is used to describe oppressive military dictatorships.

> **You Could Look It Up**
>
> **Bogus claims** promise more than they can deliver; they are lies. **Loaded terms** unfairly slant an argument. Reducing a complicated argument to mockery is called **oversimplification**.

3. Writers misrepresent the facts.

This type of bias takes many forms. First, a writer or speaker can lie outright. Or, a writer may be more subtle, inventing false data or "facts." In addition, dishonest writers often twist what their opponents have said. To misrepresent this way, they use *oversimplification*. A complex argument can be reduced to ridicule in a slogan or an important element of an argument can be skipped over.

You can partly evaluate the bias of an online source by its suffix, the last part of its URL. Here's the crib sheet.

Suffix	Meaning
com	Commercial (business or company)
edu	Education (academic site)
gov	Government
int	International organization
mil	Military organization
net	Internet administration
org	Other organizations, including nonprofit, nonacademic, and nongovernmental groups
sci	Special knowledge newsgroup

Outside the United States, domain names often end with an abbreviation for the country of origin. For example, .au is Australia, .ca is Canada, and .uk is the United Kingdom.

Each site has its own bias. A business site is going to have a different slant than a university site, for example. Any company that wants to stay in business will want to sell you a product or a service, while a university is probably seeking to disseminate knowledge. As a result, knowing the source of the site can help you evaluate its purpose and assess any possible bias.

Bias has another aspect when it comes to the web. Books don't have ads, and most of us skim magazine ads. But websites can have commercial intrusions. Not only are some websites filled with ads, the ads can also flick on and off in search engines. This makes them hard to ignore, and there's no way to rip them out.

These ads reflect the commercial nature of some websites. What you see on the screen may reflect who's footing the bill. This bias is subtle but nonetheless important.

How can you avoid being misled by biased reference materials? Here are some issues to consider as you evaluate a print or online text for misrepresentation:

- Is someone quoted out of context?

- Are facts or statistics cited in a vacuum?

- Does the quotation reflect the overall content of the source or does it merely reflect a detail?

- Has key information been omitted?

To protect yourself against biased sources and your own bias, select reference materials that reflect opinions from across the spectrum.

Take Aim: Purpose

Different sources are written for different reasons. The following chart summarizes some of the most common purposes you'll encounter. I've arranged the sources in a loose hierarchy from most to least reliable, but stay tuned for more on that.

	Source	Purpose	Authors	Reviewed
most reliable ↓ least reliable	Scholarly books and articles	Advance knowledge	Experts	Yes
	Serious books and articles	Report information	Experts; professional writers	Yes
	Newsstand magazines	Report facts	Professional writers; reporters	Yes
	Newspapers	Report news	Reporters	Yes
	Sponsored websites	Report facts; sell products	Varies	Sometimes
	Personal websites	Varies	Experts to novices	Rarely
	Listservs	Discuss topics	Anyone	No
	Usenet newsgroups	Discuss topics	Anyone	No

The most reliable sources are written by experts and have been reviewed by equally reputable readers. However, these sources alone may not be enough to make your point in print. Read on, partner.

Good Fit: Appropriateness

The value of a source depends not only on its quality but also on its use to you in a specific writing situation. *No matter how weighty and reliable the source may be, if it's not on your topic, it does not belong in your research paper.* For example, if you're writing a research paper on current events, you're going to need newspapers and magazines with the most up-to-date information, rather than books, because even the most recent ones are at least six months to a year old. You're probably going to consult websites and Usenet newsgroups as well.

Even if a source proves to be high quality and free from bias, it doesn't necessarily mean that it belongs in your research paper. For a source to make the final cut, it has to fit with your audience, purpose, and tone. It must be *appropriate* to your paper. How can you decide whether a source is suitable for inclusion in your research paper? Consider these questions:

 ◆ Do you understand the material in the source? If the source is too technical for you to grasp fully, you might not use it correctly in your paper.

 ◆ Is the source written at a level appropriate to your readers?

 ◆ Does the source have the information you need?

 ◆ Does the source suit your purpose in this research paper?

On the Right Track

When you get a nice pile of stuff, it's time to put it in some kind of order. Try these suggestions to begin sorting your research findings:

- See how each source helps you prove your thesis. If the source doesn't help support your point, it's not relevant.

- Make sure the material you found is *really* valid and can be verified in more than one source.

- Check that you have a variety of perspectives in your source material. This will help protect your paper from bias.

- See that you have material that appeals to logic as well as emotion. Remember that an effective research paper is built on logic rather than feelings.

- Decide how you will fit each source in your paper. Remember all those gorgeous shoes that pinch? Can't bear to throw them out? If the shoe and source fit, slip them on. If not, set them aside.

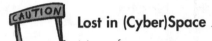

Lost in (Cyber)Space

Never force a source to fit. You can tweak your thesis a bit here and there, but never wring or wrench your point to make a source blend in.

Many sources you find won't be reliable or won't contain the information you need. Further, you will want to verify facts (such as dates, statistics, and scientific experiments) by double-checking them in at least two sources. As a result, you'll have to find many more sources than you will end up using in your paper. For instance, for a 7-page research paper, my students usually cite around 7 to 10 sources. They often have to locate as many as 25 sources to find the information they need.

Remember, all sources are not equally valid. Be sure to evaluate every source you find carefully and completely before you decide whether to use it. Be especially wary of online sources; use only reputable articles, as you learned in Chapter 13. Weak or inaccurate sources can seriously damage your research paper.

The Least You Need to Know

- Evaluate your research material to make sure it's reliable and authoritative.

- Check the authority, source, timeliness, bias, purpose, and appropriateness of each reference.

◆ When you have sufficient material, see how each source helps prove your thesis.

◆ Make sure the material is relevant, balanced, and suitable.

Integrate Research into Your Paper

- ◆ Sort and skim your material
- ◆ Use source material to support your thesis
- ◆ Blend in outside information with cue words and phrases
- ◆ Study examples

A thesis becomes persuasive when you use the best of your research to support your point. First, you decide which authorities best support your assertions. As you write, you smoothly integrate the most convincing expert opinions, specific details, and appropriate facts with your own words. You present material logically, deal with opposing arguments, qualify generalizations, and address your readers intelligently. That's what you learn in this chapter.

Sort Your Findings

You've gathered your sources and prepared a bibliography card for each one (as you learned in Chapter 4). Now it's time to fit everything in place. Here's how to do it.

1. Sort.

First, skim the sources and arrange them according to difficulty, from least difficult to most difficult to read and understand. Actually place the material in three piles. Your piles might look like this.

Easy	→	Medium	→	Challenging
Encyclopedia articles		Interviews		Scholarly journals
Newspaper articles		Books		Primary sources
Magazine articles		Surveys		Technical articles
Videos/DVDs		Charts/graphs		Academic journals

2. Read.

Read all the material. Start with the general, introductory sources first. You use these to lay the foundation for the more specialized and technical material you'll need. Then move on to the more difficult sources.

CAUTION

Lost in (Cyber)Space

No matter how great the temptation, never write on a source that you have to return to the library—even in pencil. (And none of that "I can always erase it later" stuff.)

Ask the Librarian

Write your first draft as early as possible. This gives you plenty of time to fill in the gaps by doing additional research, revising your thesis to take into account unexpected findings, or redesigning your text and graphics.

If you don't understand any of your sources because they are too academic or too technical (or just poorly written), place them on the bottom of the pile. You can return to them later. If you still don't understand them when you reread them, don't use them. Using material you don't understand *always* weakens your paper.

3. Rank.

Position each source to decide how it fits with the other sources you've gathered. Pay close attention to both sides of the issue: It's a great way to test the validity of your thesis.

4. Annotate.

Make notations on each source as you read it. Annotations are an effective way to dialogue with the source, a key step in making sure that you understand what you read. Use a pen, pencil, or highlighter if you are working on a copy of the source that you can keep. Use little sticky notes if you don't own the source and so can't write on it.

Here are some annotations to consider using, in addition to your own symbols.

Annotation	Meaning
!	Surprising point.
?	A point you don't understand.
underline/highlight	A key point.
✓	A point you may want to use.
intro	If you know, note the place
body	where you think you may want
conclusion	to use the source in your paper.

5. Take notes.

Restate what you've read to make sure you understand it fully. Take notes on the source, using summaries, paraphrases, and direct quotations as you have learned earlier in this book.

In most cases, you won't be able to tell which research information you'll decide to include in your paper—and what information won't make the cut. As a result, you'll probably end up taking far more notes than you need. Don't worry: Nearly all researchers end up with extra notes. The deeper you dig into your subject, however, the more perceptive you'll become about what you need to prove your point most convincingly.

Here's a shortcut for figuring out how much information a book contains about your topic. Look in the index. If you find several pages in a row about your topic (say, pages 45, 46, 47) rather than three separate pages (say, pages 45, 117, and 259), chances are the book with three pages in a row will give you more information. Of course, do a quick check of both books to make sure that you're not missing something good.

6. Position.

Position the source in your paper by deciding where it fits in the overall thesis and paper organization. Use your outline to help you decide. If you're not sure where a source best fits, choose two places. You'll have the opportunity to refine your placement later, but positioning information now helps you see how your paper is shaping up: how much information you have, how persuasive it is, and how much more (if any) you may need.

7. Connect.

Link each source to what you've already written. Correlate all the information to see what you have already discovered and what you still have to find. This helps you avoid repeating information.

8. Check.

Be sure that every source fits with your point and focuses on a key issue in your paper. This is a difficult process because it's tempting to include information that really doesn't help you advance your thesis just because it sounds so good. Resist the temptation to pad: Filler distracts and annoys your reader, which ultimately weakens your paper.

And never rely too heavily on any one source—no matter how good it looks. First, this can lead to bias. Second, what happens if the source turns out to be invalid or dated? Your argument can collapse.

During this process, you'll find that you're automatically changing the structure of your paper to accommodate what you're finding. Usually the changes are minor, but you may find yourself designing a radically new organization to fit the focal points and supporting details. This is fine, even desirable—as long as you're still fulfilling your assignment and creating original work.

> **CAUTION**
>
> **Lost in (Cyber)Space**
>
> Caution: If there isn't any valid opposition to your side of the topic, your topic and thesis statement won't fly. Why persuade people of something that everyone accepts as true?

Backed by the Best

How can you get the most bang for your buck by using expert opinions effectively? As an example, let's look at an excerpt from a research paper I wrote on Hester Prynne, Nathaniel Hawthorne's heroine from *The Scarlet Letter*. Here's how the paper opens.

Another Possible Source of Hawthorne's Hester Prynne

And, after many, many years, a new grave was delved, near an old and sunken one, in that burial-ground beside which King's Chapel has since been built. It was near that old and sunken grave … on this simple slab of slate—as that curious investigator may still discern, … there appeared … a herald's wording of which might serve for a motto and brief description of our now concluded legend; so somber is it, and relieved only by one ever-glowing point of light gloomier than the shadow: "ON A FIELD, SABLE, THE LETTER A, GULES." (*The Scarlet Letter*, 264).

So ends Nathaniel Hawthorne's *The Scarlet Letter*, and so begins the search for Hester Prynne's grave. Seventeenth-century Boston town officials, meticulous about keeping accurate records, nevertheless failed to record the death—or life, for that matter—of Hester Prynne, adulteress, seamstress, and ministering angel. The town officials must have been too busy surveying chimneys, keeping pigs off the streets, keeping count of the "many Miscarriages [that] are committed by Saylers … immorate drinking, and other vain expences," and granting widows permission to keep houses of "publique entertainment for the selling of Coffee, Chuchaletto, & sydar by retayle" (Nobel, 113).

The lack of official records notwithstanding, Hester's grave is more often inquired after by visitors to the King's Chapel Burial Grounds than any other, claims the custodian of that historic enclosure in a 1999 interview. Her grave is apparently sought there because Hawthorne's skillful intermingling of real and fictional people and places has led readers to believe that *The Scarlet Letter* is based on a true story. In his essay entitled "The New England Sources for *The Scarlet Letter*," scholar Charles Ryskamp establishes the fact that the supporting characters in *The Scarlet Letter*—other than Hester, Pearl, Dimmesdale, and Chillingworth, for whom we can find no real historical basis—were actual figures (258). The fictional characters assume solidity in part through their encounters with well-known citizens of colonial Boston. According to Ryskamp, Hawthorne used the most credible history of Boston available to him, Caleb Snow's *History of Boston*. …

Notice that it's not enough just to slap the information into your paper, even if you *do* surround any exact quotes with quotation marks. *All research material must be smoothly blended in and used to make a specific point.*

In this instance, I started off by citing a primary source, *The Scarlet Letter*. This shows that I know the necessary basis for the discussion. I also integrate the name of the source directly in the body of the paper ("scholar Charles Ryskamp"), use *cue words* to show how he stood behind his work ("establishes the fact that ..."), and give credit to the source in parentheses (Nobel, 113). Here's why.

Star Power

When you cite material from a well-respected source, put the author's name directly in the body of your text to get more mileage from it. Readers are impressed—and rightly so—when you cite a recognized authority. Placing the person's name in the text shows that you've done your homework, that you understand who to line up behind your argument. For example:

◆ In "Notes on the Decline of Naturalism," the <u>well-known scholar Philip Rahv</u> states that ....

◆ Testifying before Congress on the issue of unrestricted Internet access, <u>computer wizard Bill Gates</u> argued that ....

You Could Look It Up

Cue words are verbs that you use to integrate expert opinions, quotes, and other information.

Cued In

Notice that I use cue words and phrases to set off outside material. For example, I used "establishes the fact that" in my example. The two previous examples use "states that" and "argued that."

Fortunately, you've got a wide variety of cue words and phrases at your disposal. For each source, choose the cue word that expresses your exact shade of meaning. Life is difficult enough without having to hunt for cue words, so I've put together a list of the most useful ones.

Cue Words to Integrate Quotations

adds	agrees	argues	concedes
acknowledges	admits	advises	confirms
asks	asserts	believes	concludes
claims	comments	compares	considers
contends	declares	defends	denies
disagrees	disputes	emphasizes	explains

endorses	establishes	hints	hopes
finds	holds	illustrates	implies
insists	maintains	notes	observes
points out	rejects	relates	reports
responds	reveals	says	sees
speculates	shows	states	suggests

Study Examples

You've learned that when you write a research paper, you synthesize what you've read, rephrase it in your own words, and give credit to all your sources. You make a point and back it up with expert opinions. Study the following examples to make sure that you fully understand the process.

From a Paper on Nature vs. Nurture

Below are two excerpts from a research paper on the "nature versus nurture" debate. The writer presents evidence that genes more than environment determine our personalities. Study the margin notes as you read these passages.

CAUTION

Lost in (Cyber)Space _____

Never omit material from a quotation to change its meaning. Also, if you do excerpt a quotation, always be sure it makes grammatical sense after you've cut it. More on this in Chapter 16.

Integrating research:
Example #1.

1: Question sparks
reader's interest

[1] Are our traits and abilities predetermined from birth, or are they due to our upbringing and experiences? This is one of the oldest and most controversial debates in psychology: the influence of nature versus our intelligence. [2] H.J. Eysenck, Department Chair and Professor of Psychology at London University, believes that "We need genes to produce our brain and we need our environment to nourish us to grow" (Eysenck 190). Does this mean that genes or environment has a greater influence on human development? [3] The latest twin studies show that nature more than nurture determines intelligence.

2: Expert cited: source
integrated

3: Thesis statement

Integrating research:
Example #2.

1: Topic sentence

[1] The most persuasive evidence that intelligence is influenced by genetics is found in twin studies, which examine identical twins separated at birth or early in life and raised in different adoptive homes. [2] For instance, Nancy Segal, a psychologist who directs the Twin Studies Center at California State University Fullerton, asserts that "One of the most interesting findings from twin studies is that the personalities and IQs of identical twins reared together are no more similar than identical twins reared apart" (Qtd. in Pekkanen, 6).

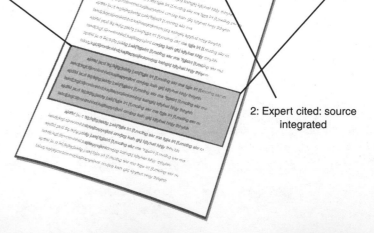

2: Expert cited: source
integrated

From a Paper on Olestra

Here is a paragraph from a research paper on Olestra, a fat substitute that humans cannot digest. This student argues that Olestra carries far more disadvantages than advantages, so consumers should use the product with care. Study the margin notes as you read these passages.

You Could Look It Up

Qtd. in, an abbreviation for "quoted in," refers to a direct quote cited in a secondary source.

Integrating research: Example #3.

1: Topic sentence

2: Summary of research: credit given

[1] Another concern arising from the consumption of Olestra is the way it removes carotenoids (pigments found in many fruits and vegetables) from the system. [2] Diets high in fruits and vegetables seem to offer protection against cancer, heart disease, stroke, and some forms of blindness (Karstadt 4). [3] Dr. Walter Willet of the Harvard School of Public Health conducted a study on this issue and concluded that "The amount of Olestra in a 1 oz. bag of potato chips will lower blood carotenoids by over 50 percent if consumed on a daily basis" (Qtd. in Cancer Weekly Plus, 8). [4] According to Dr. Willet's calculations, if Olestra sells well, it will reduce consumption of carotenoids in the US by 10 percent, resulting in between 2,000-9,800 additional cases of prostate cancer, 32,000 additional cases of coronary disease, 1,400-7,400 additional cases of lung cancer, and 80-390 cases of blindness.

3: Expert cited: source integrated

4: Paraphrase of research: credit given

Ask the Librarian

Long quotes—five lines or longer—are indented from the body paragraphs, five spaces on each side.

From a Paper on Chocolate

Following are some passages from a research paper on the advantages of chocolate. This student argues that when consumed in moderation, chocolate is surprisingly healthful. Pay close attention to the margin notes as you read these passages.

Integrating research: Example #4.

1: Opening grabs reader's attention

2: Thesis statement

[1] What an (almond) joy to find out that chocolate can actually be considered a health food! [2] Chocoholics around the world are devouring the new information researchers have uncovered: chocolate, especially expensive dark chocolate, contains substances which may enhance your overall well-being. [3] "More and more, we are finding evidence that consumption of chocolate that is rich in flavonoids can have positive cardiovascular effects," says Carl Keen, a nutritionist at the University of California, Davis (Reany). [4] At a recent scientific conference, Mr. Keen said, "We not only have observed an increase in antioxidant capacity after chocolate consumption, but also modulation of certain compounds which affect blood vessels." [5] Research has shown that flavonoids derived from a small bar of dark chocolate equal that of six apples, 4.5 cups of tea, 28 glasses of white wine, and two glasses of red wine (Reany). Perhaps we may even rewrite the old adage to be "a chocolate a day keeps the doctor away."

3: Expert cited: source integrated

4: Expert cited: source integrated

5: Summary of research: credit given

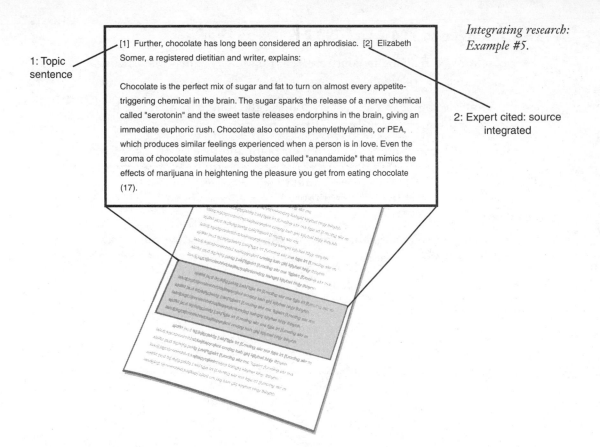

Integrating research: Example #5.

1: Topic sentence

[1] Further, chocolate has long been considered an aphrodisiac. [2] Elizabeth Somer, a registered dietitian and writer, explains:

Chocolate is the perfect mix of sugar and fat to turn on almost every appetite-triggering chemical in the brain. The sugar sparks the release of a nerve chemical called "serotonin" and the sweet taste releases endorphins in the brain, giving an immediate euphoric rush. Chocolate also contains phenylethylamine, or PEA, which produces similar feelings experienced when a person is in love. Even the aroma of chocolate stimulates a substance called "anandamide" that mimics the effects of marijuana in heightening the pleasure you get from eating chocolate (17).

2: Expert cited: source integrated

Credit Given Here

As you weave in expert opinions, facts, examples, and statistics, provide enough information so your readers can easily trace every source. You've just learned three ways to do this:

1. By placing the full citation in the body of the report

2. By integrating the source with cue words

3. By adding the documentation in parentheses

Because these methods form the basis of giving proper credit in any research paper, we'll go over them again in subsequent chapters. We'll also discuss how to use footnotes and endnotes.

The Least You Need to Know

◆ Skim, rank, and annotate your research. Rephrase the material in your own words.

◆ Position the source in your paper, connect the source to what you have already written, and correlate all the information.

◆ Be sure that every source fits with your point and focuses on a key issue in your paper.

◆ If necessary, adjust the organization of your paper to fit your thesis and information.

◆ Integrate source material by using cue words and including the names and credentials of authoritative sources.

Stop Thief! Avoid Plagiarism

- ◆ Define plagiarism
- ◆ Learn what you *don't* have to cite: common knowledge and your own original thoughts
- ◆ Learn what you *do* have to cite: quotations, opinions, and paraphrases
- ◆ Learn how to document sources to avoid plagiarism

You write a research paper to argue a thesis or present information. To make your point convincingly and provide authoritative facts and examples, you cite expert opinions from other scholars and scientists, public figures, and pundits. You use their words and ideas, giving full credit. As you write, you honor your moral responsibility to use someone else's ideas ethically and make it easy for readers to check your claims. If you fail to give adequate credit, you can be charged with plagiarism.

When you use someone else's words, ideas, or method of developing your argument in your research paper, you *must* give credit. Otherwise, you're stealing the other person's work, a crime that is called plagiarism. And whether the theft is intentional or accidental, the effect is the same—failure, disgrace, and perhaps even expulsion. In this chapter, you'll discover how to avoid literary theft by documenting your sources correctly.

What Is Plagiarism?

Everyone knows that copying someone else's paper is wrong. You know that you can't buy a paper from the Internet or take one from the fraternity/sorority files and pass it off as your own. (Well, you *can*, but you know that you *shouldn't*.) You can't download an article, study guide, or encyclopedia entry and turn it in as your own work, either. You can't swipe a chunk of someone else's scholarship and pretend that you wrote it. We all know that this type of literary theft is wrong.

But some students feel that putting ideas into their own words and providing a Works Cited page or bibliography is sufficient to avoid a charge of plagiarism.

It's not.

Other students believe that copying a passage word for word without using quotation marks is fine as long as they provide either footnotes, endnotes, or parenthetical documentation (the source in parentheses at the end of the material).

It's not.

Many students think that misunderstanding what they have to cite gets them off the hook. If they pass someone else's work off as their own by error, it's okay because it was an honest mistake.

You Could Look It Up

Plagiarism is representing someone else's words or ideas as your own.

It's not.

It's plain by now that plagiarism is more misunderstood than an erring public official. So what is plagiarism?

Plagiarism is using someone else's words without giving adequate credit. Plagiarism is …

♦ Using someone else's ideas without acknowledging the source.

♦ Paraphrasing someone else's argument as your own.

♦ Presenting an entire paper or a major part of it developed as another writer did.

♦ Arranging your ideas exactly as someone else did—even though you acknowledge the source(s).

The word *plagiarize* comes from the Latin word for kidnapper and literary theft. Plagiarism is lying, fraud, and betrayal of trust.

While plagiarism is a serious lapse in ethics as well as a cause for failure and even expulsion in some schools, documenting your sources correctly is easy. It also gives your research paper authority and credibility. Here's how to do it.

An Ounce of Prevention

One of the best ways to prevent plagiarism is to be a careful researcher. Walk this way:

◆ **Make bibliography cards.** Basically, bibliography cards are a master list of sources. When you've got a list of sources, it's much easier to track where information has come from. Use the techniques you learned in Chapter 4 for making logical and well-organized bibliography cards.

◆ **Be consistent.** So far, I've taught you the documentation system used by the Modern Language Association (MLA). I like this method of documentation because it's easy and logical. However, later on in this book I'll teach you other methods. Of course, you will use the method of documentation required by your instructor or discipline. No matter what method you use, always be consistent. If you vary documentation methods from card to card, you're more apt to get confused and misread or miscopy a source.

◆ **Take careful notes.** In Chapter 5, you learned how to take notes, including techniques for summarizing, paraphrasing, and documenting direct quotations. As you take notes, be very careful to put quotes around exact quotations. You can also write "paraphrase" or "summary" around information that you've rephrased in your own words. This will help you recall what needs to be quoted and what doesn't.

◆ **Consider color-coding.** Kick it up a notch by coding sources with colors or fonts. For example, when I handwrite notes, I use different colors to track information that I've quoted, paraphrased, and summarized. I highlight quotes in yellow and paraphrases/summaries in pink. I don't highlight my own, original ideas so I can distinguish them easily from source material. When I keyboard information, I use different fonts for different sources: **Courier New bold** for direct quotes, *Courier New italics* for paraphrases/summaries, and Courier New plain for my own words. Both methods make it a snap to distinguish sources and avoid plagiarism. Consider using my methods or creating your own variations.

◆ **Keep track of sources.** As you work, be sure to note all sources, card by card. Do not wait until you've finished a batch of cards. If you do, you're likely to get interrupted and forget what's what.

What You *Don't* Need to Document

You Could Look It Up

Document means to give credit to your sources.

So what do you have to *document* in your paper? Give credit for any information that is not common knowledge or your own original thinking. This means that you do *not* have to give a source for information you are expected to know or something that you came up with on your own. Later in this chapter, I'll show you what you *do* have to document—and how to do it.

Common Knowledge

"Common knowledge" is defined as the information an educated person is expected to know. Not to worry; you don't have to have an encyclopedic knowledge of every date, name, place, or person. You'll probably have to check a date or the spelling of a name, but you won't have to document the facts because you're expected to know them.

Common knowledge falls into many categories. For example, you're expected to know general facts about these subjects:

- ◆ Art
- ◆ Geography
- ◆ Language
- ◆ Science
- ◆ Culture
- ◆ Computer science

- ◆ History
- ◆ Films
- ◆ Music
- ◆ Literature
- ◆ Social studies
- ◆ Mathematics

Here are some examples of common knowledge that you don't have to document:

- ◆ Rosebud was the sled in the movie *Citizen Kane*.
- ◆ Leonardo da Vinci was a painter, scientist, and philosopher.
- ◆ John Maynard Keynes was likely the most influential economic thinker of the twentieth century.
- ◆ Mozart, Verdi, and Wagner all composed operas.
- ◆ Shakespeare's tragedies include *Hamlet*, *Romeo and Juliet*, and *King Lear*.
- ◆ A clone is a genetic copy of an individual organism, arrived at through asexual reproduction in which the nucleus of a cell from the body of a single parent is stimulated to start dividing by itself.

- *Quid pro quo* means "something for something; tit for tat."
- The American Revolution began in 1775 when fighting erupted at Lexington and Concord, Massachusetts.

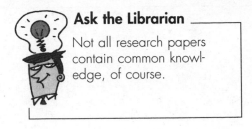

Ask the Librarian

Not all research papers contain common knowledge, of course.

How can you tell if something is common knowledge? If the fact is presented in several sources, odds are good that your readers are expected to know it. This means that you do not have to document it in your paper.

Of course, common knowledge depends on your audience. If you are writing a scholarly paper on the American Transcendental movement for a group of English professors who specialize in nineteenth-century American literature, you're going to assume a lot more common knowledge about Ralph Waldo Emerson and Henry David Thoreau than you would if you were writing the same paper for a group of brain surgeons.

Original Thinking

You don't have to document ideas and theories that you came up with on your own. You're expected to think about what you read and build on the ideas you formulate. Following is an example from a research paper on the poem *Hymn to Demeter* that Liz Fink wrote for a class at Columbia University. Notice that Liz draws from the primary source to support her own original conclusions.

> It is notable, though, that it is only after the abduction that Persephone speaks or even receives a name. *Hymn to Demeter* clearly takes place in a society where a woman's freedom and welfare is secondary to a man's political maneuvering, but subtly the poem voices a small protest. Demeter, Persephone's mother, doesn't eat or drink for nine days in her grief; as a form of action, it does nothing to rescue Persephone. It is, however, similar to how the poem as a whole acts only to recognize the horror of its society, in perhaps as futile a gesture. Demeter, with her power to withhold seed and fertility from agriculture, is nearly alone in the feminine world in holding any power, but it isn't enough to fully rescue her daughter; in the world of Homer and Herodotus, women are universally exploited pawns in a male game.

Be very careful not to cross the line between combining bits and pieces of information you read and thinking that it's your own work. It's not—it's someone else's thinking that you've merely rephrased. Original thought is just that: your own ideas that you came up with all by yourself.

Ask the Librarian

My students always ask, "What happens if I come up with something that I think is original but someone else has already thought of it?" Don't panic: Chances are that someone *has* thought of it already, but you're only expected to do a reasonable job of research, not an exhaustive one. The depth of your research depends on your purpose (class paper, Master's thesis, Ph.D. thesis, etc.) and audience (instructor, thesis advisors, etc.). Obviously, you're going to be a lot more thorough if you're doing a graduate-level research paper that involves the potential for saving lives than one for an English 101 class.

Document Quotations to Avoid Plagiarism

Now, what *do* you have to cite? You must always set off direct quotes with quotation marks and give credit to your original source. It is considered plagiarism if you copy a part of the quotation without using quotation marks—*even if you give credit.*

As you study the following examples, notice that it is not enough to put the page citation in parentheses after the information. Because the information is a direct quote, it must be enclosed in quotations.

Plagiarism

In *The Histories*, war and peace are issues of great importance; the abduction of women is not. Herodotus shrugs off rape because it is stupid after the event to make a fuss about avenging it. He quotes the Trojans, who describe rape as nothing worse than woman-stealing on both sides (4). After all, it is a story about men told through the eyes of men.

This is plagiarism because the writer fobs off someone else's words as her own. It's not enough to give credit in parentheses.

Not Plagiarism

In *The Histories*, war and peace are issues of great importance; the abduction of women is not. Herodotus shrugs off rape—"it is stupid after the event to make a fuss about avenging it"—by quoting the Trojans, who describe it as "nothing worse than woman-stealing on both sides" (4). After all, it is a story about men told through the eyes of men.

This is *not* plagiarism because the writer quotes someone else's exact words, sets them off in quotation marks, and gives full credit to the source.

Plagiarism

Additionally, perhaps even more significant than naming, the *Hymn to Demeter* features women speaking. It is significant to note that no woman speaks of an abduction or rape in *The Histories*; all the reader is left with is Herodotus saying that it is obvious that no young woman allows herself to be abducted if she does not wish to be (4). The narrator of *Hymn to Demeter*, meanwhile, depicts Persephone wailing as she is seized against her will (Homer 2). Not only is the narration sensitive to her plight (instead of overlooking it entirely to focus on its political ramifications), Persephone is allowed the chance to tell her own story. She tells of how she was forcibly abducted and Hades forced himself upon her against her will and by force (13). Her story reinforces that of the narrator's.

This is plagiarism because the writer again omits the quotation marks around someone else's words.

Not Plagiarism

Additionally, perhaps even more significant than naming, the *Hymn to Demeter* features women speaking. It is significant to note that no woman speaks of an abduction or rape in *The Histories*; all the reader is left with is Herodotus quoting, "It is obvious that no young woman allows herself to be abducted if she does not wish to be" (4). The narrator of *Hymn to Demeter*, meanwhile, depicts Persephone "wail[ing]" as she is seized "against her will" (Homer 2). Not only is the narration sensitive to her plight (instead of overlooking it entirely to focus on its political ramifications), Persephone is allowed the chance to tell her own story. She tells of how she was forcibly abducted and Hades forced himself upon her "against [her] will and by force" (13). Her story reinforces that of the narrator's.

This is *not* plagiarism because the writer quotes someone else's exact words, sets them off in quotation marks, and gives full credit to the source.

Now, reread these examples to see how smoothly the writer integrated the quotes to make her point with convincing proof. It's admirable writing.

Guidelines for Using Quotations

Use direct quotations to support what you say, not to substitute for it. Here are some additional guidelines for using direct quotations:

- **Be choosy.** Select appropriate quotations that really help you make your point. Use the quotes to nail your point.

♦ **Get the best.** Use quotations from recognized experts whose distinctive voice lends authority to your argument.

♦ **Use direct quotes.** Include direct quotations if paraphrasing them would water them down and blunt their impact.

♦ **Be careful.** Be sure to copy the quote exactly as it appears. Check and double-check your work.

♦ **Be ethical.** Change a quote only to make the narrative smooth, never to change the author's meaning to suit your purposes. Also, if you do excerpt a quotation, always be sure it makes grammatical sense after you've cut it. Use an *ellipsis* (…) to show where you have made a cut.

You Could Look It Up

Use an **ellipsis** (…) to show where you have deleted information from a direct quotation. Use **square brackets** [ ] to show that you have added a letter or word to a direct quote. Don't confuse square brackets [ ] with parentheses ( )—they are separate marks of punctuation.

♦ **Identify additions.** Show any addition to a quote in *square brackets*, [ ].

♦ **Don't overquote.** Too many quotes makes it appear that you didn't do much original thinking. It seems like you're letting other people do all the talking for you. As a general rule of thumb, no more than 25 percent of your paper should be direct quotes.

♦ **Avoid long quotes.** Many readers skip long quotes and your instructor is likely to think you're just using the long quote to pad your paper. (Hmmm … *that* old dodge.)

Document Opinions to Avoid Plagiarism

You must also document the way an author constructs an argument or a line of thinking. Thus, it is considered plagiarism if you try to fob off someone else's opinions as your own. Study these examples.

Original Source

The literary scholar George F. Whicher wrote "Emily Dickinson was quintessentially native to the region and completely innocent of literary sophistication. As a daughter of the leading lawyer of Amherst, she might normally have married a young minister or lawyer from the college he served as a treasurer but this fulfillment was denied to her. To compensate for her disaster of the heart she seems to have turned to poetry, and in single-minded concentration of what most concerned her to have immersed herself behind the hemlock hedges of the Dickinson house. Only after her death was the extent of her achievement known." (704)

Plagiarism

We can conclude that the poet Emily Dickinson was a true child of New England and very unaware of other writers. Because her father was the most respected attorney in their hometown of Amherst, Emily would be expected to be matched with someone her father knew and respected from their social class. Since she never married, however, she decided to become a writer. She worked hard but failed to achieve fame during her lifetime.

This is plagiarism because the writer puts forth someone else's opinion as her own. The writer claims that Emily Dickinson became a poet because she never got married. This is pretty radical stuff; many women thwarted in love don't turn to literary careers. Thus, paraphrasing the long quote does not make it okay; credit still has to be given to the original speaker, the literary scholar George F. Whicher. Following are two different revisions that correct the plagiarism.

Not Plagiarism

According to George F. Whicher, a Dickinson scholar, we can conclude that the poet Emily Dickinson was a true child of New England and very unaware of other writers. Because her father was the most respected attorney in their hometown of Amherst, Emily would be expected to be matched with someone her father knew and respected from their social class. Since she never married, however, she decided to become a writer. She worked hard but failed to achieve fame during her lifetime. (704)

Not Plagiarism

George F. Whicher, a Dickinson scholar, believes that Emily Dickinson became a writer because she was disappointed in love. Failing to marry—as expected of someone of her elevated social standing in Amherst—Dickinson instead devoted herself to her career to the exclusion of all else. She hid herself away from society, Whicher claims, to sublimate her disappointment in her art. Tragically, she was denied even the fame that her art brought, because her literary accomplishments were recognized only after she had died. (704)

In both examples, the writer paraphrases the original source to avoid having to insert a long quote. However, this is *not* plagiarism because the writer gives credit to the scholar who developed the critical theory, George F. Whicher. Further, the writer shows readers where to find the original source, page 704 of Whicher's book. The full citation appears in the Works Cited page, as per MLA documentation.

Document Paraphrases to Avoid Plagiarism

I've said it before but it's worth saying again: Just because you paraphrase does not mean that you can take credit for the work. You *must* still give credit for information in a paraphrase—if it is not common knowledge! You must cite the source: the book, article, web page, and so on.

It is not enough just to change a few words. Neither is it enough to rearrange a few sentences and call it kosher. It's not. Both practices can result in plagiarism. Study these examples.

Original Source

The story of Hester Prynne, heroine of Nathaniel Hawthorne's *The Scarlet Letter*, takes place in 17th century Boston. Hawthorne no doubt wandered through the King's Chapel Burial Ground when he worked in the nearby Custom House from 1839 to 1841. Tradition says that the fictional Hester Prynne is based on the original Elizabeth Pain (or Payne), who is buried in that graveyard. There is a big red A with two lions on the upper-left-hand corner of Pain's gravestone. The crest looks amazingly like Hester's gravestone, as described in the last line of *The Scarlet Letter:* "On her stone there appears the semblance of an engraved escutcheon with 'on a field, sable, the letter A gules.'"

This source comes from page 191 in a book by James Powers. The final quote comes from the last page of *The Scarlet Letter* by Nathaniel Hawthorne, page 273.

Plagiarism

Hawthorne set his romance *The Scarlet Letter* in Boston in the 1600s. The story describes characters who could be buried in the King's Chapel Burial Ground. Hawthorne had probably walked through this graveyard when he worked in the nearby Custom House in the nineteenth century. People think that Hawthorne's character Hester Prynne is based on the original Elizabeth Pain (or Payne). The two gravestones are a lot alike, since both have a big red A with two lions on the upper-left corner. Pain's gravestone looks like Hester's, as described in the last sentence in *The Scarlet Letter:* "On her stone there appears the semblance of an engraved escutcheon with 'on a field, sable, the letter A gules.'"

This is plagiarism because it does not give credit to the original source, Powers, nor to the quote from the last page of *The Scarlet Letter*. Changing the words doesn't make it your own. Below are two different revisions that correct the plagiarism.

Not Plagiarism

Hawthorne set his romance *The Scarlet Letter* in Boston in the 1600s. The story describes characters who could be buried in the King's Chapel Burial Ground. Hawthorne had probably walked through this graveyard when he worked in the nearby Custom House in the nineteenth century. People think that Hawthorne's character Hester Prynne is based on the original Elizabeth Pain (or Payne). The two gravestones are a lot alike, since both have a big red A with two lions on the upper-left corner (Powers, 191). Pain's gravestone looks like Hester's, as described in the last sentence in *The Scarlet Letter:* "On her stone there appears the semblance of an engraved escutcheon with 'on a field, sable, the letter A gules.'" (*Scarlet Letter,* 273.)

Not Plagiarism

A granite marker erected in the King's Chapel Burial Ground cites another intriguing source for Hester Prynne. According to the information on this marker, Hawthorne drew inspiration for Hester Prynne from the real-life tale of Elizabeth Pain (or Payne). On the surface, the similarities are astonishing: Both gravestones have a big red A with two lions on the upper-left corner. However, Pain was tried and acquitted for the murder of her child, whereas Prynne was tried and convicted for adultery. Nonetheless, Hawthorne had very likely seen Pain's gravestone as he walked through the burial ground on his way to his job next door at the Custom House. (Powers, 191) Perhaps Pain's gravestone sparked the idea for Hester's gravestone, which Hawthorne describes this way: "On her stone there appears the semblance of an engraved escutcheon with 'on a field, sable, the letter A gules.'" (*Scarlet Letter,* 273)

As you'll learn in Chapter 18, to create a footnote or endnotes, just add the superscript number at the end of the sentence or passage in place of the parenthetical citation.

Fortunately, avoiding plagiarism is a piece of cake: You just document your sources correctly. You give credit in your paper to the scholars who did the heavy lifting and created the primary and secondary sources that you are using to make your point.

CAUTION

Lost in (Cyber)Space

Never use both parenthetical documentation and footnotes/endnotes to give credit for the same passage. Use one or the other.

The Least You Need to Know

- ◆ Plagiarism is literary theft, passing off someone else's words or opinions as your own.

- ◆ You do not have to document common knowledge and your own original thoughts.

- ◆ Always focus on your audience when you decide what to document.

- ◆ Avoid plagiarism by documenting quotations, opinions, and paraphrases.

Part 4

Use and Document Research to Make *Your* Point

Late one night a mugger wearing a ski mask jumped into the path of a well-dressed man and stuck a gun in his ribs. "Give me your money," he demanded.

Indignant, the affluent man replied, "You can't do this—I'm a U.S. congressman!"

"In that case," replied the robber, "give me *my* money."

Here, you'll learn how to avoid *plagiarism*, literary theft. Then I'll show you how to put the finishing touches on your research paper, including writing a Works Cited page or a References page, revising, editing, proofreading, and assembling your paper.

Chapter 17

Documentation Style: Focus on MLA

- ◆ Survey different systems of documentation
- ◆ Review terms
- ◆ Learn MLA documentation
- ◆ Study a sample research paper

Back in the old days when dinosaurs roamed the earth, kids walked 10 miles uphill in the snow to school, and a dollar was worth a dollar, sources were documented with footnotes. Everyone agreed that footnotes were cumbersome to write and position on the bottom of a page, but they got the job done. They helped prevent plagiarism.

Then came the Ice Age, school buses, inflation, and endnotes. Everyone agreed that endnotes were a little easier to use than footnotes because you could put them all at the end of the paper. No more trying to position full citations and subscript numbers on the bottom of a page. Endnotes also got the job done by giving credit to sources.

Today we have global warming, cars the size of school buses, and best of all—internal documentation. It's the easiest way yet to document your sources and give full credit to the scholars and scientists who did the original research. In Chapter 16, I showed you how to use internal documentation to prevent plagiarism. In this chapter, we'll first survey different methods of documentation. Then we'll discuss the MLA documentation system in depth.

Different Systems for Crediting Sources

You've already learned the importance of giving credit to your reference sources. This is the basis of any research paper, the agreement between scholar and writer. The scholars let you use their findings to buttress your argument. In exchange, you give them credit for their insights and hard work. In addition, citing your source allows readers to follow up on your findings and thus build on *your* work.

You can choose from a number of documentation formats as you give credit to your sources. The methods have strong similarities in intent (to give credit), but some marked differences in format.

Always consult the documentation guide in your subject area when you prepare internal documentation, footnotes, endnotes, Works Cited pages, and Reference pages. Also check with your instructor to see which style of formatting he or she prefers.

Documentation Methods

The following chart shows some of the different methods of documentation and the disciplines in which they are used. There are other formatting styles as well, but space forbids inclusion of them all.

Field	Documentation System
Anthropology	*Publication Manual of the American Psychological Association (APA)* American Psychological Association
Biology	*CBE Style Manual* Council of Biology Editors (CBE)
Biomedicine	*Annals of Internal Medicine* International Steering Committee of Medical Editors
Business	Chicago Manual of Style
Chemistry	*ACS Style Guide: A Manual for Authors and Editors* American Chemical Society
Education	*Publication Manual of the American Psychological Association (APA)* American Psychological Association

Field	Documentation System
English Languages	*MLA Handbook*
Humanities	Modern Language Association
Geology	*Suggestions to Authors of Reports of the United States Geological Survey*
	U.S. Geology Survey
Law	*Uniform System of Citation*
	Harvard Law Review
Mathematics	*A Manual for Authors of Mathematical Papers*
	American Mathematical Society
Medicine	*American Medical Association Manual of Style*
	American Medical Association
Physics	*AIP Style Manual*
	American Institute of Physics
Political science	*Publication Manual of the American Psychological Association* (*APA*)
	American Psychological Association
Psychology	*Publication Manual of the American Psychological Association* (*APA*)
	American Psychological Association
Social sciences	*Publication Manual of the American Psychological Association* (*APA*)
	American Psychological Association

Agree to Disagree

The issue of documentation may seem silly, but to those of us who establish our reputations and make our living through scholarship, it's heavy-duty stuff. Below are some documentation issues you should know.

◆ **CMS.** In the humanities (English, languages, etc.), the *Chicago Manual of Style* (CMS) is endorsed by instructors who prefer full footnotes and/or endnotes rather than internal documentation.

◆ **CBE.** In the sciences, the *CBE Manual for Authors, Editors, and Publishers* is highly influential. In their latest version, the CBE (Council of Biology Editors) advocates a common documentation style for all international sciences.

CAUTION Lost in (Cyber)Space

Never mix documentation formats. Choose the appropriate format for your subject area and stick with it.

You Could Look It Up

Footnotes, endnotes, and parenthetical documentation are all ways of giving credit to the sources you used in your paper.

◆ **COS.** No matter which system of documenting you're using, you're apt to find that it hasn't kept pace with the electronic revolution. While the standard style manuals were scrambling to keep up with the flurry of websites, listservs, and e-mail, a new kid in town jumped into the fray: The *Columbia Guide to Online Style* (COS). Designed specifically for online sources, the COS system has yet to become widely accepted, however. Check with your instructor before using it.

Footnotes, Endnotes, Internal Documentation: A Review of Terms

Each discipline favors a specific documentation style. Some documentation systems require footnotes and endnotes; others prefer parenthetical documentation. Let's start with a review of definitions:

◆ **Footnotes.** A footnote is a citation placed at the bottom ("foot") of a page. It is preceded by a superscript number. The following model is written in MLA format.

> [1]Thomas R Dye and Harmon Zeigler, *The Irony of Democracy: An Uncommon Introduction to American Politics.* (Monterey: Brooks/Cole, 1987), 371.

◆ **Endnotes.** An endnote is a citation placed at the end of the entire research paper. It is preceded by a superscript number. The format is identical to a footnote.

> [1]Thomas R Dye and Harmon Zeigler, *The Irony of Democracy: An Uncommon Introduction to American Politics.* (Monterey: Brooks/Cole, 1987), 371.

◆ **Parenthetical note.** A parenthetical note gives an abbreviated form of the citation in the body of the paper. (The full citation appears in the Works Cited, References, or bibliography at the end of the paper.)

> (Dye 317)

Research papers written in the business world usually follow the rules laid down in the *Chicago Manual of Style*, whereas the humanities favor the MLA style of documentation. Therefore, when you're writing business papers, you might have to use footnotes. However, when you're writing in the humanities (English, history, foreign language, social studies, etc.), you most often use the MLA style of parenthetical or internal documentation. Let's check it out now.

The MLA System of Documentation

In most cases, MLA favors *parenthetical or internal documentation* over the traditional footnotes or endnotes. Parenthetical documentation offers an abbreviated, easy-to-use form of credit right in the body of the paper. For a complete citation, your readers can check the Works Cited page. This is a great system because it's easy for you and your readers to use.

> **You Could Look It Up**
>
> **Parenthetical** or **internal documentation** places an abbreviated form of the source within the body of the research paper rather than in footnotes or endnotes. Therefore, parenthetical documentation takes the place of traditional footnotes or endnotes.

MLA Internal Documentation

MLA documentation has two simple steps:

1. Give abbreviated credit in the text.

2. Place a full citation in the Works Cited page at the end of the paper.

Study these models to see how it's done.

Model

Step 1: Abbreviated Credit in the Text

Ghassen Nakshbendi, spokesperson for the Islamic Science Foundation in Rye, New York, said the hysteria brought "sad days for the relationship of America and the Muslim world" (Pace A6).

Step 2: Full Citation in Works Cited Page

Pace, Eric. "Muslims in U.S. Embarrassed and Indignant." *The New York Times* 20 February 1989: A6.

Model

Step 1: Abbreviated Credit in the Text

Angry Muslims have fueled a furor surrounding *The Satanic Verses* since its publication, a book which, ironically, Rushdie described as "not … an anti-religious novel … [but] an attempt to write about migration" ("Choice Between Light and Dark").

Step 2: Full Citation in Works Cited Page

Rushdie, Salman. "Choice Between Light and Dark." *The Observer* 22
     January 1989: 11.

How much bibliographic information must you include in the body of the paper when you use internal documentation? The first time you cite a source in your paper, include as much of the following information as necessary for your reader to figure out the source easily:

♦ Title of the source

♦ Writer's name

♦ Writer's affiliation

♦ Page numbers

The following passage shows the first time a source is cited. The author is important, so his name is included in the text of the paper. (The key part of the passage is underlined to make it easier for you to locate. Of course, you would not underline it in your paper.)

> In addition, many patients on Prozac began to experience personality changes over time. A new study described at the annual meeting of the American Psychiatric Association suggests that Prozac alters aspects of personality as it relieves depression. <u>Ron G. Goldman, a psychiatrist at Columbia University,</u> <u>believes that "Emotional and personality features are intertwined in depression</u> <u>so it's not really surprising that some types of personality change would accom-</u> <u>pany improvement in this condition" (Bower 359).</u>

This next example shows a paraphrase from a source also cited for the first time. Because the author isn't important, he or she isn't mentioned. Instead, the focus is on the journal from which the material was taken. (The key part of the passage is underlined to make it easier for you to locate. Again, you would not underline it in your paper.)

It has been reported that some individuals on Prozac have a decreased libido or no desire for sexual activity. <u>A study published in *The Journal of Clinical*</u> <u>*Psychiatry* in April 1994 found that among 160</u> <u>patients taking Prozac, 85 reported their sexual</u> <u>desire or response diminished after using the drug</u> <u>(Nichols 36).</u>

Lost in (Cyber)Space

Quotations have to be copied exactly as they appear, so *never* correct an error in one. If a quotation does contain an error, include the error, but add [sic] directly after the error to show that you know there's a mistake.

MLA Footnotes

Say you want to include some additional information, a comment that doesn't really fit in the body of the paper. Or say there's just no way to integrate the source in the body of the paper without making an awkward or cumbersome citation. MLA format makes it easy to deal with both situations: You just use a footnote or an endnote. Here's how to do it.

1. Put a *superscript* number at the end of the sentence or passage where you want to add the citation or comment.

2. Place the citation or comment at the bottom of the page or on a separate Endnote page at the end of the paper.

3. Number consecutively, in succession. Don't start new numbers on each page.

You Could Look It Up

A **superscript** number is raised, like this:

word¹ word² word³

Study these models to see how it's done.

Model: Adding a Source

Text:

"Oh, I am not up to discussing again that figure of fun. He is not worthy of more attention than I have granted him in my novels."

—Vladimir Nabokov on Sigmund Freud[1]

Footnote:

[1] From "Nabokov's Interview," an interview published in *Wisconsin Studies in Contemporary Literature*, vol. VIII, no. 2. Spring 1967 1 April 2003. <http://lib.novgorod.net/NABAKOW/Inter06.text>

Model: Adding a Comment

Text:

Dismissing Freud as "figure of fun" here and "the Viennese Quack" in the preface to *Bend Sinister*, Nabokov appears to have an almost Freudian obsession with denouncing psychoanalytic theory. [2]

Footnote:

[2] This denial is Freudian in that Nabokov may deny psychoanalysis precisely because it is such a key explanation of his characters' personalities and behaviors. This was suggested in Richard Lamb's "Discussing Nabokov."

Model Paper with MLA Documentation

The following paper was written by a high school student for the New York State Council for the Humanities 10th Annual Essay Contest. It won Honorable Mention. The essay contains an annotated Works Cited page. (You learned about annotating sources in Chapter 4.) Study this research paper to see how the writer integrated source material and gave full credit with MLA documentation.

The Reactions to Ayatollah Khomeini's Fatwa: Effects on Salman Rushdie and the World

Liz Fink

"Before this, other Islamic critics have accused me of being a product of the permissive society which created AIDS, and say that religious permissiveness will create a kind of religious AIDS. Some of the protesters in Pakistan have said this is somehow created by Jews in America, that Jews in America have put me up to this. So anti-Semitism is behind this as well. The point is that all they can do is hurl insults. The book doesn't hurl any insults, and frankly, I have not inflamed religious feelings. I didn't tell people to march against guns. The blood is on the hands of the people who inflamed the feelings of people who've unfortunately, have not and cannot read the book, because the book is not available." —Salman Rushdie on *Nightline*, February 13, 1989

On February 14, 1989, four months and nineteen days after the publication of *The Satanic Verses*, Ayatollah Ruhollah Khomeini declared that the book's publishers, and, most notably, its author, Salman Rushdie, were *madur el dam* (those whose blood must be shed) and anyone who was killed attempting to fulfill this decree would be hitherto regarded as a martyr (Harrison ix). This decree, known in the Muslim world as a *fatwa*, also led to several Iranian clerics pronouncing a bounty of up to five million dollars on Rushdie's head. Outraged Western nations, including the United Kingdom, where Rushdie is a citizen, wasted no time in showing their horror at the *fatwa* through diplomatic and political means. In 1999, two days shy of a decade since the publication of *The Satanic Verses*, the Iranian government announced they had no intention of harming Rushdie. These official assurances didn't end the private bounties still being offered on Rushdie's head, and today Salman Rushdie continues to live in hiding under constant police guard (Harrison x).

Rushdie lives his life in constant fear that shows little sign of abating. Angry Muslims have fueled a furor surrounding *The Satanic Verses* since its publication, a book which, ironically, Rushdie described as "not ... an anti-religious novel ...

[but] an attempt to write about migration" ("Choice Between Light and Dark"). Another interesting note is how the book's notoriety has, through mass hysteria, transcended in many ways not only what Rushdie intended but what he actually wrote. In the words of Janata MP Syed Shahabuddin in India, who supported his country's decision to ban the novel, *The Satanic Verses* is "a deliberate insult to Islam … not an act of literary creativity," maintaining that "you just have to read it" to know, but added that he himself had not (Devadas 72–73).

While there are many points of contention in the novel, beginning with its title, the inflammatory parts of the book were greatly overblown (Harrison 7–9). The hysteria was created mainly due to the need of many fundamentalists, such as Khomeini, for a scapegoat. Ironically, the negative and divisive effects *The Satanic Verses* had on the Islamic world were predominantly due to the extreme nature of the *fatwa* and the Muslim and Western reactions to it. Ostensibly just a vendetta against one author, the *fatwa* against Rushdie revealed the dangers of fundamentalism, a peril to which the world outside of the Middle East is also vulnerable. The sheer multitude of Muslim faithful who jumped to obey Khomeini's *fatwa*, something considered heinous and barbaric throughout most of the world and by many non-extremist Muslims, forced the world to open its eyes to the looming threat.

The first offense of Rushdie's most famous and infamous work is the title. *The Satanic Verses* refers to a notorious incident where Mohammed, attempting to gain regional support for his fledgling monotheistic religion, tried to grant semi-divine status to three local goddesses. Some historians said that Mohammed recanted later by saying the voice of Satan had imitated the voice of the archangel Gabriel, who relayed the Koran to Mohammed. Muslims claimed it was incendiary to draw on an incident refuted by Islamic historians.

Another insult was choosing the name Mahound, a satanic character in Christian lore, for the novel's Mohammed-like character. A passage of the novel, in way of explanation, elaborated on the choice of Mahound:

> His name: a dream-name, changed by the vision … Here he is neither Mahomet nor MoeHammered; has adopted, instead, the demon-tag the farangis hung around his neck. To turn insults into strengths, whigs, tories, Blacks all chose to wear with pride the names they were given in scorn; likewise, our mountain-climbing, prophet-motivated solitary is to be the medieval baby-frightener, the Devil's synonym: Mahound (93).

When referring to Mohammed's wives, however, Rushdie didn't hesitate to mention them by name. Of course, his decision to have a group of whores change their names and eventually their identities to those of the Prophet's wives did raise fervent objections from Rushdie's audience. His defenders cite the fact that this incident, as well as all of the passages identified as offensive, takes place in a dream sequence of a paranoid-schizophrenic character who is convinced he is the archangel Gabriel.

Perhaps the most explosive element of *The Satanic Verses* is the aspersions it casts on the validity of the Koran. Mahound's scribe, tellingly named Salman, changed some of the words supposedly dictated from Allah through the archangel Gabriel. Mahound failed to notice. Salman, explaining his actions, claimed it was too coincidental for the verses allegedly from Gabriel to infallibly be in Mahound's self-interest. The novel insinuates that the Koran is far from the pure words of Allah which faithful Muslims insist the Koran to be, that "[it] as a whole is a forgery" (Parrinder).

The exact portions of the novel considered blasphemous and offensive are often unclear; what is clear is what happened upon the publication of *The Satanic Verses* by Viking Penguin in Britain on September 26, 1988. A little over a week later it was banned in India, and by the end of November, Pakistan, Saudi Arabia, Egypt, Somalia, Bangladesh, Sudan, Malaysia, Indonesia, and Qatar followed suit, with South Africa canceling a book tour amidst threats of violence and arson. There were several book burnings and demonstrations in Britain and a riot in Islamabad, Pakistan where a crowd attempted to storm the American embassy. In Britain, it was suspected that the riots were stage-managed by the leaders of Muslim organizations who were in a position to know enough about the book to influence their less-informed compatriots, "referring to the fact many of the novel's opponents hadn't actually read it. In the case of the Islamabad riots, the Jamaat-i-Islam party almost certainly helped instigate, with a clear goal of inciting religious fervor to weaken the prime minister, Benazir Bhutto, whom they were bitterly opposed to because of her gender (Harrison 7–8).

Despite the religious fervor reminiscent of Europe in medieval times created by the minions of Muslims who continue to attempt to obey the Ayatollah's *fatwa*, many Muslims objected to the extremity of a measure so clearly stifling the freedom of expression and clouding Western views of Muslims. Ziauddin Sardar argued that Salman Rushdie "plundered everything" he (Sardar) held dear because he "rewrote the life of Prophet Mohammed and tried to seal it in his own secularist image." He did, however, argue just as vehemently about the horror of the Ayatollah's *fatwa* as he did about the grievously offensive nature of Rushdie's novel: "The Ayatollah blurred the distinction between image and reality ... [he] created an image of authentic Islam where the *fatwa*, even though it has no basis in the Koran, was legitimate" (Sardar).

Sardar wasn't alone in bemoaning the implications of the Ayatollah's *fatwa*. Seyyed Hossein Nasr, a premier Shiite Muslim scholar in Washington, said: "We are outraged at the pronouncements of Khomeini and the fundamentalists because Islam is a religion of tolerance of opinion, of discussion, of dialogue. It's not really a closed religion." Ghassen Nakshbendi, spokesperson for the Islamic Science Foundation in Rye, New York, said the hysteria brought "sad days for the relationship of America and the Muslim world" (Pace A6).

Many Muslims disagreed with and even felt deeply insulted by many parts of *The Satanic Verses* but still don't support its banning, let alone the holy murder of its author. Many feel they were victimized in the ensuing tumult when shocked Westerners fell into the trap of characterizing all Muslims as fanatic fundamentalists. As Sardar said, "the mayhem that followed echoed the Malay proverb which says that when two elephants fight it is the grass that gets trampled. For the past decade, I have been the grass in between."

Large numbers of Muslims, including Sardar, condemned denying Rushdie's freedom of expression. Interestingly, Sardar also cited the unwillingness of anyone in the West to publish any of his criticism of *The Satanic Verses*. As Sardar was forced to conclude, "Freedom of expression is a one-way street."

The clearest victim in the outcry over *The Satanic Verses*, however, remains Salman Rushdie himself. As the editors of *The New Republic* said in a 1989 article, "Two Cheers for Blasphemy": "We are hearing a lot about the hurt feelings of Muslims, particularly from the representatives of Muslim organizations on American television. But it is Rushdie, not Khomeini, who is running for his life" (6–7).

Rushdie continues to live in hiding, with Scotland Yard supplying him with a twenty-four hour guard. Rushdie declared that he regained his Muslim faith and publicly disavowed "any statement in my novel *The Satanic Verses* uttered by any of the characters who insults the prophet Mohammed, or casts aspersions upon Islam, or upon the authenticity of the holy Koran, or who rejects the divinity of Allah" (Harrison 11). He promised not to allow a paperback edition or further translations to be printed as well. Despite all of this, Khomeini remained steadfast:

> Even if Salman Rushdie repents and becomes the most pious man of time, it is incumbent on every Muslim to employ everything ... to send him to hell. Imperialist mass media were falsely alleging that if the author repented, his execution order would be lifted ... this is denied, 100 percent ("Khomeini Spurns Rushdie Regrets").

Even the 1998 announcement by Iranian foreign minister Kamai Kharrazi that the Iranian government would cease attempting and encouraging the murder of Rushdie and would dissociate itself from the bounty on Rushdie's life didn't mean Rushdie could come out of hiding. Kharrazi didn't address the consensus view of Iranian clerics that the death sentence against Rushdie is a *hukm*. A *fatwa* is only valid in the lifetime of the religious authority who issues it, while a *hukm* is valid beyond his death. Ayatollah Abdallah Javadi-Amoli said in February 1997: "This is not a *fatwa* which died with the death of the religious leader who issued it … It is a *hukm* which is permanent and it will stay in place until it is carried out" (The Library Institute).

Initially after Kharrazi's statement, Rushdie was confident that "the whole issue will now very rapidly fade into the past" (The Library Institute). Sadly, he was quickly proven wrong. No number of apologies, professions of faith, announcements by the Iranian government that they are no longer after his life, and Muslim backlashes against Khomeini's decree will make it any more likely that the only death Salman Rushdie has to worry about is old age.

Rushdie finally waxed bitterly over the apparent triumph of what many have interpreted as fundamentalist suppression of expression. "How fragile civilisation is; how easily, how merrily a book burns!" he said ("Choice Between Light and Dark").

The hysteria over *The Satanic Verses* was fueled only superficially by the novel itself. While there were certainly points of contention in Rushdie's work, they were of no more a grievous nature than those in *The Last Temptation of Christ* and other works of fiction for which the lives of the author and publishers weren't threatened and entire nations didn't institute bans. Many motives made fanning fundamentalist fires politically expedient, particularly in Pakistan and Khomeini's Iran. Very quickly other issues became entwined with the arguments inherent in Rushdie's work; during the Islamabad storming of the American embassy, for instance, rioters sported placards protesting Israel and the American support the novel received. The example the West set, that freedom of expression erodes the power religion holds over the populace, is also responsible. Reactions to the extremity of measures undertaken by Muslims led to widespread international condemnation as well as degraded relations between the Middle East and the West. It also spurred Westerners to class all Muslims as equally extreme as the adherents to Khomeini's *fatwa*. Additionally, it furthered schisms within the Muslim world between moderates and extremists.

Ayatollah Khomeini's *fatwa*, though ostensibly aimed only at Rushdie and his novel's publishers, quickly sensitized the world. All of Europe, particularly the

British, reacted swiftly against the threat on Rushdie's life. The European foreign ministers in 1989 met and condemned the *fatwa* as "an unacceptable violation of the most elementary principles and obligations that govern relations among sovereign states" (Ibrahim). The United States, too, realized the threat in the call to murder Rushdie. Representative Stephen J. Solarz asked, "Are we taking any steps to protect those American citizens who might be vulnerable?" (Friedman). The danger was increased even more when a man called a Bombay news media and threatened to blow up British Airways flights serving India until Britain gave up Rushdie (Randal). The danger faced by Rushdie is also faced by the rest of the world. If he is vulnerable for alleged blasphemy, who is safe? The world grappled with that question in the immediate aftermath of the issuance of the *fatwa*, and, shaken, was compelled to conclude the answer is no one, least of all Westerners who complacently thought geographic isolation was a sufficient barrier from the fanaticism they thought the world left behind with the Crusades.

After falling from almost thirty thousand feet, Salman Rushdie's heroes found themselves unwittingly caught up in a struggle between good and evil in the forms of newfound identities representing Satan and Gabriel. The issues weren't quite so clear on a black and white scale, however, as politics corroded the initial conflict between liberty and repression and the extremity and bias of some influenced the world. Ultimately, though, Salman Rushdie and his Whitbread prize–winning novel were just as inadvertently caught in an equally epic struggle as the heroes of *The Satanic Verses:* they became pawns in the battle of fundamentalism and Western democracies, of destroying the opposition in a religious fervor or glorifying in diverse opinions through freedom of expression.

Works Cited

Devadas, David. "Salman Rushdie: Political Scapegoat." *India Today* 31 October 1988: 72–73.

A very interesting article, particularly in illustrating how few of Rushdie's criticizers had read his novel.

Harrison, James. *Salman Rushdie.* New York: Twayne Publishers, 1992.

This book provided biographical information on Rushdie and information about the fatwa *affecting his life, but its analysis of his work lacked insight.*

Ibrahim, Youssef M. "Reply to Khomeini." *The New York Times* 21 February 1989: A1, A8.

This article had excellent details about the reactions in the Western world to the fatwa.

"Khomeini Spurns Rushdie Regrets and Reiterates Threat of Death." *The New York Times* 20 February 1989: A1, A6.

This article reinforced the Ayatollah's unwavering conviction in the righteousness of his decree.

The Library Institute of Human Relations. American Jewish Committee December 1998.

This article provided a few facts, but it editorialized too much and wasn't extremely helpful.

Pace, Eric. "Muslims in U.S. Embarrassed and Indignant." *The New York Times* 20 February 1989: A6.

This article was fantastic in quoting Muslims who opposed the fatwa *and showed the faults in classifying all Muslims as extremists.*

Parrinder, Patrick. "Let's Get the Hell Out of Here." *London Review of Books* 29, September 1988: 11–13.

This fascinating book review of The Satanic Verses *has some insight into the novel's meaning.*

"Passages Muslims Condemn from 'The Satanic Verses.'" *The New York Times* 16 February 1989: A6.

This article was very basic and served as a summary for points of contention in the novel.

Randal, Jonathan C. "Rushdie's Book Burned in Britain." *The Washington Post* 18 January 1989.

While the primary focus of this article was the burning and banning of The Satanic Verses—*events that were documented better in other sources—I found the portions about Rushdie's shock over the controversy noteworthy.*

Rushdie, Salman. "Choice Between Light and Dark." *The Observer* 22 January 1989: 11.

Rushdie's defense of his own work was helpful. It was also interesting how he emphasized the novel's focus was not to critique religion, but to write about migration. He reinforced his desire to have the work read as fiction.

Rushdie, Salman. *The Satanic Verses.* New York: Viking Penguin Inc., 1988.

Reading the novel is absolutely critical to understanding the controversy.

"The 'Satanic Verses' Uproar." *Nightline*, Show No. 2016. 13 February 1989.

This interview showed the flaws in the arguments of opponents to The Satanic Verses *and the fact that logic didn't matter to many of them.*

Sardar, Ziauddin. "The Satanic Verses Was Not Only Blasphemous; Worse, It Fueled Western Prejudices Against Muslims." Statesman and Nation Publishing Company 2 October 1998.

This article was fascinating as its author protested to the novel while objecting to the fatwa. *It was also powerful to read how he bemoaned the fate of moderate Muslims who fell prey to stereotypes.*

"Two Cheers for Blasphemy." The *New Republic* 13 March 1989: 7–9.

This is a strongly written article explaining the injustice created by denying Rushdie's freedom of expression and how the peril presented by fundamentalists exists for the entire world.

The Least You Need to Know

◆ Each discipline favors a specific documentation style. Use the method of documentation expected in your field.

◆ Footnotes, endnotes, and parenthetical documentation are all ways of giving credit to sources you used in your paper.

◆ In MLA documentation, you place an abbreviated credit in the text and a full citation in the Works Cited page at the end of the paper.

◆ Use footnotes in MLA documentation to include a comment or give credit to a source that cannot be included in parentheses.

Documentation Style: Focus on APA and CMS

- ◆ Master APA documentation
- ◆ Distinguish between APA and MLA documentation
- ◆ Learn CMS documentation
- ◆ Study a sample research paper written with APA documentation

As you learned in Chapter 17, different areas of study use different documentation formats in research papers. The APA system is used in research papers written in the social sciences: anthropology, education, home and career skills, linguistics, political science, psychology, and sociology. In this chapter, you'll first learn how to use this method of documentation to give credit to all your research sources. Then I'll show you how to use CMS (*Chicago Manual of Style*) documentation, a system used in the humanities. It's based on footnotes/endnotes rather than internal documentation.

The APA System of Documentation

The psychologists at the American Psychological Association created APA documentation, but not to worry: It's as easy as the MLA system to use. As with MLA documentation, the APA system has two simple steps:

1. Give abbreviated credit in the text.

2. Place a full citation in the References list at the end of the paper.

The abbreviated credit can be placed right in the body of the text or in parentheses at the end of the passage, just as it's done in MLA. You can use as much or as little of the reference material as you need, as well.

In both systems, a page number must be given for direct quotations. However, the MLA system omits the designation *p.* or *pp.* before the page numbers; in the APA system, page numbers must be preceded by *p.* or *pp.*

There's a minor difference in the bibliography as well. In the MLA system, the list of sources at the end of the paper is called "Works Cited," but in the APA system it's called "References." There are some minor but important differences in format between these two pages, as you'll learn in Chapter 19.

APA vs. MLA Formats

The following chart highlights the main similarities and differences between the MLA and APA methods of documenting sources.

Feature	MLA	APA
Giving credit in text	Author's name used in text	Author's name used in text
	Date may be included	Date *always* included
	Credit may be in ( )	Credit may be in ( )
	Page number not preceded by *p./pp.*	Page number *always* preceded by *p./pp.*
Complete source list at the end	List called "Works Cited"	List called "References"
	Date goes near end of citation	Date goes in the front of citation, after author's name

Model Internal Documentation in APA Format

Study these models to see how it's done.

Model

Step 1: Abbreviated Credit in the Text

According to Almond and Powell (1966), the majority of the people who support our current two-party system claim that the parties bring together the ideas and standards of many different people, and give the voters a unified policy that they can associate with, a concept that Almond and Powell call "interest aggregation" (p. 98).

Step 2: Full Citation in References Page

Almond, G. & Powell, G. (1966). *Comparative Politics, A Developmental Approach.* Boston: Little, Brown and Company.

Model

Step 1: Abbreviated Credit in the Text

We have gotten more than we expected in our imperfect government, because the battle for control of the government continues to seesaw back and forth between the two rival camps. But there is hope in sight: Voters are drifting away from the two parties and registering as nonpartisan voters (Dye & Zeigler, 1987).

Step 2: Full Citation in References Page

Dye, T. & Zeigler, H. (1987). *The Irony of Democracy: An Uncommon Introduction to American Politics.* 7th ed. Monterey: Brooks/Cole.

Although you can distribute the documentation throughout the passage, the APA parenthetical notes should be as brief and inconspicuous as possible.

From the Reference Desk

According to the U.S. copyright law, authors own their own words as soon as they are "fixed in any tangible medium of expression, now known or later developed, from which they can be perceived, reproduced, or otherwise communicated, either directly or with the aid of a machine or device." Under the Fair Use section of the copyright law, copyrighted material can be used in other documents without infringement of the law "for the purposes of criticism, comment, news reporting, teaching (including multiple copies for classroom use), scholarship, or research."

The CMS System of Documentation

Footnotes and endnotes are another form of documentation used in research papers. The folks over at the *Chicago Manual of Style* set the standard for those who favor footnotes. As always, check the requirements in your field before you hitch your wagon to a footnote style. Some instructors detest footnotes/endnotes, whereas others embrace them.

As you learned in Chapter 17, a footnote is a bibliographic reference indicated by a number in the text. You write the same number on the bottom of the page, followed by the complete citation. An endnote is identical in form to a footnote, but the complete citation is placed at the end of the paper on a separate page labeled "Endnotes."

Here are the general guidelines for CMS footnote/endnote use:

◆ Choose either endnotes or footnotes. You can't have both.

◆ Place each number at the *end* of the material you want to credit.

◆ Use superscript Arabic numerals. These are raised a little above the words.

◆ Indent the first line of the footnote or endnote five spaces. All subsequent lines are placed flush left.

◆ Single-space each footnote; double-space between entries. This is done automatically in most software programs.

◆ Number footnotes or endnotes consecutively from the beginning to the end of your paper.

◆ Use a new number for each citation even if several numbers refer to the same source.

◆ Leave two spaces after the number at the end of a sentence. Don't leave any extra space before the number.

Writing Footnotes/Endnotes in CMS Format

Because we're doing the two-step, here are the two steps you need to follow to write a footnote in CMS format. (It's a snap to do, too.)

1. In the text of your paper, place a raised number *after* anything you need to document.

2. On the bottom of the page on which the note appears (footnote) or on a separate page at the end of the paper (endnote), write the full citation. Place the raised number *before* the citation.

Format for Citing Books

The basic CMS footnote/endnote citation for a book looks like this. You would place this information on the bottom of the page for a footnote or at the end of the entire paper for an endnote.

Footnote number. Author's first name and last name, *Book Title* (place of publication: publisher, date of publication), page number.

Example

⁵George Orwell, *Animal Farm* (New York: Harcourt, Brace & Company, 1946), 15.

Format for Citing Periodicals

The basic footnote/endnote citation for a magazine, newspaper, or journal looks like this:

Footnote number. Author's first name and last name, "Article Title," *Periodical Title*, date, page number.

Example

³Martha Stewart, "Watching Paint Dry Is Fun to Do," *Home and Hearth*, 18 June 2004, 61.

Format for Citing Electronic Sources

The basic footnote/endnote citation for an electronic source looks like this:

Footnote number. *Name of Web Page*. Available from web address; INTERNET.

Example

¹²*King Lear*. In *MIT Complete Works of Shakespeare*. Available from http://mitshakespeare.edu; INTERNET.

Model Footnotes in CMS Format

Use the following models as you write your own footnotes and endnotes. The first model shows a direct quotation credited with a footnote:

Model

Step 1: Note in Text

No one supposes that an actual bundle of papers prepared by a surveyor named Jonathan Pue ever existed. However, it is nevertheless "far from certain that no real historical basis exists for Hester."⁶

Step 2: Footnote

[6] Charles Boewe and Murry G. Murphey, "Hester Prynne in History," *American Literature* 32 (May 1960), 202–294.

So you can compare, here's how the same passage looks when credit is given through parenthetical documentation:

No one supposes that an actual bundle of papers prepared by a surveyor named Jonathan Pue ever existed. However, as Charles Boewe and Murray G. Murphey remarked in their article "Hester Prynne in History," it is nevertheless "far from certain that no real historical basis exists for Hester" (203).

The following model shows you how to use a footnote to document the way an author constructs an argument or a line of thinking.

Model

Step 1: Note in Text

Others have tried to find out if Hawthorne based Hester on actual historical facts. The most striking is the case of Hester Craford, punished for "fornication" with John Wedg. She confessed and was ordered severely flogged. The punishment was postponed for a month to six weeks after the birth of her child, and it was left to Mayor William Hawthorn to see it carried out. The woman's first name and the judge's last name—he was, of course, Hawthorne's ancestor, the infamous "hanging judge" of Salem who refused to repent his role in the 1692 witchcraft hysteria—suggests that Hawthorne must have used this case as the basis for his novel.[7]

Step 2: Footnote

[7] Michael Bell, *Hawthorne and the Historical Romance of New England.* (Princeton: Princeton University Press, 1971), 61.

To compare, here's how the same passage looks when credit is given through parenthetical documentation:

Others have tried to find out if Hawthorne based Hester on actual historical facts. The most striking is the case of Hester Craford, punished for "fornication" with John Wedg. She confessed and was ordered severely flogged. The punishment was postponed for a month to six weeks after the birth of her child, and it was left to Mayor William Hawthorn to see it carried out. The woman's first name and the judge's last name—he was, of course, Hawthorne's ancestor, the infamous "hanging judge" of Salem who refused to repent his role in the 1692 witchcraft hysteria—suggests that Hawthorne must have used this case as the basis for his novel (Bell, 61).

You can use footnotes or endnotes not only to acknowledge a source but also to add observations and comments that don't fit into the body of your text. The model below shows you how to use a footnote to add additional information or a comment that you need. The process is the same in MLA and APA documentation.

Model

Step 1: Note in Text

He returned in March of 1839 and settled into the routine of his new job as measurer of coal and salt for the Boston Custom House.[9]

Step 2: Footnote

[9]The installation of the new Democratic administration of Martin Van Buren, the chosen candidate of old General Jackson, opened up some opportunities for both Franklin Pierce, newly elected to the Senate, and Jonathan Cilley, then a congressman. Both began to search for some suitable administrative post for their friend. In the end they were successful, for Bancroft (an influential politician) offered Hawthorne a choice of positions. In January, Hawthorne accepted the post of measurer at a salary of $1,500 a year.

Ask the Librarian

Use an *ellipsis* (three evenly spaced periods) to show that you've omitted part of a quotation. Don't use an ellipsis at the beginning of a sentence; just start with the material you're quoting. If you omit more than one sentence, add a period before the ellipsis, to show that the omission occurred at the end of a sentence.

Model Paper with APA Documentation

The following paper was written for a high school government class. It uses APA-style documentation.

No Choice in Government

Charles Rozakis

A civil war is raging in our country right now, yet few of us even realize it. The two sides are both well known, and more importantly, they have the job of running our country. For years now, the Republicans and Democrats have been at each other's throats, claiming that the ideas of their political opponents will harm the United States more than help it. However, it is this political infighting which is the true bane of America. This two-party political system which we Americans are so proud of is the cause of more trouble than most of us realize.

The Democratic party as we know it has been around since 1792, when they were known as the Republican Party, or sometimes the Anti-Federalists. The group was originally formed as an opposition to the Hamiltonian Bank of the United States (U.S. Gov't, 1978, p. 247). The Democrats picked up their current name when Andrew Jackson became president, and for much of this early period, they were in control of the government. However, as slavery became a larger issue, the Democrats tried to skirt the issue and never took a firm stance on it. This partially gave rise to the Republican party, the only party to have anything definite to say regarding slavery (U.S. Gov't, 1978, pp. 247–252).

The Republicans did not call for the abolition of slavery, just the prohibition of the practice in any state where it was not already present. The Republicans grew quickly, but did not win the presidency until Abraham Lincoln was elected in 1860. Shortly afterward, the Civil War began, and was won by the Union, led by Lincoln. The Democrats, incidentally, opposed the war and thought it would turn out to be a failure (U.S. Gov't, 1978, pp. 255–258). Much like the Democrats before the war, the Republicans controlled the government, with the Democrats as their only real opponents. From this point on, these two parties would remain the main competitors for dominance of the government, with only brief showings from other minor parties trying to establish a foothold in the political arena.

The Democrats have usually been advocates of strong government support of the people, intervening whenever help is thought to be needed—whether the help is wanted or not. This includes extensive social programs to help out the less-fortunate citizens of the country, but these numerous social bureaucracies lead to a larger government. In turn, this larger government results in increases in taxes to pay for the new departments that need to be created. The Democrats are also proponents of progressive ideals and the equality of all people, a somewhat socialistic stance.

The Republicans, on the other hand, tend to favor little government intervention. Instead, they rely upon the people to help themselves, and help only when asked. This is one of the subtle but most important differences between the two parties. Republicans also tend to be more tradition oriented, clinging to old ideals and standards even when the world is changing around them. Capitalism and social Darwinism (economic survival of the fittest) run strong in the Republican party, which may be a reason why they try to be as unobtrusive in the lives of the people as possible.

The majority of the people who support our current two-party system claim that the parties bring together the ideas and standards of many different people and give the voters a unified policy, a concept that Almond and Powell call "interest aggregation" (Almond & Powell, 1966, p. 98). However, with only two major political parties, people are forced to assume that there are only two opposing viewpoints. If you believe in Item A of the Democratic party, you must therefore be a supporter of Items B, C, and D. This package deal may not encompass all an individual's beliefs. Suppose an affluent gay businessman was asked to choose between a typical Republican statesman and a typical Democratic statesman. Republicans and their fundamentalist Christian backers are for the most part intolerant of homosexuality but are in favor of entrepreneurs. Democrats, while being supposedly more tolerant of gays, are also in favor of substantially higher taxes for those who earn more. How does this man choose between his economic well-being and his social well-being?

The two parties lend themselves to black or white thinking; you either believe in this policy, or the other. There is no in-between. This black or white thinking has led to the factionization of our country, with people flocking to one political pole or the other. The common words one hears regarding political stance are "conservative" and "liberal," which are associated with Republicans and Democrats respectively. Very rarely do we hear of people being "moderates" because this implies that the person is indecisive.

As a result, voters often go into the polling booth with one thought in mind: vote for Party A. People are not voting for candidates or their ideas; rather, they are voting for which side of the political spectrum the candidate is on. This is most frequent in minor elections with relatively unknown candidates. Because the voter does not know either of the candidates, he votes for the one in the Democratic slot or the Republican slot, regardless of the candidate's qualifications.

The Democrats and Republicans are so well-entrenched in our lives and in the political system that it is very difficult for an independent candidate or minor party to be noticed. Congress is dominated by these two parties, with only a small number of independents holding office. Interestingly, Congress has not seen more than one independent in office simultaneously since 1979. Hawaiians had an independent as their mayor for some time, Frank Fasi. However, Fasi was a member of both the Democratic and Republican parties before he formed the

Best Party. The United States is frequently spoken of as the Land of Opportunity, but how can someone establish herself as a politician if she isn't a member of one of the two prominent political parties?

The credibility of our future statesmen is frequently under scrutiny, due to the constant mudslinging that occurs during election time. Every time an election year rolls around, we see slanderous material on the television and in the newspapers. The material is often researched and paid for by the opposition. The Republicans and Democrats are guilty in the extreme of this. The people have been told (by the Democrats, naturally) that the Republicans want to take away educational grants, welfare, and Social Security, and give tax breaks to the rich, all of which are all bent truths. The Republicans want to reform some of these social programs and are not in favor of raising taxes for the wealthy. Our Democratic president has come under constant fire for being a liberal. Since when was that a crime? Surveys show that voters are becoming increasingly disgusted with the mudslinging campaigns, but do the candidates stop? Of course not, because they've got an election to win.

Fortunately, there is hope in sight, as voters are drifting away from the two parties and registering as nonpartisan voters (Dye & Zeigler, 1987, p. 186). I hope this is a sign that we are trying to get away from political parties as a whole, but chances are it means that we'll be seeing a third party arise in the near future. Although it's not the perfect solution to our problem, it is a step in the right direction. Will we ever be rid of political parties? Probably not, but I will leave my faith in the wisdom of George Washington who warned against "the baneful effects of the party spirit generally" (qtd. in U.S. Gov't, 1978, p. 242). I hope others see this wisdom as well.

References

Almond, G. & Powell, G. (1966). *Comparative Politics, A Developmental Approach*. Boston: Little, Brown and Company.

Dye, T. & Zeigler, H. (1987). *The Irony of Democracy: An Uncommon Introduction to American Politics*. 7th ed. Monterey: Brooks/Cole.

The U.S. Government: How and Why It Works (1978). New York: Britannica Books.

The World Almanac and Book of Facts (1995). New Jersey: Funk & Wagnalls.

The Least You Need to Know

◆ As with MLA documentation, the APA system has two simple steps: Give abbreviated credit in the text. Then place a full citation in the References list at the end of the paper.

◆ CMS format uses footnotes/endnotes to show sources.

◆ To create a footnote, put a number in the text right after the source. Write the same number on the bottom of the page, followed by the complete citation.

◆ Always check with your instructor to see which documentation system to use.

End Game: Prepare "Works Cited" and "References" Pages

- ◆ Discover the three main types of source lists
- ◆ Survey general rules for source lists
- ◆ Learn how to prepare an MLA Works Cited Page
- ◆ See how to format an APA References page

You're almost there, partner. Just a few more matters to attend to and you'll be ready to hand in your research paper. In this chapter, I first give you the general rules for formatting your sources. Then I show you how to assemble an MLA-format Works Cited page. Then we parallel-play with an APA-format References page. Let the fun begin!

The Three Main Types of Source Lists

Your sources will be listed in the back of your paper in one of three ways: a Works Cited page, a References list, or a bibliography. Here's how they compare:

◆ A *Works Cited* page is an MLA-formatted list of all the works you *cited* in your paper. "Cited" means that you made specific reference to the sources in the text of your paper. The reference can be in parenthetical documentation or footnotes/endnotes—it makes no difference at all.

You Could Look It Up

A Works Cited page is an MLA-formatted list of all the works you cited in your paper. A References list is an APA-formatted list of all the works you cited in your paper. A bibliography, in contrast, is a list of all works you *consulted* as well as *cited* in your paper.

◆ A *References* list is an APA-formatted list of all the works you *cited* in your paper. A Reference list is the same as a Works Cited list but in a slightly different format.

◆ A *bibliography*, in contrast, is a list of all works you *consulted* as well as *cited* in your paper. Thus, a bibliography is longer than either a Works Cited page or a References page.

In most cases, you just need a Works Cited or References page. However, you may be asked to prepare a bibliography as well. Be sure to check with your instructor so you know which format to follow.

Overall Guidelines

Whether you're preparing a Works Cited page, a References page, or a bibliography, be sure to follow the format exactly. Here are six customary rules that hold for both citation formats:

1. Entries are arranged in alphabetical order according to the author's last name.

2. If the entry doesn't have an author (such as a web page, encyclopedia entry, or editorial), alphabetize it according to the first word of the title. Ignore the articles *a*, *an*, and *the* when they begin the title.

3. Forms for documenting web sources are still evolving. If you're not sure how to document an Internet source and can't find a format in this book, use common sense and include as much information as your reader will need to locate the source easily.

4. Indent the second and all subsequent lines five spaces. That's usually one tab.

5. Follow the formatting exactly. Pay close attention to punctuation and spacing because even a minor variation in formatting can result in misreading. This may seem minor, but instructors notice errors in bibliographic entries because they read so many research papers.

6. The date in a bibliographic citation is written in European style, with the date *before* the month, rather than *after*. For example: 6 November 2004.

Below are the guidelines for preparing a Works Cited page (MLA format) and a References page (APA format).

Prepare a Works Cited Page: MLA Format

Recall that a Works Cited page provides a complete citation for every work you *cited* in your research paper. This means that you referred to the sources in direct quotes, paraphrases, or summaries.

Here's an overview of the specific MLA formats for the Works Cited page. Notice that the indentation is the reverse of footnote/endnote form.

Citing Books

Book with one author.

> Author's last name, first name. *Book Title.* Place of publication: publisher, year of publication.

> Example:

> Dune, Lavon. *Nutrition Almanac.* New York: McGraw-Hill, 1990.

Book with two or three authors. Notice that only the first author's name is inverted. This is done for alphabetical order.

> First author's last name, first name and second author's first name, last name. *Book Title.* Place of publication: publisher, year of publication.

> Example:

> Hamstring, Thomas and John Viceroy. *Baseball Almanac.* New York: Random House, 2004.

Book with three or more authors. You can write all the authors or only the first one and then write *et al.* ("and others") for the rest of the authors. This is the preferred form.

> Author's last name, first name, et al. *Book Title.* Place of publication: publisher, year of publication.

Example:

Lucatelleri, Guiseppi, et al. *Learning Italian*. New York: Scholastic, 2003.

An author and an editor. Be sure to include the author's name, the title of the book, and then the editor. Use the abbreviation Ed. whether there is one editor or many.

Author's last name, first name. *Book Title*. Ed. editor's name. Place of publica tion: publisher, year of publication.

Example:

Twain, Mark. *The Collected Short Stories of Mark Twain*. Ed. Lisa Laughlin. Boston: Allyn & Bacon, Inc., 1999.

An editor but no author. Give the name of the editor or editors, followed by ed. (if one editor) or eds. (if more than one editor).

Editor's last name, first name. ed. *Book Title*. Place of publication: publisher, year of publication.

Example:

Devlin, T'aysha, ed. *The Poetry of the City*. New York: Gold Seal Publishers, 2004.

A book issued by a corporation. Give the name of the corporation as the author, even if it's the publisher as well.

Name of the corporation. *Book Title*. Place of publication: publisher, year of publication.

Example:

IBM. *Know Your Computer*. New York: IBM, 2003.

A book in a series. After the title, include the name of the series and series number.

Author's last name, first name. *Book Title*. Name of the series and series number. Place of publication: publisher, year of publication.

Example:

Neu, David. *Liz Fink*. Twayne's United States Authors Series 124. Boston: Twayne, 1990.

A selection reprinted in an anthology.

> Author's last name, first name. "Title of Selection in the Book." *Book Title*. Editor's name, ed. Place of publication: publisher, year of publication.

Example:

> Kogan, Dore. "Gene Families: The Taxonomy of Protein Paralogs and Chimeras." *Genetic Innovation*. Gresheti Hamlei, ed. New York: Broadway Books, 1999.

Pamphlet. Cite a pamphlet the same way you would a book.

> Example:

> Gordon, Marla Meg. *You and the Law*. Eugene, OR: Consumer Information Group, 2003.

Ask the Librarian

If the page numbers in an article are not consecutive, cite the first page number followed by a plus sign (+).

Citing Periodicals

Article citation with an author. You may have some or all of the following information. For example, the citation may not include a date, a volume, or a number. Only include the information that is available. *Never* make anything up!

> Author's last name, first name. "Title of the Article." *Magazine* day, month, and year of publication, volume, number: page numbers.

Example:

> Dorans, Audrey. "Butterfly Wings It With a Few Genes." *Science News* 23 November 1996, Vol. 150, No. 21: 324–25.

Article citation without an author.

> "Title of the Article." *Magazine* day, month, and year of publication, volume, number: page numbers.

Example:

> "Developmental Biology: Possible New Roles for HOX Genes." *Science* 12 December 1997: 278–80.

Editorial.

> "Title of the Editorial." Editorial. *Newspaper* day, month, and year of publication, section: page number.

> Example:

> "The Importance of Donating Blood." Editorial. *The Cleveland Plain Dealer* 23 June 2004, sec. C:2.

Review. To indicate that an article is a book, movie, or play review, write "Rev. of" before the work being reviewed. Use the abbreviation "dir." for the director.

> Author's last name, first name. "Title of the Review." *Magazine* rev. of *Name of Book, Movie, or Play*, dir. name of director. *Name of Publication* day, month, and year of publication: page numbers.

> Example:

> Goldish, Meish. "The Karen Ziemba Story" Rev. of *Steel Pier*, dir. Chaya Rosen. *The New York Times* 1 August 1998: 17.

Citing Government Documents

Begin the citation with the branch of the government that issued the document (national, state, local) and follow it with the name of the government agency. (The GPO is the government's publishing company.)

> Branch of government. Issuing agency. *Title of the Document.* Publishing information. Washington: GPO, date.

> Example:

> President's Commission on the Assassination of President Kennedy. *Hearings Before the Senate*. Washington: GPO, 1964.

Citing Interviews

Name the subject of the interview, followed by *Personal interview* or *Telephone interview*. Then comes the date.

> Subject's last name, first name. Personal interview. Day, month, and year of interview.

Example:

Greene, William T. Personal interview. 1 September 2004.

Citing Speeches or Lectures

Name the speaker, the title of the speech, the name of the occasion or sponsoring organization, the location, and the date. If you don't have all this information, provide as much as possible.

> Speaker's last name, first name. "Title of the Speech" name of occasion. Place of speech, day, month, year.

Example:

> Fink, Debra. "Tennis for the Beginner" Long Island Regional Tennis Association Yearly Meeting. Huntington, New York 6 June 2004.

Citing Radio Shows and TV Shows

Identify significant people involved with the production, followed by their role: Writ. (writer), Dir. (director), Perf. (performer), Narr. (narrator), Prod. (producer).

> "Title of Performance." *Name of TV or Radio Show.* Writ. name of writer. Dir. name of director, Perf. name of performer. Narr. name of narrator. Prod. name of producer. Sponsoring agency. Place of filming, day, month, year.

Example:

> "Writing Careers." *Live with Regis and Kelly!* Narr. Vivian Herterford. Prod. Linda Softy. Fox News, New York, 4 February 2004.

Citing Electronic Sources

Electronic sources are often missing key information such as the author and date. As mentioned earlier, use whatever information you can find for your citation.

General web page.

> Author's last name, first name (if available). "Title." Publication date. Date of your access. <web address>

Example:

Bürglin, Thomas R. "The Homeobox Page." Biozentrum of the University of Basel, Switzerland. 27 August 2004. http://copan.bioz.unibas.ch/homeo.html>

Electronic Listserv, newsgroups, Usenet newsgroup, and bulletin boards.

Author's last name, first name (if available). "Title." Date the source was posted. The medium (online posting). Name of the network. Date of your access. <online address>

Example:

Race, Janice. "Calorie Restriction." 20 June 2003. Online posting. Calorie Restriction for the Purpose of Retarding Aging Newsgroup. 7 July 2003. <news.calorie.fdale.edu.>

E-mail. Give the sender's name, a description of the document, and the date of the communication.

Sender's last name, first name, "Description of the document." E-mail and name of correspondent. Date of the document.

Example:

Small, Geoffrey, "Hawaii 5-0." E-mail to Violet Blue. 17 August 2003.

Periodicals available on both CD-ROM and in print. Include in your citation all the information you would for a print magazine, as well as the publication medium (CD-ROM).

Author's last name, first name. "Article Title." *Magazine* date: page numbers. Title of CD-ROM. Publication medium. Name of the distributor or vendor. Electronic publication date.

Example:

Engel, Diane. "Midwest Realities." *Time* 1 December 1998: 34+. Midwest Voices. CD-ROM. InfoTrak. March 2004.

Periodicals available only on CD-ROM.

Author's last name, first name (if known). "Article Title." *CD-ROM title*. Edition. Publication medium (CD-ROM). Distributor or vendor, city of publication, publisher, date of publication.

Example:

"Rocks and Gems." *Compton's Interactive Encyclopedia.* 2003 ed. CD-ROM. Cambridge, Massachusetts, 2003.

Prepare a Reference Page: APA Format

Recall that American Psychological Association (APA) documentation is used in the social sciences, including anthropology, education, home economics, linguistics, political science, sociology, and, of course, psychology.

Citing Books

The typical APA reference for a book includes the author's last name, followed by initials rather than the first and middle names. The date is placed in parentheses, followed by the title of the book, and a period. Then come the place of publication, colon, publisher, and a period. The second and all subsequent lines are indented, as with the MLA citations. For example:

Book with one author.

Author's last name, first initial. (year of publication). *Book Title.* Place of publication: Publisher.

Example:

Rozakis, L. (1999). *The Complete Idiot's Guide to Shakespeare.* New York: Alpha.

Book with two or three authors. Notice that APA documentation uses the ampersand (&) between each author's name in the References list.

Author's last name, first initial, & author's last name, first initial. (year of publication). *Book Title.* Place of publication: publisher.

Example:

Hamstring, T., & Viceroy, J. (2004). *Baseball Almanac.* New York: Random House.

Book with three or more authors. In APA documentation, write all the authors. You can use et al. for a parenthetical reference, but you have to list all the authors on the References page.

Author's last name, first initial, & author's last name, first initial, & author's last name, first initial, & author's last name, first initial, & author's last name, first initial, & author's last name, first initial. (year of publication). *Book Title.* Place of publication: publisher.

Example:

Lucatelleri, G., & Mello, F. & Schmidt, H. & Cotton, I., & Betts, A. & Tyree, Q. (2003). *Learning Italian.* New York: Scholastic.

One or more editors.

Editor's last name, first initial, & editor's last name, first initial. (Eds.). (year of publication). *Book Title.* Place of publication: publisher, year of publication.

Example:

Sylban, T., & Duiz, P. (Eds.). (2004). *The Collected Short Essays of Harve Laine.* Boston: Allyn & Bacon, Inc.

A selection reprinted in an anthology.

Author's last name, first initial. (year of publication). *Book Title.* In name of editor (Ed.), Title of Anthology (pages of selection). Place of publication: publisher.

Example:

Neu, D. (2004). Liz Fink. In A. Drevin (Ed.), *Twayne's United States Authors Series* (pp. 79–92). Boston: Twayne.

Citing Periodicals

The basic APA periodical reference looks like this:

Author's last name, first initial. (year, month). Title of Article. *Title of Periodical,* page numbers.

Example:

Mallory, J. (1999, May). Sing Your Way to Happiness. *American Educator,* 49–50.

Notice how the name, date format, title, and page numbers differ in APA and MLA formats.

Article citation without an author.

> Title of article. (year, month). *Title of Periodical*, page numbers.

> Example:

> Developmental Biology: Possible New Roles for HOX Genes. (1997, December). *Science*, 278–80.

Citing Electronic Sources

Provide the same information you would for the print source: author, date of posting, title of article/web page, publication information. Then identify the medium, the date you accessed the site, and the web address.

General web page.

> Author's last name, first initial. (date of posting). Title of web page. [information about source]. Retrieved date from the World Wide Web: <web address>

> Example:

> Cardillo, L. (1999, January). Holes in Space. [Article posted on website Cardillo]. Retrieved 10 January 2004 from the World Wide Web: <http://oposite.stcsi. edu/pubinfo/ RP/35/>

Ask the Librarian

Note that *On line* is spelled as two words in APA format, one word in MLA format.

E-mail. APA documentation treats e-mail as personal communication. As a result, no mention is made of any e-mail in the References list. However, you should cite e-mail in the body of your paper, using parenthetical documentation.

Movies/videotapes.

> Director's last name, first initial. (Director). (year of movie). *Title of Movie*. (Film). Place of production: studio.

> Example:

> Craven, W. (Director). (1987). *Nightmare on Elm Street* (Film). Hollywood, CA: Paramount.

A Note on Formatting

Let's talk formatting. Here's how your Works Cited page or References page should look:

◆ **Title.** Center the title (Works Cited or References) on the top of the page, about an inch from the top. Don't underline, bold, or italicize it.

◆ **Numbering.** Don't!

◆ **Spacing.** Start each entry flush left. Indent all subsequent lines of an entry. As with the rest of your paper, double-space each entry on your Works Cited page.

The Least You Need to Know

◆ Use the correct type of source list for your field of study. A Works Cited page is MLA style; a Reference list APA style.

◆ Formats for documenting web sources are still evolving. If you're not sure how to document an Internet source and can't find a format in this book, use common sense and include as much information as your reader will need to locate the source easily.

◆ Follow the formatting exactly. Pay close attention to punctuation and spacing.

◆ Don't number the entries.

Chapter 20

Spit and Polish

- Add frontmatter and endmatter, as needed
- Revise and edit carefully
- Keyboard your paper
- Proofread with an eagle eye

In this chapter, you learn how to include any necessary text in the front (called frontmatter) and text in the back (called endmatter or backmatter). Then I show you how to improve your research paper by editing and proofreading it. At the end of the chapter, you get an opportunity to read a model research paper that contains endmatter.

Endmatter and Frontmatter

You may have some endmatter after your Works Cited or References page. Endmatter includes the following:

- **Graphics.** Graphics are charts, maps, graphs, figures, and photographs. You can place each graphic at the appropriate place in the text or group them at the end. Choose the method that best satisfies the reader's requirements and expectations.

- **Glossary.** A *glossary* lists and defines technical terms or presents additional information on the subject. For example, the book that you are reading right this minute contains a glossary, called Appendix A.

Lost in (Cyber)Space

Visuals you took from an outside source must be documented the same way you would credit any other source.

Depending on the subject of your research paper and the course requirements, you may need to include specific materials before the body of your paper as well. Frontmatter includes a title page, table of contents, foreword, preface, and abstract. They are arranged in the following order. Here's how to prepare each one.

◆ **Title page.** At the minimum, include the title, your name, and the date. Depending on your audience, you may also need to include the person for whom the paper was prepared (such as an instructor or a client), the title of the class, and a reason the paper was written.

◆ **Table of contents.** List the paper's main divisions. Be sure to label each section of the paper to match the headings on your table of contents.

◆ **Foreword.** Relax: You don't write the foreword. Rather, in most instances, the foreword is written by an expert in the field and serves as an endorsement of the contents. Check out the foreword in this book for a model.

Ask the Librarian

Keyboard your table of contents last so you will know the page numbers to include.

◆ **Preface.** Here's where you write your acknowledgments. This is your thank-you page.

◆ **Abstract.** As necessary, write a one-paragraph summary of the contents of your research paper. An abstract is most often required in technical or scholarly papers.

Checklist

Use the following checklist to make sure that you've taken care of the technical aspects of assembling your research paper.

Frontmatter

Title Page

❏ Did you write your name, your instructor's name, and the date on the title page?

❏ Did you include any additional information required by your instructor, such as the title of the class?

❏ Did you center the title?

❑ Did you capitalize only the major words in the title?

❑ Did you remember not to underline or italicize the title?

Table of Contents

❑ Did you include a table of contents, if required?

❑ Do the page numbers on the table of contents match the numbers in the body of the report?

Other Frontmatter

❑ Do you need a foreword? If so, is it complimentary?

❑ Do you need a preface? If so, have you acknowledged everyone you should include?

❑ Do you need an abstract? If so, is it concise but complete? Does it have the appropriate tone? Is it the correct length?

Body

❑ Did you number the pages and place your last name before each number?

❑ Are the pages in the correct order?

❑ Did you use the correct documentation format as required by your instructor, such as MLA, APA, or CMS?

❑ Did you use a consistent document style and not switch between styles mid-stream?

❑ If you used any footnotes, did you number them correctly? Does each number in the text correspond to the appropriate footnote or endnote?

Endmatter

❑ Did you include a Works Cited or References page?

❑ Is your list of works in alphabetical order?

❑ Did you indent the entries correctly?

❑ Did you include any other required endmatter?

Revise and Edit Your Research Paper

Revising and *editing* doesn't mean that you didn't do a fine job on your rough draft or that you're not a good writer. In fact, just the opposite is the case. The finest writers tend to do the most revising. The very word *revise*, meaning "to see again," shows that this process involves judging and rethinking your first thoughts to make improvements.

You Could Look It Up

Revising and **editing** are evaluating your writing to find ways to make it better. The process involves deleting, adding, replacing, and moving words, sentences, and passages in the text.

It's important that you step back from your work and see it with a fresh and impartial eye. As you revise and edit, try to be objective about your work, to judge it as others would.

From the Reference Desk

Thinking of asking a friend or lover to read your drafts to help you edit them? It's a great idea from your standpoint, but your reader may not be as enthusiastic. British prime minister and writer Benjamin Disraeli (1804–1881) had a standard reply unmatched for diplomatic ambiguity for people who sent him unsolicited manuscripts to read: "Many thanks; I shall lose no time in reading it."

Consider Audience and Purpose

As you begin to revise your research paper, think about your *audience* and *purpose* for writing. Remember that your *audience* is the people who will read your paper. To meet their needs, ask yourself, "What does my audience know about my topic?" Recall that your *purpose* is your reason for writing. To focus on the purpose, ask yourself, "What am I trying to accomplish in my research paper? Am I explaining or persuading?"

After you understand how the revision and editing process works, you'll find the process relatively painless and even interesting. Let's start by seeing how deleting material can often make your writing stronger.

Revise by Deleting

In every bloated research paper, there is a concise research paper trying to get out. Your job is to write the concise research paper that says it all. Often, as much gets left out as put in. An effective writing style shows an economy of language.

Delete material that's off the topic or repeats what you've already said. As you revise, look for ways to tighten your sentences by removing extraneous material that clogs your writing. The following chart provides some examples. The underlined text should be deleted to improve the writing.

Look For	Revision
Repetition Bring it to a <u>final</u> close.	**Cut the unnecessary material.** Bring it to a close.
Filler <u>The point that I am trying to make is that you should</u> never miss a <u>good</u> chance to edit your <u>own</u> research paper.	**Cut the fluff.** Never miss a chance to edit your research paper.
Unnecessary modifiers The <u>big, huge,</u> massive cloud <u>completely</u> covered <u>over</u> the sun.	**Select the best modifier.** The massive cloud covered the sun.
Passive voice Falling asleep is done by the average person in seven minutes.	**Active voice** The average person falls asleep in seven minutes.

Revise by Elaborating

Effective research papers use relevant support to bring the topic to life, prove the point, and engage the reader(s). As we have already discussed, this "support" can be details, facts, definitions, examples, statistics, and quotations. Adding them to a draft is called *elaboration*.

As you read your draft, see where you need to add more detail to make your point clearly and persuasively. Use the following chart to help you focus your exploration.

You Could Look It Up

Elaboration is adding details to support your main idea.

Problem	Solution
Facts missing	*Add hard data.*
Point unclear	Research papers require specific facts, dates, examples, and expert opinions to make your case or explain the topic fully.
Lack of sensory details	*Add details drawn from the senses.*
Vague writing	Focus on things you can see, smell, touch, taste, and hear.

Revise Punctuation

Punctuation creates meaning just as words do. Try it yourself on the following letter by adding the punctuation you think is necessary. (You'll have to add capitalization, too, to show the start of a new sentence.)

> Dear John
>
> I want a man who knows what love is all about you are generous kind thoughtful people who are not like you admit to being useless and inferior you have ruined me for other men I yearn for you I have no feelings whatsoever when we're apart I can forever be happy will you let me be yours
>
> Mary

Following are two variations. See how the change in punctuation drastically alters the meaning in each example.

Version 1

> Dear John,
>
> I want a man who knows what love is all about. You are generous, kind, thoughtful. People who are not like you admit to being useless and inferior. You have ruined me for other men. I yearn for you. I have no feelings whatsoever when we're apart. I can forever be happy—will you let me be yours?
>
> Mary

Version 2

> Dear John,
>
> I want a man who knows what love is. All about you are generous, kind, thoughtful people, who are not like you. Admit to being useless and inferior. You have ruined me. For other men, I yearn. For you, I have no feelings whatsoever. When we're apart, I can forever be happy. Will you let me be?
>
> Yours,
>
> Mary

So don't neglect the little guys—commas, periods, semicolons, and colons—as you focus on revising the words, phrases, and sentences in your research paper.

Revise by Rewording

Other times, you'll have to select new words to get your meaning across. When you revise by rewording, you replace words and revise sentences to make your writing accurate and fresh. Here's how to do it:

- ◆ Look for words that you used too often.

- ◆ Replace repeated nouns with pronouns.

- ◆ Substitute other repeated words with synonyms.

- ◆ Ditch empty, overused adjectives such as *excellent* and *nice*.

- ◆ Sharpen your writing by finding the precise word you want, not a close relative.

Revise for Unity

To make your writing more succinct, you can also combine related sentences to create unity and coherence. When you revise for unity, also look for sentences that are off the topic. Add *transitions* to join related ideas. A transition can be a word (such as *also*) or a phrase (such as *for example*) that shows how ideas are related. Each transitional word and phrase indicates a slightly different shade of meaning, so choose your transitions as carefully as you choose your peaches.

Here's an example of sentences revised for unity, thanks to transitions. (The transitions are underlined.)

Flabby

The Vikings consumed a bucket or two of vibrant brew they called "aul" (ale). The Vikings headed fearlessly into battle often without armor or even shirts. The term *berserk* means "bare shirt" in Norse. The term took on the meaning of their wild battles.

Fit

<u>After</u> consuming a bucket or two of vibrant brew they called "aul" (ale), the Vikings would head fearlessly into battle, often without armor or even shirts. The term *berserk* means "bare shirt" in Norse, and <u>eventually</u> took on the meaning of their wild battles.

You Could Look It Up

A **transition** is a word or phrase that links related ideas. Examples include *also, in addition, for example, specifically,* and *on the other hand.*

Correct Errors

So far, we've concentrated on revising stylistic issues, but errors in grammar, usage, and mechanics can also seriously affect your ability to communicate your point—not to mention seriously reduce your grade.

Everyone has difficulty in certain areas, so pay special attention to the grammar and usage issues that drive you around the bend. That said, here are some of the most common errors I find in my students' research papers:

1. Commonly confused words (such as *their/there/they're*)

2. Dangling participles

3. Misplaced modifiers

4. Spelling errors

5. Run-on sentences

6. Fragments (incomplete sentences)

7. Illogical sentences

8. Lack of parallel structure

9. Wrong case (I vs. me, for instance)

10. Unclear pronoun reference

11. Misused adjectives and adverbs (*good* vs. *well*, for instance)

12. Errors in agreement of subject and verb

CAUTION

Lost in (Cyber)Space

Spell checkers can help you catch some types of spelling mistakes, but they're useless with misused and often confused words. Grammar checkers, on the other hand, are of little use. These programs usually cause novice writers to make more errors than they had before!

Type and Proof

When you're satisfied with the content and style of your research paper, you're ready to type up the final copy. You know that appearance matters, so you're going to make sure that the final copy speaks well of you.

Keyboarding

Use standard 10- or 12-point fonts such as Times Roman, Courier, or Helvetica. Avoid fancy, elaborate fonts, because they're unprofessional and a pain in the neck to read. Also avoid stylistic elements that might distract readers, such as excessive highlighting, boldfacing, or boxes.

Double-space the text and unless specifically requested to do so, don't right-justify (align) your paper. The right margins should be ragged.

The Final Shine: Proofreading

It goes without saying (but I'm saying it anyway) that you'll very carefully proofread your final document. Of course, you've already revised and edited the paper at each stage.

Carefully reread your paper for errors in the following areas:

- Spelling
- Capitalization
- Words omitted
- Typographical errors
- Indentations
- Spacing
- Words used twice
- Formatting errors

Model Paper

The following paper was written for an undergraduate engineering class at Princeton University. Notice the appendix and visuals, useful in a technical and/or scientific paper.

The "Electro" wireless key—30 amperes capacity.

Samuel Morse
Charles Rozakis

Samuel Finley Breese Morse (1791–1872) developed a practical version of the telegraph. He took Joseph Henry's idea, improved on it, and put it into use. The scientific portion of this paper will focus on the invention and workings of the telegraph; the social part on Morse code, the idea of connecting the continent, and the various effects of politics and society from the ability to communicate over long distances; and the symbolic portion on the resonance of Morse code in today's society and Morse's impact on the world of art *(The Innovators* 67).

When examining the scientific aspect, one must start with Joseph Henry, the innovator who invented the telegraph. His work built upon Volta's battery design, Ohm's experiments with electricity, and Sturgeon's invention of the electromagnet. Working with a horseshoe electromagnet, Henry demonstrated that one could get a large magnetic force with a small voltage by increasing the number of turns of wire around the iron core (*The Entrepreneurs* 220).

(Current in amps) × (number of turns) / (Length of core) = flux density or IN/L_C = flux ϕ

Henry's telegraph integrated this electromagnet design, which created a strong magnetic force and allowed messages to be sent over long distance.

However, Henry had no desire to turn his invention into an innovation that the world could use. That responsibility fell to Samuel Morse who, at the time, had also been working on an idea for sending messages over long distance using wires. In 1835, he set up a laboratory at NYU where he experimented with electricity. However, as he was an artist, not an engineer, his lack of mechanical skills and knowledge of electromagnetism made building a working system extremely difficult. To compensate for this, Morse formed a partnership with Leonard G. Gale, a colleague who had worked with Henry. Gale used Henry's idea to overcome Morse's biggest problem—a lack of magnetic force. By greatly increasing the number of turns of wire and the battery voltage, the two men were able to send a signal over ten miles of wire (*The Entrepreneurs* 83).

In *The Entrepreneurs*, Billington traces how Morse patented the telegraph in 1842, and on March 3, 1843, Congress granted him $30,000 to build a trial line between Baltimore and Washington. Ezra Cornell strung the wire, and the following year the first message went through and long-distance communication became a real possibility (56).

For the social aspect, it is important to note that the telegraph played a major part in connecting the continent. Not only did it allow fast communication over large distances for the first time, but it also made train travel safer and more efficient. The telegraph made it possible to synchronize clocks at distant train stations and make accurate schedules. It also allowed stations to tell each other where each train was and thus help prevent accidents. Together, the telegraph and the railroads reduced isolation and increased mobility, speeding up life in the United States (*The Innovators* 167).

Morse code can be considered the first modern information system. Morse's dot-dash system (shown in the appendix) is a simple means of communicating messages with as few errors as possible; even when errors occur, the message is still understandable. Morse code came into wide usage and was still common during World War II (Phillips 118).

The businesses that controlled telegraph lines had a major impact on society. Western Union was once called "the only American corporation of truly nation-wide scope." Not only did companies like Western Union create many jobs, but people like Ezra Cornell then turned around and used that money to form Universities. The profits from the telegraph industry went into education, which led to the next generation of innovations.

Even though it's rarely used now, Morse code still resonates symbolically. Almost everyone knows the three-dot, three-dash, three-dot code for S.O.S., which is still widely used as a distress call. In fact, almost any sort of signal in patterns of three is considered a call for help (Phillips 24).

In *The Innovators*, David Billington notes that Morse also made a mark on art. When he went to Europe seeking support for the telegraph, he discovered Louis Daguerre and the new art of photography, which he brought back to America. Further, Morse appears in a central, prominent position in Christian Schussele's *Men of Progress*, clearly indicating that he was a driving force in the march of progress (94). As an innovator, Samuel Morse took the ideas of many people and gathered them into a workable network that helped connect the continent. He gathered engineers, monetary backers, and politicians to make the telegraph a success, and had a significant impact on the scientific, social, and symbolic aspects of the modern world (*The Innovators* 178).

Appendix

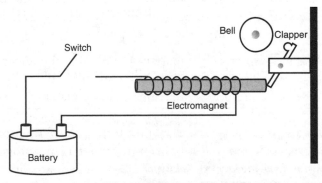

A Schematic Diagram of Henry's Telegraph

From Billington, The Innovators, *p. 128.*

International Morse Code

Letter	Morse	Letter	Morse	Digit	Morse
A	.-	N	-.	0	-----
B	-...	O	---	1	.----
C	-.-.	P	.--.	2	..---
D	-..	Q	--.-	3	...--
E	.	R	.-.	4	....-
F	..-.	S	...	5	.....
G	--.	T	-	6	-....
H	....	U	..-	7	--...
I	..	V	...-	8	---..
J	.---	W	.--	9	----.
K	-.-	X	-..-		
L	.-..	Y	-.--		
M	--	Z	--..		

Letter	Morse	Punctuation Mark	Morse
Ä	.-.-	Full-stop (period)	.-.-.-
Á	.--.-	Comma	--..--
Å	.--.-	Colon	---...
Ch	----	Question mark (query)	..--..
É	..-..	Apostrophe	.----.
Ñ	--.--	Hyphen	-....-
Ö	---.	Fraction bar	-..-.
Ü	..--	Brackets (parentheses)	-.--.-
		Quotation marks	.-..-.

If the duration of a dot is taken to be one unit, then that of a dash is three units. The space between the components of one character is one unit, between characters is three units, and between words seven units. To indicate that a mistake has been made and for the receiver to delete the last word, send .... (eight dots).

From www.soton.ac.uk/~scp93ch/morse/index.html

Works Cited

Billington, David P. *The Innovators*. John Wiley & Sons, Inc. New York. 1996.

Billington, David P. *The Entrepreneurs*. Department of Civil and Environmental Engineering, Princeton University. 2000.

Perera, Tom. *Telegraph & Scientific Instrument Museums*. http://chss.montclair.edu/~pererat/telegrap.htm

Phillips, Stephen Christopher. *Morse Code and Phonetic Alphabets*. http://www.soton.ac.uk/~scp93ch/morse/index.html

The Least You Need to Know

- Add frontmatter and endmatter to your research paper, as needed.
- Consider your audience, purpose, and content as you revise and edit.
- Revise by deleting irrelevant material and adding necessary elaboration.
- As you revise, use punctuation to make your meaning clear.
- Revise for unity by combining related sentences, deleting sentences that are off-topic, and adding transitions.
- Keyboard and proofread carefully.

Glossary of Research Terms

abstract   A brief summary of an article.

almanac   A book published yearly that contains useful and interesting facts about the seasons, U.S. states, countries of the world, sports, and so on.

angle brackets < >   When placed around a text, angle brackets indicate that all the characters within the brackets must be treated as a single unit, without any space between them.

annotated bibliography   A bibliography or Works Cited page that includes your analysis of the sources.

APA   The American Psychological Association, a professional organization of psychologists that created a system of term paper documentation.

archivist   A specialized librarian, knowledgeable about a special era, collection, or historical figure.

atlas   A book of maps or charts.

bibliography   A list of all works you consulted as well as cited in your paper.

bibliography cards   Cards on which you note all the information you need to document a source.

bogus claims   A form of misrepresentation in which the writer uses research to twist the truth.

brackets [ ]   A mark of punctuation used to enclose information in a direct quotation.

call number   A book's classification number. The Dewey Decimal system, the Library of Congress classification system, and the SuDocs system each use a different set of call numbers.

circulate   A library term for "items that leave the building."

classification systems   Used by libraries to track, shelve, and retrieve the materials in their collections.

computerized database   A bibliographic computer file of reference sources.

cue words   Verbs that you use to integrate expert opinions, quotes, and other information.

diary   A personal, day-by-day account of events, experiences, and observations.

dictionary   An alphabetical reference list of the words in the language. Abridged dictionaries are one-volume books that contain the most common words; unabridged dictionaries are multiple-volume books that contain all the words in a language. Everyday dictionaries are abridged.

documentation   Giving credit to your sources.

ellipsis   The set of three spaced dots (...) used to show that you have omitted something from a direct quotation.

encyclopedia   A collection of articles on many topics.

exposition   Writing that explains. An expository research paper summarizes facts about a topic.

federal depository libraries   Libraries that have been designated as recipients of federal documents. Partial federal depository libraries receive only some of the documents, depending on their needs and storage capabilities.

footnotes, endnotes, and parenthetical documentation   Different ways of giving credit to sources you used in your research paper.

full-text article   An article that is complete.

Internet service provider   A company that provides access to the Internet. They are abbreviated ISPs.

interviews   Meetings arranged to obtain information by questioning a person or group of people.

loaded terms   Terms that unfairly slant an argument.

location prefixes   A letter or series of letters before the call number that show a book is shelved in a special area of the library or has restricted borrowing privileges.

meta-engines   A group of search engines all in one.

MLA   The Modern Language Association, a professional organization of English and foreign language professors that developed a system of documentation for research papers.

netiquette   The system of appropriate behavior that governs the Internet.

note cards   Cards on which you record important information for your research paper in an easy-to-use manner.

open stack   Libraries that allow patrons access to the materials; closed stack libraries do not. Thus, in a closed stack library, patrons cannot browse the stacks, much less remove materials themselves.

oversimplification   Reducing a complicated argument to mockery.

paraphrase   A restatement of a passage in your own words. A paraphrase may be longer, shorter, or the same length as the original.

parenthesis ( )   A mark of punctuation used to enclose additional information in a text.

parenthetical or internal documentation   A form of citation in which an abbreviated form of the source is placed within the body of the research paper rather than in footnotes or endnotes. Therefore, parenthetical documentation takes the place of traditional footnotes or endnotes.

periodicals   The general term for newspapers, magazines, academic journals, and any other material published on a regular schedule.

persuasion   Writing that appeals to reason, emotion, or ethics (or the sense of right and wrong).

plagiarism   Representing someone else's words or ideas as your own. It is literary theft.

primary sources   Source material based on direct observation or participation.

qtd. in   An abbreviation for "quoted in"; refers to a direct quote cited in a secondary source.

refereed journals Periodicals that have undergone a peer review process, the articles carefully checked for content. This results in a dependable scholarly research source.

reference list An APA-formatted list of all the works you cited in your paper.

research paper A long essay in which the writer reports his or her research findings. A research paper can also be called a library paper, a term paper, or a thesis.

revising and editing Evaluating your writing to find ways to make it better.

search engines Computer programs that work with your browser to find information on the web. After you type a keyword or phrase into your browser's dialog box, a search tool looks for web pages that have your keyword(s). You get the results, called hits.

secondary sources Research sources created from primary sources.

spam Junk e-mail.

subject The general content of a research paper.

summary A relatively brief, objective condensation of a passage.

superscript number A raised number used with a footnote and/or endnote. A superscript number looks like this: word[1].

survey A sampling of opinions used to approximate what a complete collection and analysis might reveal.

tabloids Newspapers measuring about 11×15 inches and known for their lavish photographs and sensational content.

thesis The writer's hypothesis, theory, or opinion. Also called the thesis statement.

topic The specific issue being discussed in a research paper.

transition A word or phrase that links related ideas. Examples include *also, in addition, for example, specifically,* and *on the other hand.*

vertical file A filing cabinet or series of filing cabinets in which pamphlets are stored.

vetted material Articles, books, and other material that has been read and reviewed for inclusion. Databases that are vetted are composed of carefully selected high-quality articles and information.

working bibliography A list of the sources you plan to use.

working outline   An outline that shows how you will organize the information in your research paper. You revise the outline as you research and draft to accommodate new information and your rethinking on the topic.

Works Cited page   An MLA-formatted list of all the works you cited in your paper.

World Wide Web (abbreviated WWW)   A network of pathways through the Internet that connects "pages" of material—whatever can be sent electronically.

Model Research Papers

Use these research papers for models of style and format.

Model Paper 1

The following paper was written for an undergraduate class at Princeton University. It was chosen for presentation at an international scholarly conference.

The Golem in Comic Books
Charles Rozakis

Comic books have always been a literary medium unto themselves. Though they share qualities with novels, fantasy literature, and comic strips, they are a category all to themselves. The golem legend in comics has taken a different path from that in modern novels, and while it shares some common characteristics with fantasy role-playing games (such as *Advanced Dungeons & Dragons*), there are many differences.

One of the most interesting changes to the golem from the early legends to comic books is the appearance of the golem. (Which is not surprising, as comics are such a visual medium to begin with.) In all of the comics except Jaime Morgan Roberts' *Golem*, the golem appears as a statue made of stone or clay that moves. This common theme in comic books is a major departure from the legends. This, I believe, originated in Gary Gygax's early *Dungeons & Dragons* books in the early 1970s. When he set the golem into his fantasy world, there were four varieties—the mud or clay golem, which is basically the one we're familiar with; the flesh golem, which is essentially Dr. Frankenstein's monster; and the iron and stone golems, which, like the clay golem, where inanimate material brought to life. And so that their nature would be obvious, Gygax decided that clay golems looked like animate clay statues. This idea was picked up by comic writers and artists at the time.

The legendary golem looked like a normal person, not like a clay statue. In the Babylonian Talmud, Rabbah creates a man and sends him to R. Zera. R. Zera does not know that the man is a golem until he speaks to him and receives no answer. This implies that the man looked normal—if he looked like a clay statue, R. Zera would have known his origin on sight. Also, the third-grown calf created by R. Hanina and R. Oshaia must have looked like a flesh-and-blood calf. It's highly unlikely that the two rabbis would eat a calf-shaped thing of mud.

The modern novels, for the most part, seem to have taken a different path from the comics in terms of appearance. In *The Sword of the Golem*, Joseph Golem is large and off-putting, and his skin has a slightly earthen tone, but he looks otherwise completely human. This is true of many of the stories of Rabbi Loew's golem.

The purpose of the golem in comics is always practical. No one ever makes a golem in a comic book for the spiritual aspect or "just to prove they can do it." The common purpose for the golem is to protect the Jewish people or act as an agent of vengeance. This theme is the same as the modern tales of the Golem of Prague, where Rabbi Loew creates the golem to protect the Jews of the ghetto, so that they will not have to fight. This is quite different from Ashkenazi Hasidic legends, in which the golem was created and then immediately unmade, its only purpose to show how righteous the creator was.

The one other major theme that appeared in a number of comic books was the idea that the golem would receive the soul of another person. This appears in *Strange Tales*, *The Invaders*, and *Detective Comics*. This has no connection to the original golem legend, and is perhaps the comic books' greatest departure from the original golem stories.

The first appearance of the golem legend in comics that I could find was in *The Incredible Hulk* #134, published in 1970. Roy Thomas crafted a story called "Among Us Walks … the Golem" in which the Jewish peasants of Morvania are persecuted by a dictator named Draxon. A little girl meets the Hulk, and mistakes him for the golem her father has told her stories of. When her father finds out, he recalls the story of the golem of Prague, and wonders if the Hulk could be the Morvanians' golem. In the end, persuaded by the little girl, the Hulk fights for the people and defeats the dictator, then crushes the "Imperial Amulet" that had served as the symbol of Morvania's monarchy. The man exclaims, "This is a sign! You were our golem!" To which the Hulk replies that he's going, and wanders off wondering exactly what a golem is.

The Hulk fits the physical description of a golem very well, with his massive, off-putting, inhuman appearance; superhuman strength; and near-invulnerability. This is a halfway point between the golems that can be mistaken for human, and the golems that look like mobile statues. The Hulk's features, though green and grotesquely over-muscled, are essentially human—in fact, if not for his green skin and hair, he'd probably look very much like any description of Rabbi Loew's golem.

The next appearance of a golem in comic books is in *Superman* #248, published in 1972. Len Wein's tale "The Man Who Murdered the Earth" features the evil scientist Lex Luthor creating a creature called the Galactic Golem. Luthor describes his creation, "Like the legendary golem of old who was forged from bits of clay, I have molded a man-thing that'll be more than a match for my old 'friend'—Superman!" The creature, created of "galactic matter," is incredibly strong and tough, but has no mind of its own and cannot speak (though Luthor can speak through it using a microphone). Unable to destroy it, Superman lures the creature out into space. The Galactic Golem returns in *Superman* #258 (published later in 1972), in "Fury of the Energy-Eater." Returned to Earth, now able to speak, the golem challenges Superman again, and ends up covered in ferrous metal and stuck to the Earth's magnetic north pole.

The Galactic Golem really has little to do with the traditional golem legends, though the idea that Luthor created the golem out of cosmic "clay" is based in them. In this case, however, pseudo-science creates the golem and, in turn, traps it—magic and mysticism don't play a part at all.

Len Wein wasn't done with golems, though. In *Strange Tales* #174, he and Roy Thomas introduced The Golem   The Thing That Walks Like a Man. Introduced in "There Walks a Golem," the creature was Judah Loew's creation, which had wandered into the desert and been buried in sand after peace was brought to Prague. Uncovered by an archeologist and his young assistants, the golem seems a statue. When soldiers wreck the camp and shoot the old archeologist, he manages to bring the golem back to life before he dies. The golem then jumps to the task of saving the assistants from the soldiers. But strangely enough, it appears that the golem has received the soul of the archeologist—the golem has "inherited" the twinkle in his eye.

In *Strange Tales* #176–177, Mike Friedrich took over the script and introduced a villain named Kaballa, an evil magician who sent demons to capture the golem. But the golem gains new powers whenever his charges are threatened, and defeats the demons several times. The word "emeth" appears on the golem's forehead near the end of #177 (in English letters, not Hebrew) and the narration tells the reader that the "truth" that motivates the golem is not fear, hate, or even justice, but a love for those he needs to protect. Kaballa is then seen plotting his next move—If the golem's power comes from his emotional affinity for these people, Kaballa will eliminate them.

These comics use a lot of the aspects of the original legends, but with some new ideas as well. Here, Judah Loew's golem was chiseled from stone rather than shaped from clay, and rather than being put to rest in the attic of the Altneushul, it ends up buried in a desert, presumably in the middle east. The change that I find most notable is that the golem is not awakened by the archeologist's intoning of the 221 gates, but by his teardrop. This is an interesting idea, that it wasn't the magic formula or God's intervention that animated the golem, but human emotion and need. (The idea of tears animating the golem was also in the Hulk story—the little girl's tears motivated the Hulk to act.) It is interesting that none of this golem's power seems to come from God. There is no mention of the Shem being put in his mouth, and Kaballa talks about him drawing power from the earth. Perhaps this can find its roots in the "Tellurian power" that Scholem mentions (Idel 41), "those powers inherent in the brute material which enter into the constitution of the Golem." Near the end of issue #177, as I mentioned above, the narration says that the truth that motivates the golem is love. This is a far cry from "YHVH ALHYM AMTh" ("God the Tetra-grammaton is truth") appearing on the forehead of Jeremiah's golem (Reuchlin 139).

The other thing of note in *Strange Tales* #177 is that the issue begins with a two-page rendition of the story of the Jew who let his golem grow too large. The footnote cites Scholem's *On the Kabbalah and Its Symbolism* as the source for the legend. This implies that artistic license, not misinformation, was the cause of the discrepancies between these comics and the original legends—the authors were obviously doing their homework.

Roy Thomas's last twist of the golem legend appeared in *The Invaders* #13. Set during World War II, this story takes place in occupied Poland. The Invaders have come in search of Jacob Goldstein, who was studying occult books and looking for a way to liberate the Jewish ghetto. Soon, in ancient Kabbalistic (sic) texts he finds the secret to creating a golem. Jacob pours a mysterious liquid called "heavy water" on the clay he's prepared, writes "emeth" on its forehead, and when lightning strikes the building, a 10-foot-tall, stone-skinned doppelganger of Jacob emerges from the rubble. After rescuing a young girl from a Nazi soldier, the golem frees the captive Invaders and knocks the Nazi general off a rooftop. When asked who he is, the golem rubs his forehead, accidentally wiping out the "e" from "emeth," and transforms back into Jacob Goldstein.

This story seems more similar to the Hulk comic than the golem legends. Jacob Goldstein has not created new life, in fact has not achieved a creation of any sort. He himself transforms into a large, super-strong, stonelike being. This is not very different from the gamma bomb accident that transformed Bruce Banner into the Hulk. But while his method (studying the Laws of Creation, forming the figure from clay, writing "emeth" on the forehead, etcetera) is similar to the original legends, the end result is not really a golem.

The next time a golem had a starring role in a comic was in 1982, when Mendy Enterprises started publishing *Mendy and the Golem.* This series, aimed for young children and marketed as the world's only kosher comic book, features a family of Jews (the Kleins) and their golem, Sholem. The stories are very tongue-in-cheek, and interspersed in the comic are "Torah Tales," "Stories of our Sages," and kid-friendly Jewish law. Sholem appears as a silent, faceless block of granite that protects and obeys the Kleins.

Mendy and the Golem puts the golem in the place of servant and protector of the Jews, as he appeared in most of the stories of Judah Loew. Sholem is super-strong, hard as a rock, and apparently very heavy (he dives into a lake at one point and the resulting wave puts out a huge fire). This comic doesn't seem to touch on the original legend of the golem or his creation at all. (I would have liked to see a copy of *Mendy and the Golem* #10, in which Dr. Hardheart builds an evil golem that looks like Sholem to rob banks.) Though I think Gersham Scholem would probably have found it quite funny that this comic's golem is named after him.

Batman encountered a golem in *Detective Comics* #631–632, a two-part story called "The Golem of Gotham." The story features an old Jewish man, Saul Zweimer, who is a Holocaust survivor. Frightened by Neo-Nazi activity in Gotham City, he makes a golem. The old man still mourns the death of his friend Jacob, who was taken away by the Nazis on Kristallnacht. The man's thoughts in the narration boxes are all directed to Jacob, leading us to believe that the old man didn't make it out of the Holocaust with all of his wits intact. Soon, the silent, mud-caked humanoid strikes the old man and runs amok into the night. Batman loses his first battle with the golem, which is superhumanly fast, strong, and tough. However, Batman notices the word "emeth" on the creature's forehead, and, being the world's greatest detective, determines that the creature is a golem. He traps it under a fallen statue and forces the old man to erase the "e" from "emeth" and destroy the golem.

The creation of the golem in this book is closer to the legends than any of the other comics. The old man circles the clay, reciting the 221 combinations of alphabets from the Book Yetsirah, then he recites the permutations of the letters with the letters of the tetragrammaton, and writes "emeth" on the forehead of the golem.

The projection of creator onto creation is also very evident. As we learned from the Talmudic stories, man is incapable of perfect creation because his iniquities separate him from God. In this story, the old man's delusions, fear, and guilt for betraying his friend Jacob are projected onto the golem. The golem, in turn, hallucinates SS officers, is incredibly violent, and perhaps even contains a little of Jacob's spirit. Because his creator is a little eccentric, the golem goes crazy—it is an imperfect creation.

As a side note, both this story and the one from *Strange Tales* use 221 gates, rather than 231. I am at a loss to explain where the number came from, as the *Strange Tales* story was written before Idel's article that uses that number.

At the end of the story, Batman says, "There's only room for one golem in this town." He's implying that the purpose of the golem was to be a protector and agent of vengeance in Gotham City, a position that is already filled by Batman. The golem and Batman are very similar, both being "superhuman" to a degree, and both being created out of fear, to inflict fear on others. Batman took that identity because his parents were killed by a mugger, and he wished to become a creature "that all men fear" (Secret Files). Saul created the golem because he was afraid of the neo-Nazis, and tells his golem, "The point was to let him tell his friends that the ghetto now has a terrible protector!" The two cannot coexist, because they are essentially the same creature.

This idea leads directly into *Ragman* #5–6. This story, titled "Feet of Clay," introduces a very intelligent but silent golem. Apparently this golem was created by the same Rabbi who created Ragman's special suit. Using the suit of rags drains power away from the golem, for apparently the two cannot coexist. The golem's thoughts tell the reader that it existed for forty years, fighting evil and earning the right to be "more human." It thinks, "In another year or two, I would have been completely human! I would have been able to speak! I will not return to clay!" The Rabbi sums up this dual existence as such: "In fighting the golem, you fight yourself! Perceive him as a monster and that monster will be you!" When the golem's friend Betty wipes the "emet" off his forehead, he dissolves and his power goes into the Ragman.

The idea of the golem needing to "earn" a higher soul by fighting evil is new. In the legends, though there was great debate about what sort of soul a golem had, if any, there was never any talk of him gaining a higher one. However the golem was made, that was how he would stay—there would never be anything to "earn."

The destruction of this golem is a very interesting scene; as Ragman realizes he must "Erase the truth," the golem thinks that it's not so easy to erase the truth. His response is that the power of the truth is the power of love. As in *Strange Tales*, the idea is that not "God is truth" but "Love is truth" and a golem draws its power from those it loves and needs to protect. As the golem dissolves, it finally gets a voice to say, "Betty, I love you." This love then becomes new power for Ragman.

The other thing to note about the golem's destruction is that Betty erases the entire word, not just the "e." Rather than truth becoming death, truth becomes nothing at all, and the golem ceases to exist.

Jaime Morgan Roberts's *Golem* departed from most of the running themes in comics. A magician named Eliphas Crowley (perhaps a reference to occultist Aleister Crowley) steals a scroll from a museum and uses it to create a golem. Unlike other comic golems, this one looks human and has "emet" written on his forehead in Hebrew. Also, while the golem initially cannot speak, it learns how by reading a woman's mind. In addition, it is mentioned that the golem will grow each day until it's uncontrollable, and if the scroll Crowley used had the Shem written on it, then this is the only comic book where God's power fuels the golem.

The backup story in this comic is even more interesting, if a bit disturbing. It takes place at Hitler's armored fortress in World War II. A golem is charging into the place, killing Nazi soldiers left and right. When the golem reaches Hitler, it explains that it is undead, returned to life by an old Rabbi, and is there as an agent of vengeance. Hitler then exclaims that no Jewish demon will kill the master of the arian (sic) race, and shoots himself.

What this does have in common with the other comics is the golem's superhuman abilities, and his purpose. In the first story, he is a protector and serves the man who created him. In the second, he is an agent of vengeance for the Jewish people. He is much more of the "artificial superman" that Rabbi Loew's golem is usually shown as, supposed with the same danger of losing control.

The final comic-book golem I would like to mention appears in *The Books of Magic* #8. Tim Hunter, destined to be the greatest magician the world has ever known, meets a golem created by another magician. Being held up by one arm and being in a rather unpleasant mood, Tim tries to cheer himself up by drawing a happy face on the golem. He then magically renames the golem "Happy" and binds it to his service. The magician's other servant then says to Tim, "That was, like, impossible, what you just did. You know that? You can make golemim, or you can unmake 'em, but you can't change 'em." This implies that there are set rules in magical practice that determine the creation of golems, and that Tim's power is so great, he is able to ignore those rules as he pleases.

This leads back to the *Advanced Dungeons & Dragons Monster Manual*. The golem Tim encounters was created by a magician (not a Rabbi) as a guardian and protector. It fits Gygax' description of the creatures very well, and shows where comics and fantasy literature come together once again.

Golems continue to have a place in comics today, but only as small pieces of the original legends. The modern incarnation of Supergirl was formed out of "protomatter" and brought to life by advanced science. The heroin Wonder Woman was formed by her mother, Hippolyta of the Amazons, out of clay and given life by the ancient Greek gods. She is perhaps the closest thing to a golem in comics today, being an artificial person, a defender of the oppressed, and a superhuman gifted by the gods (Secret Files).

Works Cited

Babylonian Talmud bSan 65b—Page 65 in our packet.

Books of Magic, The #8. "Altars." DC Comics. New York, NY. 1994. (Collected in *The Books of Magic—Summonings*, available at most comic stores or from www. silverbulletcomicbooks.com)

Detective Comics #631-632. "The Golem of Gotham." DC Comics. New York, NY. 1991.

Gygax, Gary. *Advanced Dungeons & Dragons Monster Manual*. TSR Games. Lake Geneva, WI. 1978.

Idel, M. "Introduction." *Golem*, pp. XV–XXXI.—Page 39-47 in our class packet.

Incredible Hulk, The #134. "Among Us Walks … The Golem." Marvel Comics Group. New York, NY. 1970.

Invaders, The #13. "The Golem Walks Again!" Marvel Comics Group. New York, NY. 1976.

Jaime Morgan Roberts's *Golem* #1. Pop Art Productions. St. Quincy, MA. 1994.

Mendy and the Golem #9. "Home on the S-s-st-range!" Mendy Enterprises. New York, NY. 1983.

Ragman #5-6. "Feet of Clay." DC Comics. New York, NY. 1992.

Reuchlin, *De Arte Cabalistica*, Liber Tertius—Page 139 in our class packet.

Secret Files at http://www.dccomics.com/. Click the "Secret Files" button on the right, then click the button for the appropriate character.

Strange Tales #174, 176, 177. "The Golem—The Thing That Walks Like a Man!" Marvel Comics Group. New York, NY. 1974.

Model Paper 2

The following paper was written for an undergraduate literature class at Princeton University.

Psychoanalysis and its Discontents:
Nabokov's Critique of Psychotherapy in *Pnin*
Elizabeth Landau

"Oh, I am not up to discussing again that figure of fun. He is not worthy of more attention than I have granted him in my novels."

—*Vladimir Nabokov on Sigmund Freud*[1]

From the above quotation, we see a mocking, disdainful side of Vladimir Nabokov that peeks through many of his novels—his contempt for Freudian psychology. Dis-missing Freud as a "figure of fun" here and "the Viennese Quack" in the preface to *Bend Sinister*, Nabokov appears to have an almost Freudian obsession with denouncing psychoanalytic theory.[2] Freud may not be worthy of more attention than Nabokov gives him in his books, but many of his novels such as *Pnin* do give Freud a great deal of attention. Nabokov's denial of psychoanalysis, however, may have legitimate roots outside of Freud's own theories. In examining Nabokov's exaggerated, satirical portrayal of psychoanalytic principles in *Pnin*, we see that Nabokov may have legitimate concerns not about the theories themselves, but how they can take on an almost totalitarian[3] character in a world where therapists dictate social norms. Freudian psychology, as well as other notions of therapy, impose fixed notions of behavioral drives and stages of human development, seeking to reform those who do not conform. Psychotherapy, Nabokov shows us through his characterizations of the Winds, imposes a rigid set of norms that, when taken to the extreme, threaten individuality and creativity.

Victor's parents' comical infatuation with the notion that their son must conform to Freud's notion of the Oedipal complex impedes their ability to relate to him; they treat him as more of an insane patient than a son. Waiting for their son to display Oedipal tendencies,[4] Liza and Eric "in their capacity of psycho-therapists, did their best to impersonate Laius and Jocasta, but the boy proved to be a very mediocre Oedipus" (87–88). The notion of literally impersonating Lainus and Jocasta is obviously ridiculous—in mythology Oedipus killed his father Lainus and married his mother Jocasta, a tragedy no parents would want to experience. But here Nabokov reminds us that Freud's Oedipus complex, which the reader may take for granted as part of human development, is equally undesirable from a rational perspective. Nabokov's description of the complex the Winds expect Victor to have—they believe "every male child had an ardent desire to castrate his father and a nostalgic urge to re-enter his mother's body"—seems repugnant and far-fetched in these terms (90). Obviously, one would expect a man whose son has literally "an ardent desire to castrate his father" to be quite concerned about his own safety; a mother whose son has the "nostalgic urge" to return to her womb should also be concerned about his sanity. But though Nabokov's literal spin on the Oedipal complex exaggerates Freud's general principles, the Winds' disappointment that Victor is only "mediocre" with respect to Oedipal tendencies reveals the Winds' totalitarian imposition of psychotherapeutic norms on their son's childhood development. That they classify Victor as a "problem child" because he "did not reveal any behavior disorder" seems contradictory, but in a society where the "triangle of Freudian romance" is "modish," the seemingly pathological Oedipal complex is a prerequisite for conformity (90). Victor is no longer his therapist-parents' son; he is "their little patient" (92). In this almost totalitarian culture of the therapeutic, those who do not display a particular pathology are considered sick outcasts.

As the tyrannical parents of such an outcast, the Winds attempt to stifle their son's creativity to force him conform to their psychoanalytic models of development. When Victor proves to be a mediocre Oedipus, Dr. Wind has his son tested "psychometrically," assuming that his son's behavior will conform to the examinations' possible diagnoses (90). But because Victor possesses genuine creativity and artistic imagination, the tests cannot classify him according to traditional psychological models. Nabokov mocks the therapists' irrational dismay at these results:

> The seven-year-old subject scored on the so-called Godunov Drawing-of-an-Animal test a sensational mental age of seventeen, but on being given a Fairview Adult Test promptly sank to the mentality of a two-year-old. How much care, skill, inventiveness have gone to devise those marvelous techniques! What a shame that certain patients refuse to co-operate! ... The Sterns reported that "unfortunately the psychic value of Victor's Mind Pictures and Word Associations is completely obscured by the boy's artistic inclinations" (90–92).

Victor's scoring as an adult on the drawing test and as a two-year-old on an "Adult" test reveals fundamental flaws in the tests themselves—clearly, for an imaginative artist and creative thinker, these tests do not yield useful information about a person's mental abilities or health. For therapists who believe so strongly their categorization of children, however, such anomalous results suggest a lack of cooperation. Rather than praise Victor's independent thinking, the therapist laments the abuse of the tests, to which they believe all children conform in some way. Artistic inclinations inhibit a person's ability to conform to fixed notions of mental health, notions that Nabokov criticizes by satirizing the Winds' treatment of their son.

Eric Wind's vision of a society based on group therapy further exemplifies this totalitarian aspect of psychotherapy that Nabokov fears. Though not necessarily Freudian, the idea of a therapy where the people share their intimate feelings in groups is another popular form of psychotherapy:

> Professor Chateau affirmed that Dr. Wind even called Siamese twins "a group." And indeed progressive, idealistic Wind dreamed of a happy world consisting of Siamese centuplets, anatomically conjoined communities, whole nations built around a communicating liver" (51–52).

Dr. Eric Wind values the group over the individual, envisioning a world in which all people look alike, think alike, and even literally share the same anatomy. That Siamese twins are "a group" shows Wind's only concern is the functionality of the entire conjoined being, not individuals. His vision of the ideal world, then, is one in which there is no individuality or creativity but a group of identical beings that literally share the same life force. Clearly, this anatomically totalitarian regime does not allow for artists or creative thinkers like his son Victor or Pnin. But Nabokov takes the analogy one step further. Not only is there no creativity in this group-therapy society that Pnin calls "a kind of microcosmos of communism," group members give up their right to have private feelings (52). Pnin laments, "Why not leave their private sorrows to people? Is sorrow not, one asks, the only thing in the world people really possess?" (52). If everyone shares the same feelings, then even suffering is no longer an individual's own possession. The totalitarian regime of psychotherapy seeks to take people's sorrows and reform them, taking for granted that individual sorrows are unique. In light of Nabokov's maxim that "genius is nonconformity," group therapy obliterates the very notion of genius altogether (89).

Nabokov said he was not out to put forth any social message, but by criticizing Freud and other psychotherapeutic values, he necessarily critiques ideas that constituted, and still constitutes, an integral part of popular culture and popular conceptions of mental health in society. Though he does exaggerate the attitudes of therapists in *Pnin*, the satire conveys the essence of what can make psychotherapy a dangerous element of society. If parents subscribe too fervently to fixed notions of how their children should behave, they are apt to misdiagnose a disorder or completely stifle a child's creativity. Group therapy may have a cathartic effect, but when carried to the extreme, it removes the element of privacy from one's own thoughts and feelings. Nabokov challenges us to treat mental health as unique to each person rather than subscribe to popular notions such as the Oedipal complex. As Nabokov put it in an interview, "Let the credulous and the vulgar continue to believe that all mental woes can be cured by a daily application of old Greek myths to their private parts. I really do not care." This attack may seem haughty, but as we have seen, it is warranted if society uses such notions of conforming to Greek myths to stifle the individuality and creativity of its members.

Endnotes

[1] From "Nabokov's Interview," an interview published *in Wisconsin Studies in Contemporary Literature*, vol. VIII, no. 2. Spring 1967 1 April 2003. <http:// lib.novgorod.net/NABAKOW/Inter06.text>

[2] This denial is Freudian in that Nabokov may deny psychoanalysis precisely because it is such a key explanation of his characters' personalities and behaviors. This was suggested in Richard Lamb's "Discussing Nabokov."

[3] I use the term *totalitarian* somewhat loosely, in the spirit of the *Merriam-Webster* definition—"based on subordination of the individual to the state and strict control of all aspects of the life and productive capacity of the nation, especially by coercive measures."

[4] Generally, the Oedipal complex dictates that a son display fear and hostility toward his father and a repressed sexual desire for his mother. Symptoms could include a range of repetitive behaviors. See "Sigmund Freud's Theories."

Works Cited

Lamb, Richard. "Discussing Nabokov." *Slate*. April 2, 2003. <http://slate.msn.com/id/2000072/entry/1002648/>.

Nabokov, Vladimir. *Bend Sinister*. New York—Vintage Paperback, 1990.

———. *Pnin*. New York—Vintage Paperback, 1989.

"Nabokov's Interview." 1 April 2003. <http://lib.novgorod.net/NABOKOW/Inter06.txt>.

"Sigmund Freud's Theories." *Pagewise*. 2 April, 2003. <http://allsands.com/Science/castrationphall_rxj_gn.htm>.

Model Paper 3

The following paper was written for an undergraduate science class at Princeton University.

The Origin of Oxygen in the Earth's Atmosphere
Charles Rozakis

This paper is intended as an overview of how the earth's atmosphere transformed from a concoction of sulfur, chlorine, methane, and ammonia into the 78 percent nitrogen and 21 percent oxygen it is today. I will discuss how the change occurred, the time scale, and the various forms of evidence that scientists used to come to these conclusions.

The earth's atmosphere initially consisted of hydrogen and helium gas. These gasses, being too light for Earth's gravity to hold and subject to high-energy radiation, were "boiled off" into space, and gradually replaced by gasses expelled in volcanic eruptions. This process is known as "outgassing," and among these gasses were carbon dioxide, chlorine, methane, nitrogen, water vapor, ammonia, and various sulfur compounds. Additionally, some water entered the system from icy comets that hit the earth. Eventually, a new atmosphere was formed, in which carbon dioxide was in much greater concentrations than it is today, and oxygen was probably less than 1 percent of the atmosphere (Carslaw 2–5).

Then, somewhere between 2.1 and 2.5 billion years ago, significant amounts of oxygen began accumulating in the atmosphere. One of the major causes of this change came from cyanobacteria, the first organism capable of photosynthesizing. These bacteria then trapped much of the carbon and released oxygen into the atmo-sphere. While some of the carbon removed from the atmosphere in this way was re-released during decomposition, some of it remained as part of the increasing bacteria population, and some was buried by sediments, to later become fossils. The oldest fossils of such bacteria are from 3.8 billion years ago, which implies that this buildup of oxygen was a gradual process at first. The first single-celled plants appeared approximately 2.1 billion years ago, which seems to coincide with the most rapid rise in oxygen (Carslaw 5–7).

The other cause of the change was from the chemical separation of water molecules into oxygen and hydrogen. This is called photochemical dissociation, and it refers to the breakup of water molecules by ultraviolet radiation. Until recently, scientists had no method to determine what proportion each process may have contributed to this rise in oxygen.

Another question, which Catling (839) raises, is why oxygen accumulated as it did. After all, in the modern atmosphere, atmospheric oxygen concentrations remain relatively constant. This is because, as I mentioned before, carbon trapped during photosynthesis is generally able to return to the atmosphere through decomposition. The high-energy radiation present at the time of the early atmosphere comes into play again here. Much of the hydrogen released by breaking apart water molecules was then lost into space, as the original hydrogen/helium atmosphere had been. This resulted in a net increase in atmospheric free oxygen.

The addition of so much oxygen in the atmosphere allowed for the development of the earth's ozone layer, which permitted the expansion of terrestrial life by shielding organisms from the most damaging effects of ultraviolet radiation. High-energy radiation interacted with oxygen molecules in the upper atmosphere and formed ozone.

An often-noted observation is that the pre-oxygen atmospheric conditions were necessary for life to form; however, when photosynthetic organisms released significant quantities of oxygen into the atmosphere, the accumulation of oxygen and ozone destroyed those conditions. Life could only begin in a system where free oxygen would not react with it and high-energy radiation could reach it to cause reactions. But life could only flourish in an oxygen-rich atmosphere where it could perform aerobic respiration and was protected from damaging radiation.

One can learn about this rapid rise in oxygen in the atmosphere from sedimentary deposits. They seem to indicate that the change was during the Early Proterozoic, approximately 2.3 billion years ago, but various estimates for this accumulation of oxygen in the atmosphere range from as early as 3.5 billion years ago to as late as 2.0 billion years ago. Geologists know from banded iron formations in 2.2-billion-year-old rocks that significant quantities of oxygen were present at that time—enough, at least, to oxidize the iron in the rocks in a process akin to rusting. However, the fossil record is filled with gaps, so these formations cannot tell scientists how much oxygen was present or where it came from. This period, from the earliest-known rocks, 3.9 billion years ago to 2.2 billion years ago, provides very limited knowledge about the atmosphere and about life.

On a similar note, one source of better information about this time period could be biologically mediated isotope distributions in the geological record. However, there are a number of problems with this method, mostly stemming from the fact that rock sequences from this time period are hard to find, usually poorly preserved, and mostly highly metamorphic. The information from ancient biologic signatures, when altered by a metamorphic event, is essentially destroyed (Paytan 626).

These studies of reduced and oxidized iron and uranium minerals, and some later studies of microfossils and ancient soils, led to many researchers becoming convinced that atmospheric oxygen underwent a dramatic increase in concentration between 2.2 and 2.4 billion years ago. But some geologists remained skeptical because the geochemical and biological data allowed room for alternative interpretations (Kasting 819).

Paytan discusses a method of using sulfur-containing minerals to assist in timing the evolution of atmospheric oxygen. One way to track oxygen in the ancient atmosphere involves discerning a recognizable signature in rocks that originated from chemical processes in the atmosphere—in this case, from the oxidation of sulfur-bearing gases. From variations in the four most common isotopes of sulfur that were incorporated into sulfide and sulfate minerals in the rocks, the scientists were able to infer that the atmosphere 2.45 billion years ago had limited free oxygen and was the main arena for chemical reactions involving sulfur. When oxygen became a major component of the atmosphere, sulfate-reducing bacteria became active in the then sulfate-rich oceans. Using radiometric dating, researchers determined that sulfur isotope ratios of Archean sulfides and sulfates differ from those of younger sediments. Paytan presents several possible explanations for this—the most likely (and most popular) being that these odd ratios resulted from gas-phase photochemical reactions such as photolysis of SO_2.

What this essentially comes down to is that more research is needed, as scientists are currently unable to make firm conclusions concerning the environmental evolution of the Archean Earth from these data. Paytan and Kasting both comment on additional studies that could be useful. We have a fairly good idea of how the atmo-sphere evolved, but more research is needed to prove it, and to give a more accurate timescale.

Works Cited

Carslaw, Ken. "The Origin of the Atmosphere." February 10, 2001. http://www.env.leeds.ac.uk/envi1280/lecture_notes_carslaw1/

Catling, David C., Kevin J. Zahnle, and Christopher McKay. "Biogenic Methane, Hydrogen Escape, and the Irreversible Oxidation of Early Earth." *Science* 293—839–843 (Reports).

Kasting, James F. "The Rise of Atmospheric Oxygen." *Science* 2001 293—819–820 (Perspectives).

Paytan, Adina. "Sulfate Clues for the Early History of Atmospheric Oxygen" *Science* 288—626–627 (Perspectives).

Index

C

D

S

Y–Z

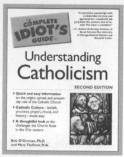

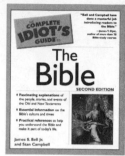

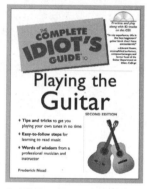

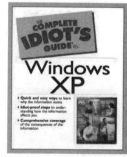

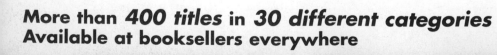

About the Author

Laurie E. Rozakis, Ph.D., earned her Ph.D. in English and American literature with "distinction" from the State University of New York at Stony Brook. A professor of English at Farmingdale State College, Dr. Rozakis has published more than a hundred books and scores of articles. In addition to *The Complete Idiot's Guide to Research Methods,* her publications include trade books, young adult books, textbooks, biographies, reference books, articles, and scholarship. Her latest books include *The Complete Idiot's Guide to Grammar and Style, Second Edition, The Complete Idiot's Guide to College Survival,* and *Super Study Skills* (Scholastic).

Dr. Rozakis frequently appears on television, including *Live with Regis and Kelly!*; the *CBS Morning Show*; the *Maury Povich Show*; *Fox Good Day, New York*; *Metro Relationships*; and *Fox Personal F/X.* Her career and books have been profiled in *The New York Times*, the *New York Daily News*, *Time* magazine, and the *Chicago Tribune.*